Margaret Crump

IN THE LINE OF DUTY

IN THE LINE OF DUTY

The Story of Two Brave Men

BY LARRY STURHOLM
AND JESS ROE

A DOUBLEDAY-GALILEE ORIGINAL
DOUBLEDAY & COMPANY, INC.
GARDEN CITY, NEW YORK
1980

Grateful acknowledgment is made by the authors for permission to quote from Helen Steiner Rice's "But He Who Makes a Sacrifice," copyright © by Gibson Greeting Cards, Inc.

ISBN: 0-385-15396-1
Library of Congress Catalog Card Number 79-8552

Printed in the United States of America

First Edition

This book is dedicated to my Lord and Savior, Jesus Christ; to my wife, Jeanne, who took her marriage vows, "in sickness and in health," very seriously; and to three great children, Mike, Christine, and Susan.

Also, I wish to express my sincere appreciation to all of the doctors, nurses, aides, and orderlies who patiently took care of Mike and of me, to all of our relatives and friends who gave me support and help when I really needed it, and to all the people who, knowingly or unknowingly, gave me strength to keep going.

And very special thanks go to James E. Davis, who taught me the meaning of true friendship, and to Magdalen Goergeny, who got me going again: a great therapist and a good friend. And last but not least, to my friends Larry Sturholm, who wrote the book, and Johnny Howard, who had the idea.

God bless all of you.

Jess H. Roe

FOREWORD

News reporters tend to be a bit skeptical. It seems to be a prerequisite for the job, but it is also something of a handicap in terms of vision. You become used to living in a world of hard facts and concrete evidence. The daily demand of "Show me" or "Prove it" can limit your horizon.

There is, I believe, a real danger of becoming too cynical toward your fellow man. Life and death, suffering, and even human relations can lose their meaning. This seems to be especially true in dealing with religion.

Personally, I find discussing religion uncomfortable. While I am willing to admit the "possibility" of an Almighty God, it is extremely difficult to come to grips with truly accepting Him into my heart. There are no hard facts or concrete evidence that would make a commitment easy.

Because of those unsettling feelings, I was somewhat hesitant about working with Jess and Jeanne Roe on the story of their life, even though I recognized they had overcome tragic and difficult circumstances. Although the factual aspect of the story represented no problem, being a newsman I experienced a tremendous amount of apprehension about dealing with their religious evolution and the role Jesus Christ played in their lives.

I first met Jess and Jeanne in the fall of 1977. At the time they lived in the small farming community of Dundee, Oregon, about thirty miles southwest of Portland.

A mutual friend of ours, John Howard, had been badgering me for over a year to at least go out and talk to the Roes about their life. Each time the subject was raised, I argued that religious stories should be written by religious persons. I insisted that I was a doubter and that would pose problems in terms of developing a credible work. Still, John persisted and finally I realized that he was not going to let the subject drop until I met them.

One Sunday afternoon we drove out to Dundee. It was a typical

Oregon fall: cloudy, windy, and rainy—not unlike Hawaii during a hurricane.

To say I was uneasy was an understatement. I had been told Jeanne and Jess were born-again Christians. As someone who had never met a born-again Christian, or understood what the term meant, I wasn't sure what to expect. At the very least, I expected to meet an overly enthusiastic Bible-quoting couple who would insist upon giving me a pop quiz on the apostles. At worst, they might be insistent upon saving my soul.

Armed with these trepidations, I entered their home, taking care that John led the way.

What I discovered was two very warm, very happy people. For the first fifteen minutes not one word about religion was spoken. Finally I felt compelled to broach the subject and I was surprised by their response.

They were born-again Christians, that was true, and they enjoyed discussing their God and how He had entered and changed their lives. They did not, however, feel compelled to burden others with a long dialogue about how everyone must find God.

"We are always willing to offer encouragement to those who ask for it, and we feel rewarded if that encouragement bears fruit," Jess explained. "But our own discovery of the Lord was a personal thing. We decided on our own to open our hearts and ask Him in. I don't think there is any other way. You have to want it. No amount of talking or cajoling can be as effective as someone simply opening his heart. So we happily talk about how God has changed our lives, and we hope our example will help others."

That explanation impressed me deeply. In a few sentences they had put religion in a perspective that even a hardened newsman could appreciate. The uneasiness that I had experienced melted away during the next three or four meetings. Finally I developed a genuine interest in the Roes, not so much for their story, but because of the warmth and friendship they offered.

To say that I have been born again would be misleading. But because of the friendship that has developed between myself and the Roes during the writing of this book, I can honestly say I have experienced a new attitude toward religion. Where before I was too cynical to look for Him, I now am forced to take a second look, to explore a new direction.

Where that might lead is certainly difficult to say, but my association with the Roes has been a very pleasant experience. They would be the first to insist that they are average people who lead an average life. Perhaps that is true, but there were many obstacles for them to conquer in order to lead their "average" life.

As their faith has encouraged and sustained them, the Roes' example of confronting and defeating those obstacles should offer encouragement to others. I know it did for me.

LARRY STURHOLM
Salem, Oregon
1979

IN THE LINE OF DUTY

PART ONE

CHAPTER ONE

The pheasant came sailing majestically out of our neighbor's field and dropped silently into our freshly planted garden for its late-afternoon feeding. It was obvious he was confident of his surroundings. He'd been a regular customer since Jeanne put the garden in three weeks earlier. Whatever it was Jeanne had planted, it certainly agreed with him. The ring-necked rooster waddled up and down the neatly hoed rows past the corn, lettuce, and cucumber seeds, finally stopped at the sunflower and began scratching. Occasionally he'd turn toward the house as if to say, "Love your salad bar."

Luckily for him, both Jeanne and I had given up hunting. But as we watched him dig around in the freshly planted section, I had some second thoughts and suggested Jeanne get the shotgun. With one shot, she would save her garden and solve the question of what to have for dinner.

Finally, in a desperate move to save the corn, Jeanne charged out of the house, grabbed a handful of rocks, and took out after the rotund bird. He didn't appear overly concerned as the first two rocks sailed harmlessly over his head and the third fell pathetically short of its mark. He finally gave ground, however, when Jeanne charged him, screaming and yelling as she ran. It took him a few feet to get airborne, but he finally lifted off the ground and disappeared into a nearby pasture, scolding us as he went. The garden had been saved, but Jeanne's voice would be a bit hoarse for the next few days.

A few years before, the bird would have been dinner, but over the years we have changed our attitude toward God's creatures and toward God Himself. Looking out from the deck of our new home, about twenty miles south of Portland, we both marvel at how wonderful God has been to us. In the past twenty-five years, we've laughed, cried, experienced joy and pain, and still count some tremendous people as our friends.

When Jeanne and I were first approached about the possibility of describing our lives to others, we wanted to say no. It wasn't necessarily a matter of being humble, since we did live through some experiences that others might consider difficult. But neither of us felt those experiences were unique—such things happen to many families—nor did we think our lives might serve as an inspiration to others. It was just the lives God had chosen for us, and they have been good ones. And there was the uneasiness of baring all of our foibles to unknown readers. But as a year passed, and again we were asked to share our lives with God with others, it occurred to us that perhaps this was God's will, that He wanted the story to be told.

After much soul-searching, we finally agreed, assuming that once the story had been told, no one would want to publish it. What follows is just another of the surprises that God has given us over many years.

Accepting God did not come easy for me, nor did it come suddenly in a flash of light or with the trumpeting of angels. It came only after much stubbornness on my part and much patience on His.

There are many who admit to His presence, at least to an awareness of His presence, and these are good people, people I believe God will bring to Him when the time arrives. But that's not exactly what I mean by accepting the Lord into your heart, and I'm trying to define my personal experience only because acceptance of God will undoubtedly mean many things to many people, as it should. I believe God reveals Himself by whatever means is available: that He did not lay out a specific blueprint for His children to follow in order to find salvation. It is not what you say or how you say it that counts, it is what is in your heart. To follow a formula would make it too easy. Again, this is my understanding of the Lord and how I found peace.

Acceptance to me literally means knowing God, knowing Jesus Christ, and believing They are always with you and love you as a member of Their family. It's a matter of opening up your heart without reservation. "The light shines in the darkness; but the darkness has not understood it." (John 1:5; New International Version)

It's also the ability to love your fellow man and accept him for what he is without feeling the emotions of envy or repulsion; to be able to shake the hand of the President of the United States and then offer the same hand to one less fortunate than yourself with the same degree of enthusiasm as you offered it to the President. The Lord is with us, there is no doubt in either of our minds, but it wasn't always like that for me. In earlier years there were many doubts and many temptations.

Jeanne and I had gone to West Linn, Oregon, High School together, but were never more than nodding acquaintances. It wasn't until the Christmas of 1945, after I had been discharged from the Army Air Corps, that we met at a holiday dance and began to date. After that we were constantly together and married the following May. By the fall of 1947 Mike had come into the world. Our first daughter, Chris, arrived in 1949 and Susan (everyone calls her Sus) was born in 1951.

By the time Sus was born, I had been on the Portland police force for almost two years. Before joining, I sold farm machinery for the Oregon Grange and found the job interesting, but not necessarily challenging. The people I met were honest, hardworking, and cheerful, but there was little excitement in discussing the pros and cons of cover crops. Occasionally an old high school friend, Moon McMullin, who had joined the force two years earlier, would drop by and try to badger me into taking the entrance exam. Moon held the exam score record, and I would always tell him the only reason I didn't take the exam was to ensure his record would stand for a few more years. Moon had been a straight-A student, majoring in chemical engineering at Oregon State University. But in the middle of his senior year, Moon got into a heated argument with one of his professors and stomped out of the class and college and right into the Portland Police Department. Moon could be extremely impulsive at times, and once he made up his mind, no one on earth could talk him out of it.

This good-natured badgering went on for five or six months and I'm not really sure how the good-natured prodding pushed me into action. But one day, while I was in downtown Portland on business, I found myself walking past the Central Precinct. The next thing I knew, I had inquired about the next testing date and had signed up. There was no obligation—just come in and take the test. Moon's mark remained intact, but I did finish fourth out of 120 applications and the department offered me a position as a patrolman.

Things seemed to steamroll along and the next thing I knew I was a rookie policeman walking a beat in downtown Portland, but not without strong objections from Jeanne. She was unhappy with my decision from the start and tried on a number of occasions to talk me out of it. Despite her foot-dragging, once the ball started rolling I knew I wanted to be a policeman. Jeanne must have sensed my determination and finally resigned herself to the fact. In 1950 policemen still walked beats, and many residents knew their local policeman by his first name.

It was a new and exciting world for a guy who a few months before thought fast-paced living was selling two hay balers in a day or getting into a heated discussion over the merits of a John Deere tractor versus a Ford or International Harvester. Back then, I believe, policemen had more public support and they seemed to receive more community respect and appreciation for the job they were doing. A lawsuit brought against a policeman was almost unheard of, and because of that many times policemen were able to correct civil matters and domestic problems on the scene rather than dragging them before the courts.

Many times today, with civil suits hanging over them like a double-edged sword, policemen seem to have been maneuvered into a position of becoming much like private citizens: they're afraid of getting personally involved! I'm sure I'd think twice about trying to help solve, say, a domestic quarrel. Today I'd be more inclined to leave it up to the courts rather than run the risk of a lawsuit dealing with the murky problem of constitutional rights. Even the Supreme Court can't agree on the subject, so what chance does a policeman have?

I'm sure we did things that would have turned an American Civil Liberties Union attorney purple with indignation in our efforts to follow the spirit of the law rather than the letter. And I'm sure there were times when authority was abused. But that always seems to be the case when humans deal with other humans. By and large, however, I personally think laws were better enforced and society better served when policemen were allowed more freedom to act.

And it seemed that the judges were a little more willing to take corrective action rather than dishing out a slap on the wrist. That was especially true of "Jailin' Jake" Quillan. Everyone knew exactly where they stood with Jailin' Jake. If you had done your best to enforce the law and keep peace, you knew Jailin' Jake would support you. If you were a bit remiss in the performance of your duties, you were apt to get a severe tongue-lashing from the judge while the defendant was given the lightest possible penalty allowable under the law. That is, unless the defendant had been arrested for drunk driving or contributing alcohol to minors. Jake was especially tough on those violators.

His young son had been killed by an intoxicated driver, and from that day forward Jailin' Jake waged an unrelenting war against alcohol. He vowed publicly that within his jurisdiction such offenders would be put away for as long as the law would allow. He felt it was his job to protect the public. When either a driver or contributor of alcohol came before him, the gavel came down heavily and without mercy. But not without humor.

Jake would sit on the bench and listen to excuses and pleas for mercy with an unsympathetic ear. Occasionally, as the defendant pleaded his case, Jake's eyes would wander toward the skylight, or he would fiddle with a desk drawer or click a ball-point pen against his teeth to pass the time. Finally, with an exasperated sigh, he would cut the defendant off short. "I've heard enough, one hundred and ninety days! Next case."

Jake's courtroom was always full, especially when word got out that a drinking case was being heard. Policemen who were at the courthouse to give testimony in other courts would hurry over to Jake's courtroom for the trial; off-duty courtroom clerks would show up, and so would idle attorneys.

One case that had drawn a rather large gallery involved a Chicago resident I had arrested on New Year's Eve for being drunk on a public street, handing out whiskey to teenagers, and striking a police officer. He had flattened my partner with a haymaker during the arrest; and striking a police officer, to Jake's way of thinking, was just one step below contributing or drunk driving.

Unfortunately for the Chicago man, no one had warned him about Jailin' Jake's animosity toward liquor. When asked how he pleaded to the charges, the man launched into a strong defense of his actions.

"Your honor," he said in a rather officious manner, "I think there are a number of extenuating circumstances which should be considered by the court. First of all, I'm a visitor from out of state and—"

Jake quickly cut the man off. "I'm not interested in whether you're from out of state, sir!" The words were delivered in a gruff, threatening manner. "I want to know how you plead to the charges!"

"Your honor, I was celebrating New Year's Eve." There was a noticeable drop in the confidence of his voice. "Ah, I probably had too much to drink. You know how those things can get out of hand, and I wasn't aware that those around me weren't twenty-one."

"Sir, this court has a number of cases on its docket for today! How do you plead?" Jake's neck colored a bit as he looked down at the defendant. The thinly veiled threat in Jake's voice had obviously unnerved the man.

"Well, ah, yes. I mean, I guess I plead guilty to being drunk and contributing to minors, your honor. But it was New Year's Eve!" he whined.

"I don't know about Chicago," Jake responded sarcastically, "but here in Portland it's not a tradition to punch our policemen on New Year's Eve! Did you hit the arresting officer?"

To ardent Jailin' Jake followers, it was obvious that he was quickly losing what little patience he had. The last question had been delivered with an icy blast that could be felt in the back row of the courtroom.

The man was sweating profusely, and the confidence he had earlier shown quickly disappeared. He stammered nervously as he continued.

"The officer was being unnecessarily rough and was pushing me around." Jake's eyes lifted absentmindedly toward the skylight as the man tried to justify his actions. "Your honor, I'm guilty, I admit that. But I would like you to consider that I'm a visitor here and, ah, not familiar with your laws." The man's voice dropped off noticeably as he saw his plea was having no effect on the judge. "I, ah, would like to"—he coughed nervously—"throw myself on the court's mercy."

"The court's mercy" had been lost on everyone but the court clerk, since the words had been delivered in a whisper of fear.

Jake leaned over his desk and looked down at the clerk. "What? What did he say?"

The clerk began to laugh, realizing that asking for mercy in Jailin' Jake's court was like Pharaoh's asking God not to part the Red Sea. "He's throwing himself on the mercy of the court because he's a visitor, your honor." You could hear stifled snickering ripple through the room.

Jake's face turned a deep shade of red. "You come into Portland, make a public nuisance of yourself, strike one of our policemen, and expect this court to show you mercy? If this is the way you act in Chicago, then stay there! You say you're not familiar with our laws! Well," Jake said, leaning over his desk and scowling angrily, "I'm going to give you some time to learn them. Ninety days! Next case!"

"Ninety days!" the man whined. "Your honor, give me a break!"

This time the judge spoke through tightly clenched teeth, barely able to control his anger. "Young man, I did give you a break! I could have given you a hundred and eighty days! A hundred and eighty days!" Jake pounded his fist on the desk after each word.

That was Jailin' Jake Quillan. He was high on every policeman's list. He believed in swift justice and disliked forcing policemen to stand around waiting to testify. He knew most of us had to come in on our days off, and he also understood that most of us worked a second job on those days off.

Soon after coming on the force, I discovered that most policemen had at least one part-time job and usually two or more in order to make ends meet. I was no exception. I came on the force at a starting salary of $245 a month, and my house payment was $100. On top of that, I was supporting a family of four, and later five, and found it necessary to hold down as many as four jobs at one time. One day I'd turn in my blue uniform for a butcher's apron, another day I'd drive a cab, or work at the post office during the Christmas rush. Three days a week I filled in as a Lake Oswego patrolman. But the most demanding job, in terms of time and physical exertion was what my Portland patrol partner, Jim Davis, and I called "The Red Rock Express."

Davis was a year younger than I; he was single, stood six feet, was muscular, had a square face, and wore a closely cropped crew cut. He also wore a perpetual mischievous grin and had a talent for finding new ways to get into trouble with the precinct commander. And when he got into trouble, I was usually standing next to him when the ax fell.

One of our constant downfalls was "The Red Rock Express." In the early fifties a reddish volcanic rock was popular with homeowners and contractors. It was used for retaining walls and rockery around homes. Seeing a chance to cash in on a current trend, Jim and I bought a twenty-four-foot '51 GMC flatbed truck and went into the red-rock-hauling business.

It was a twelve-to-fourteen-hour round trip from Portland to the rock quarry near Redmond in central Orgeon. In the snowy winters the drive took as long as twenty. Today, with straighter roads, it's probably a leisurely four-and-a-half-hour drive. But back then a straight stretch of highway was maybe a hundred yards long. We'd get off duty at midnight, change clothes, and head out for Redmond. We'd load rock all morning, return to Portland by two in the afternoon, unload it, and get to the station just in time to go back on duty. To survive, we'd take turns driving and sleeping, both in the truck and in the patrol car. It was tough, hard work, but there's a certain satisfaction that exhaustion from honest labor brings.

Still, it was tough on the family. I might go two or three weeks without seeing the children, and many times I saw Jeanne only long enough to kiss her before collapsing into a deep, exhausted sleep. To use an old cliché, we were like ships passing in the night.

The whole family was terrific about my absence, though. Many mornings I'd wake up staring at a note written by Mike and Chris that they had pinned to my pillow before leaving for school. Sometimes I'd find one under my coffee cup or tucked neatly into the toe of my shoe. "Hi, Daddy. Did you catch any crooks? We love you!" it would read and there would be a stick drawing of a policeman arresting a villain. I did the same, leaving notes in their lunch boxes telling them to study hard or reminding them to help their mother with the household chores. It was a demoralizing thing to realize your children were growing up and you weren't around often to enjoy it. Fortunately Jeanne was a good mother and watched over them, making sure they grew up correctly. She accepted my long hours of work. She understood I was trying to make things easier for her and the children. But, later, when work gave way to drinking, she stopped being tolerant.

Our "Red Rock Express" got Jim and me into a lot of trouble around the precinct. Not because we were moonlighting, but because we were constantly going off our assigned beat or district to look at new equipment for the business. A memo had been sent around to all precincts expressly forbidding officers from going off their district. The consequence would be a three-day suspension without pay that everyone could ill afford.

Despite the threat, we continued to "expand our district boundaries" the way General Patton had conducted "reconnaissance in force" when ordered to stay put. Hearing about a bargain on a used truck, one night we wound up four miles off our district. No sooner had we pulled up to the truck dealership than an apartment manager came dashing across the street.

"Officers," he pleaded, "you've got to help me! One of my tenants is tearing his room apart!"

We both knew that if we investigated and were forced to make an arrest, or if the manager wanted to file charges, we'd have to file a report that would show we were considerably off our district. Davis began to sweat a little as the thought of three days' pay raced through his mind.

"Ah, look, we really can't help you," he said as sympathetically as possible. "Why don't you call the police." As the words escaped his mouth, he turned sheepishly toward me and shrugged his shoulders helplessly.

The manager's mouth fell about a foot in disbelief. "But you are the police!" he whimpered in confusion.

"Gotcha." I grinned at Davis and put on my hat.

"Please hurry. This guy is destroying my apartment, and I just had it remodeled!"

We were trapped into helping the manager, so with heavy hearts we got out of the car and followed him into the apartment. As it turned out, remodeling was a new coat of paint, but we could hear a lot of shouting and furniture crashing down the hallway. On the way in, we decided the best approach would be to try and calm everyone down, reach some kind of agreement, and then retreat as quickly as possible. Under no circumstances did we want to make an arrest. An arrest or any other action that would demand a report would have been like taking a full-page ad in the newspaper announcing: "We Have Been off Our District! Please Suspend Us!"

The tenant was certainly upset and had vented some of his anger on the furniture and directed a number of extremely descriptive phrases at the manager, who had just raised the rent following the "remodeling." Although the tenant was only average-size, which gave Jim and me an obvious edge, he was boiling mad and ready for a fight. When he saw us walk in, with the manager hanging safely in the background, he became more belligerent, now directing his ire at us as much as at the manager.

Policemen are supposed to be thick-skinned, but there are limits. Jim's thick skin was a bit sensitive, and after he'd listened to a constant barrage of colorful adjectives directed at the two of us, his temper was on the rise. It was only a matter of seconds before it would reach the explosion point.

"Jim, calm down! Remember, we can't afford to make an arrest."

Jim's face twisted with frustration, but he didn't react, and I turned my attention toward the tenant. It took a few minutes, but finally the guy began to quiet down a bit. He still kept chipping away at us, however—sneering at how the manager was getting us to do his dirty work, implying that we were just trained dogs doing a job. The manager, meanwhile, was aggravating the situation by warning the tenant that he'd have us throw him out in the street.

Finally, after some fast talking, we got a reluctant agreement from the tenant that instead of tearing the place apart because he felt the increased rent was unfair he'd contact an attorney. He also agreed to pay for the broken furniture, but it was obvious he was still livid and having a difficult time checking his temper.

Under the impression we had at least defused the situation enough to make a hasty retreat back to our district, we started to leave. But just as we did, the manager decided to fire a parting shot.

Still safely behind us, he poked his hand between us, waved a finger at the tenant, and yelled threateningly, "And if you cause any more trouble, these officers will come back and throw you in jail!"

That was the last straw. The tenant took a wild swing at the manager, but hit me. Jim finally had an excuse to release his pent-up anger and almost climbed over my back in a frantic effort to get to the tenant. The fight was on. Jim and I went crashing into the room and for the next five minutes were thrashing about trying to subdue him. There was now no way out. We had to make the arrest. And all the way back to the precinct, the tenant was raging in the backseat, screaming obscenities in our ears, while we were mourning the loss of three days' pay.

Fortunately, that evening the night sergeant, "199 percent" Fitzsimons, was in a good mood. He had earned the title of 199 percent for his total devotion to strict adherence to the rules. He wouldn't bend them for anyone for any reason. This night, however, because the tenant was now loudly directing his wrath toward policemen in general, Fitzsimons felt we had done a public service regardless of where we were at the time of the arrest. He ignored our rather transparent excuse and gleefully booked the troublemaker, giving us only a mild verbal reprimand and an unofficial pat on the back.

Davis and I constantly found ourselves in difficult straits. Sometimes, as in the apartment incident, we were the victims of circumstances, merely innocent bystanders in the path of history. But for the most part we were guilty as charged. We had a knack for running into supervisors while off-district, and occasionally our horseplay would draw attention to us. Like the night we started chasing each other around the precinct building with a bottle of perfume. The chase went upstairs, downstairs, and around the building. Finally, with Davis screaming at the top of his voice not to throw the perfume on his freshly dry-cleaned uniform, we burst into the patrol briefing room, where the next mayor of Portland was delivering a campaign speech.

We were halfway through the room before we realized what we had done and immediately froze. The mayor-to-be, Terry Schrunk, stood there with a perplexed expression on his face while the blood drained from our own.

There was a brief period of deadly silence; then Jim turned to Schrunk and grinned. "We're just getting in shape for the Policemen's Ball, Terry," he said and raced out the door with me in hot pursuit.

Neither of us was surprised when the ax eventually fell. We were told that we both needed stabilizing influences for the good of our careers and that by no stretch of the imagination could either of us be considered a stabilizing influence. So, for the good of the department, we were banished to opposite ends of the city.

I had been on the force four years and it was now 1954. Pressures were beginning to build, but I didn't know how to cope with them. Policemen seldom see the public at its best. Either citizens need help or they are causing trouble. There is seldom a middle ground. At first you're shocked by all the problems people have and you try to help. After a while the magnitude overwhelms you and you begin to think there is no solution. Then you become callous and begin making sick jokes about people's tragedies as a subconscious means of releasing the frustrations of what you believe is a hopeless situation. When I first came on the force, I recall, I watched an old man searching through a restaurant garbage can for something to eat. I leaned up against a wall and began crying. Four years later I could have watched the same old man and made wisecracks about him.

After the callous stage, you begin to drink in search of a quick escape. What had been slowly building over the past year was now beginning to accelerate. Before the transfer I might have gone out once in a while for a social drink with a few of my fellow officers, but the pace began to pick up. At the time of the transfer I would go out maybe three nights in a row, once every other month. The first night would be just for a social drink, the second night the social drinking was extended for a few more hours, and by the third night I would drink to get falling-down drunk. I would become mean and surly as the hostility I had been harboring toward society, which I had managed to suppress while sober, came violently to the surface.

These drinking sessions touched off some heated arguments at home. Jeanne had never complained about the long hours away from the family when I was working or testifying in court. (Many officers had to give up their normal days off in order to testify about arrests or citations issued.) But now, when I came home drunk, she found it difficult to contain her anger. The arguments always ended with my apologizing and promising not to do it again. But the drinking binges were increasing as 1954 merged with 1955.

My new assignment only intensified the situation. I was transferred to one of the toughest areas of Portland, the Albina District. A few years before, it had been a wide-open area. Gambling, prostitution, drugs, and violence were a nightly occurrence; decency and honesty never appeared at night. You quickly learned that humans were never to be trusted, that everyone was suspect.

The only bright spot was my partner, Lee Stockdale. Stockdale was a living legend. Before he was assigned to the Albina District, policemen had quite literally been run off the streets by the local rowdies. That ended when Stockdale arrived. He was a tough, gruff, stockily built man who administered justice with his fists as much as he did by the book. Today he would have been the target of a hundred lawsuits, but in 1955 the only way to survive as a policeman was to be tougher than the opponent and to impose eye-for-an-eye justice. During one tavern brawl there must have been fifteen men fighting when we pulled up to the front door. But when I started to get out of the car, Stockdale just smiled and said, "That's okay, pard, I can handle this one. One riot, one cop."

He walked over to a nearby alley, picked up a sturdy two-by-four, swung it a couple of times as Mickey Mantle might in order to get the feel of the wood, then stomped inside. For a couple of minutes there was a lot of hollering and glass crashing, but then things became ominously quiet. Three men came flying out the door and landed on the pavement. A voice came from somewhere inside the tavern: "You're under arrest. Don't move till I get out there!" It was an order and no one moved until Stockdale reappeared. He leaned into the car and smiled: "You got the next one, pard."

Another time, just before Lee retired, we were parked on a major avenue watching traffic. A memo had come down to all patrols warning that unless traffic citations were brought up to a "respectable level" it would be assumed that officers weren't doing their job. The term "quota" wasn't used, but the implication was there. This drove Stockdale up the wall since he felt he needed to devote every minute on duty to keeping the lid on his district. He argued that he couldn't keep tabs on the criminals and at the same time hand out traffic tickets. His argument fell on deaf ears until one night when he decided to make his point.

We had been at the corner only a few minutes when a Rose City transit bus ran a red light. Under normal circumstances, it was a common occurrence, which was ignored. But this time Lee ordered me to give chase.

"What?" I asked in bewilderment.

"Pull him over! He blew the light."

"But that's a bus!"

Stockdale grinned. "He's a citizen, just like everyone else. Get 'im! We need to get our citations up to a respectable level."

It took us a few blocks to flag the bus down, since the driver undoubtedly thought we were after someone else. He was totally incensed when Stockdale started writing out the ticket.

"What are you doing?" he screamed.

Stockdale looked up from his ticket book. "Writing you a ticket, neighbor. You ran a red light!"

"But I'm a bus driver. We always run the lights!"

"Not tonight."

The driver was beside himself and walked around screaming and yelling that Stockdale couldn't do this, while the passengers watched in amusement.

You always knew when Stockdale's patience was wearing thin because he would use the term "neighbor." For those who knew him, that was a signal not to push any further. It was a telltale sign the driver was not aware of.

"I don't care what you write," the driver snapped, "I'm not going to take it."

Stockdale smiled coldly, ripped the ticket out, and handed it to the driver. "Here you go."

The bus driver shook his head. "I won't accept it!"

"Neighbor, you better take it. I've already written it." The driver hadn't noticed the icy tone of Stockdale's voice, but I had and stood there wondering what was going to happen next.

"I'm not going to accept that ticket! You can't give me a ticket! This is ridiculous," the driver snorted and started to get back on the bus.

"Hold it right there, neighbor. Take this ticket or else!"

"What ya going to do, take me in?"

Stockdale was a big man, but moved with the quickness of a cat—a very strong cat. In one swift movement, Stockdale had the driver by the scruff of the neck and was dragging him back to the patrol car.

The passengers, about twenty of them, stared out the window, their eyes bulging at the sight of their driver being dragged away while Stockdale was yelling, "You, neighbor, are under arrest!" With that, Stockdale opened the back door of the car and tossed the confused driver inside.

I stood there along with the passengers, my mouth gaping. "What about the bus?"

Stockdale looked over at the driverless bus and shrugged his big shoulders. "I'm not a bus driver. Are you?"

"No."

"Well, then I guess it stays there until another bus driver comes along." You could hear the amusement in his voice. "We got ourselves a traffic citation to worry about."

"Yeah, but the passengers!"

Stockdale shook his head. "That's the bus company's problem. They run buses, we write tickets." That ended the discussion. We jumped in the car and headed for the precinct while the passengers sat in the bus wondering what was going to happen. The driver was booked for refusing to accept a traffic summons and for resisting arrest. A few hours later, the bus company finally managed to get a new driver for its stranded bus and passengers. After that arrest, memos urging officers to keep their traffic tickets up to a respectable level were never sent to Stockdale's district.

Humorous moments were few and far between, however. On the average night, we'd investigate wife beatings, shootings, knifings, and death in all forms. Young children, the same age as Mike and Chris, were out wandering the streets looking for their parents, or they'd roam the streets in gangs. During the last few months, depression was a steady companion and, as the depression increased, my spiral toward alcoholism accelerated.

The spiral spun almost completely out of control on February 18, 1956. Stockdale and I were on duty late in the evening when we heard a police call about two officers who had been injured in a car accident in northeast Portland. Vern "Boots" Stroeder and Roy Meizner were veteran police officers who were well liked throughout the department.

Arriving on the scene, we knew immediately there was no hope that either could have survived the crash. You couldn't even tell what kind of a car it had been. They had been hit broadside by a car traveling eighty miles an hour. They never knew what hit them. As I stood there watching the flashing ambulance lights and listening to the muddy voices coming out over the two-way radio, and the road flares that cast an ominous red pall over the twisted metal, I had a premonition that I'd be next. That feeling stayed with me for the next two months—regardless of the amount of alcohol I consumed to drown it—and in those days before I'd met Christ I did drink a lot.

CHAPTER TWO

For close to six years, I worked every night shift in the police department, and during that time I observed the worst possible human traits brought out in full force each night. My emotions and empathy for mankind dried up and disappeared in a cold, unfeeling gray fog. Death and suffering became commonplace and I found myself viewing human suffering with an emotionless and uncaring eye. Violence and a disregard for life and dignity seemed normal, decency and love abnormal. I became suspicious of those offering a helping hand. No one was above suspicion.

For me to recognize this evolution of my attitudes toward the entire human race was shocking enough, but then to discover that I was rapidly becoming part of that godless world I was hired to suppress created absolute panic. I was slowly sinking in a sea of filth and degradation. Looking into the mirror each day, I saw my transformation from a caring person into a callous, unloving man drifting toward alcoholism. Without a strong wife like Jeanne, my marriage would have ended months before. Looking back at that moment of my life, I realize she was the only thing that stood between me and total disaster.

I felt so helpless as the days blurred together into meaningless periods of living. God gives each of us just so many days, and I was giving no thought to how I was using them. They were just wasted days; I spent them with no more thought than one might give to taking out the garbage.

Those days were squandered as easily as an alcoholic spends money to buy wine. And the end result was much the same: a dull empty feeling, a sickening realization that things were out of control. Then panic set in when, in frustration, I began to sense I couldn't stop my slide downward.

I managed to slow the downward slide some by getting a transfer to a day shift job: giving out parking tickets. It was not exactly your glamour police assignment, but it got me away from the growing nightly depression and back into the light, where I had an opportunity to meet and associate with normal people once again.

This was a time before meter maids, and all parking tickets were issued by motorcycle policemen. In Portland the parking-ticket patrol, dubbed the "paper hangers," patrolled the streets on three-wheeled cycles. Since I was low man on the totem pole in terms of seniority, I naturally got the oldest motorcycle: one with mechanical brakes that grabbed only intermittently. Every time I applied the brakes, they grabbed about once every three or four revolutions of the wheel. The tires would dig into the pavement each time the brakes took hold, leaving rubber marks that looked as if I was attempting to send Morse code. There would be a rubber mark, then a blank space, another mark or two, another blank space, and so on. It goes without saying, I was not ecstatic about the bike's performance. But at least I was on days.

Days meant in the evening I could have dinner with my family, which was a luxury for all of us. The temptation to drink was lessened a great deal when I realized the entire family was waiting for me. For the first time in six years the family was together. We got reacquainted with our friends and neighbors. Jeanne enjoyed fixing the dinners and I enjoyed playing with the children. Baseball season was just about to begin, and Mike was getting ready for Little League tryouts. Chris talked excitedly about school, and Sus was making plans for her first year in school the coming fall. It had taken a long time, but I knew we were finally starting to put some order back into our lives. It would last exactly ten days.

Handing out parking tickets is not considered to be a prestigious job. Basically, you do the same thing for eight hours: fill out tickets, write down license plate numbers, tuck the ticket under the wiper, and then move on to the next car. Most "paper hangers" issued between 150 and 180 tickets a day. But, as a rookie, I never got past 80. Mostly I spent much of my time drinking coffee and then listening to my stomach gurgle as I rode around my district.

The week before I joined the parking-ticket patrol, the weather had been awful. Rain came down in buckets, and I was prepared for the worst. But on the day I reported for duty, the skies suddenly cleared and marked the start of an early and hot summer. I reported for work on April 3, 1956.

After ten days of issuing parking citations, I knew I had stumbled onto one of the most boring jobs ever devised by mankind. But if I was bored, at least I was bored in nice weather, and nice weather on a motorcycle isn't half bad.

Friday the thirteenth marked the completion of my ten days. It was a beautiful morning, and KEX radio disc jockey Barney Keep cheerfully announced that temperatures would reach the high seventies and that the sunshine would last for at least another week. Jeanne announced that she was planning a big dinner in honor of my day shift job.

I smiled as I started up the motorcycle and shouted over its roar, "Be careful and don't burn dinner. Remember, it's Friday the thirteenth!"

"You be careful!" she admonished as I roared off down the road.

Her warning had been delivered with a more serious tone than mine, since Friday the thirteenth had not been kind to me in the past. When I was thirteen (there's that number again) there had been a big February snowstorm in the Portland area. A foot of snow blanketed the Lake Oswego golf course, and after dinner most of the neighborhood kids headed out for the course and a steep hill along one of the fairways.

Although my mother was reluctant at first to let me go, I managed to wear her down after an hour of constant pleading. When I finally got to the hill, it was dark. Only the snow reflecting moonlight that filtered down through the clouds offered any light at all. That, of course, did not deter the twenty or more youngsters and adults who zoomed down the hill. It was about a hundred yards down to the base. To the right of the sled run was a stand of trees, while on the left was a clump of rocks, so the object was to stay in the middle. However, in the dark it was a tricky proposition. To add to the problem, the run angled slightly to the left, and if you overcompensated for the rocks you ran the danger of hitting the trees, which is exactly what I did.

A friend and I went down together, with the friend riding on top of me. The snow was flying up into my eyes, and I couldn't see ahead more than a foot or two. I heard him say, "Turn it right!" Then there was a kind of white flash inside my head and that was it. I had collided with a small tree. My friend escaped without any injuries, but the impact broke every rib on my right side; my right arm was broken in two places; the shoulder blade and collarbone were shattered, a rib ripped a hole in my lung; and my heart was pushed downward.

For three days I lay unconscious, and for the first two days doctors gave me a less than fifty-fifty chance of surviving. During those entire three days I can recall only one thing: a recurring dream that remains vivid to this day. In the dream, I was attempting to wade across a river to a beautiful island I had never seen before. I was drawn to the island because of the most incredible colors. They were spectacular. Everything on the island was in brilliant colors. In most cases, vivid colors generate excitement or a feeling of activity, but there everything was so peaceful and tranquil. I wanted desperately to reach the island and began wading across the river. But halfway there I found the water too deep and was forced to turn back. I'm not sure how many times I tried to cross the river, but each time it was always the same: I would get halfway and the water would become too deep. I was never allowed to cross over to the island.

Twenty years later, I was faced with another Friday the thirteenth, but I had no superstitious feelings about the day. I traveled around the downtown Portland area handing out my own form of "bad luck" greetings to parking violators and enjoyed the warm sunshine. I could almost taste the round steak Jeanne had promised. Just after five, I had to make one final round in order to check two tow-away zones. One was on the east side near the Willamette River waterfront.

Since it was almost quitting time, Wayne Bergstrom offered to go along for the final check in order to speed things up. Both of us were looking forward to a beautiful weekend with our families. It had been a quiet day and the weather forecast was still predicting good weather for the next week.

Traveling south on Grand Avenue (a major artery on Portland's east side), we turned west on Morrison, heading toward the Willamette River. Morrison was bumper-to-bumper with rush-hour traffic. We were going against the traffic and laughed at the long line of cars, wondering how anyone ever came up with a term like "rush-hour traffic." Heading west on Morrison, you travel down a gentle slope, which tends to increase your speed. As we approached Third and Morrison and a set of eight railroad tracks, there was an old two-story brick building on the right that blocked our view of any train on the first set of tracks.

Just before reaching the brick building, I glanced down to shift from first to second. At that split second, an engine came out from behind the two-story building. When I looked up again, I wasn't any more than fifty feet away and I was still picking up speed. At that moment I was probably traveling between twenty and twenty-five miles an hour.

I immediately jammed on the hand brakes, but it seemed to have little effect on my speed. Wayne Bergstrom hit his brakes at the same time, but his cycle was equipped with hydraulic brakes and he came to rest about two feet from the engine. By this time the engineer had seen us and hit his brakes. All I could hear was the frightening sound of metal shrieking against metal.

My mind began shouting, "My God, I'm going to hit the train! I'm going to hit the train!" I clutched the hand brake harder, but the mechanical brakes were grabbing intermittently and I could feel the tires dig into the pavement, then continue to roll toward the train, which seemed to be growing larger by the second.

Realizing I could not avoid hitting the engine, I tried to lay the motorcycle over on its side so it would hit the engine first. I turned the front wheel sharply to the left. On a two-wheeled cycle, this would have forced the bike to slide over on its side and slip out from under me, leaving me to bounce along behind it on the pavement. But my three-wheeler didn't slide over on its side. Instead, with the front wheel turned, the brakes grabbed the pavement once more and the effect was disastrous. It turned the cycle into a catapult. The rear end of the bike flipped forward and literally threw me under the train. I could still hear the metal wheels screaming against the metal rails and I saw those wheels coming toward me. My mind was screaming, "Oh, God, I'm gonna get run over!"

Then there was a white flash and I was unconscious. Bergstrom later told me that I had been thrown between the wheels and crashed into a metal box toward the back end of the engine. I'm not sure just how long I was out, probably no more than a minute or two, but when I regained consciousness the cycle was behind me, wedging me up against that metal box. The cycle engine was roaring wide open. Apparently, when I was thrown off, I twisted the accelerator handle and it stuck.

My mind was totally disoriented as I lay there. I couldn't remember what had happened. There was no pain yet and the world made absolutely no sense. Then I noticed my feet were hanging directly over my head. My legs had been bent backward and pushed up over my head. The impact had folded my body like a piece of paper. All I could think of was "That's a heck of a place for my feet to be."

My mind continued in a fog as my body moved into shock. The cycle engine continued to race noisily, and I could hear voices that seemed a long distance away. I heard someone say they had to get me out of there, but I wasn't sure who they were talking about. I lay there staring at my feet, struggling to regain control of my life. My right hand had been shattered by the impact and for the first time I realized I had been hurt. Through the blood I remember seeing an odd white substance, which I later discovered to be bone. By the time I began to understand what had happened, the pain arrived for the first time and I passed out.

For the next twenty minutes I drifted in and out of consciousness. At times the voices would be loud or sharp, other times they would be distant and weak. Seldom did anyone make any sense to me as my brain concentrated on fighting the pain that built like a tidal wave and swept over my body. I felt a flash of heat rush to my head and I was out again.

The next time I awoke, I was flat on my back and people were staring down at me. Some wore expressions of concern, others seemed curious. I could feel someone tugging at my right arm.

"What's the matter?" My question was asked in a surprisingly weak, soft voice. I remember at the time the softness of my voice, and it frightened me. I had watched so many people die while speaking softly.

The man working on my arm ignored the question, but began talking to me. "I'm a doctor. You've banged your arm up pretty good. The artery has been cut, but I think I've got it stopped. The ambulance is on its way. Just lie back and relax."

He continued to talk, and somewhere in the distance I could

hear the siren, but then everything began to whirl around and I dropped back into the blackness and the voices became muffled again. The siren still seemed to be off in the distance when I came to, but after collecting my thoughts I realized I was inside an ambulance. An attendant was staring at me, and I felt the plastic oxygen mask pressing against my nose and cheeks. Out the side window I could see the steel girders of a bridge flying by. The sky was still blue and puffy clouds dotted the horizon. I thought to myself, "What a beautiful day," and passed out again.

The persistent tugging at my coat sleeve dragged me out of the unconscious fog and back into the world of pain. I was lying on an operating table, and a man in a white uniform was gingerly trying to pull my coat off. My right hand was nothing but a mass of blood and bone.

"Well, I see you've come around," he said in what seemed like an oddly cheerful voice. "Sorry about the pain, I can't seem to get this sleeve off."

The pain returned and increased in intensity with each tug. "Cut it off! Just cut it off," I gasped.

As they worked on me, I tried to piece together the sequence of events as a means of keeping my mind occupied and away from the bolts of pain flashing through my body. I suddenly discovered I had a terrible urge to go to the bathroom and laughed as I recalled how many cups of coffee I had had during the morning and afternoon breaks.

Jeanne

The afternoon had been extremely busy for me. Mike and Chris came home after school and immediately went outside to play. Sus was busy banging pots and pans together on the kitchen floor while I put the finishing touches to dinner. It was such a beautiful spring day. Of course, everyone is partial to their own region, but I sometimes find it difficult to believe anywhere else could be as beautiful as Oregon in the spring.

At six-thirty, I called the children in and had them wash up for dinner, thinking Jess would be home at any minute. I had one ear turned toward the driveway, half expecting to hear his motorcycle chugging into the yard. You could hear that motorcycle a half block away.

By a quarter to seven I began wondering where he was, since he was usually home not later than six-forty. He was almost like clockwork, and he knew I was fixing a special dinner. However, after six years of night shifts, I knew I could live with his being a few minutes late. At seven I decided he must have been held up with some extra paper work and told the kids to go ahead and start eating. Mike gave a loud sigh of relief. He had been badgering me from the moment he walked in the house about when we were going to eat. Mike seemed ready to eat twenty-four hours a day.

I sat down at the table with the children and we talked about the events of the day. Mike noted with a great deal of satisfaction that there were only thirty-two more days until summer vacation. Chris was sure it was thirty-six, and the argument was on. Sus would switch from one side of the argument to the other as if she were watching a tennis match, and the discussion raged until someone went for the calendar. They were both wrong. It was forty-three days.

Chris and Mike had just finished eating when the front door bell rang. At the door were two policemen I had never seen before.

"Are you Mrs. Jess Roe?" one of them asked.

I felt my stomach tighten slightly. "Yes."

The officer glanced down at his feet for a split second and then cleared his throat. "Ah, Jess has been in an accident and we were sent to take you to the hospital." He looked in at the children. "Is there someone nearby who could take care of the kids?"

"How badly is he hurt?" The tightness in my stomach was slowly developing into a hard knot.

"We don't know, Mrs. Roe. We were just sent out here to pick you up. Is there someone who can watch the kids?"

I took a couple of deep breaths to calm myself and collect my thoughts. "Yes," I said, trying to regain control of a mind that buzzed with alarm. "Ah, my neighbor. I'm sure she'll watch them. Just a minute." I called Lois Koellermeier and told her what had happened. She came immediately, and within five minutes we were on our way to the hospital.

I sat there in the backseat for a moment studying the two officers, trying to gauge their expressions for any hint of Jess's condition. "Are you sure you haven't heard anything about Jess?" My palms were beginning to sweat, and I could feel the clamminess covering my body as my nerves tightened. I found it somewhat reassuring that the policemen sent were two I didn't know. Normally, if an officer had been killed, the department would send a close friend.

The officer who had come to the door turned and offered what I'm sure he thought was a reassuring smile. "I'm sorry, Mrs. Roe. We really don't know anything at all. We were off duty at the time of the accident and didn't even hear the radio call. We were just told to come out and pick you up. We'll be at the hospital in a few minutes. I'm sure everything is all right."

Actually, the officers weren't being completely honest with Jeanne. Although they hadn't heard the original radio call on the accident, many, including them, had heard a report about someone's being Dead-on-Arrival at Good Samaritan Hospital, which was where I had been taken. Since the radio call didn't identify the person (a victim of another traffic accident), word quickly spread that I had been killed. Nothing had been officially announced, but the two officers taking Jeanne to the hospital were burdened with the uncomfortable impression that they were escorting a widow.

Meanwhile, I had been cleaned and patched up as much as possible in the emergency room and had been wheeled into X-ray for a lengthy photo session. They probably took enough pictures to fill a family album. The pain, which had been centralized in my hand and back, was now spreading throughout my body. My head throbbed from a deep cut in the back, every joint screamed in agony, and it even hurt to breathe. Taking stock of my condition, I was a bit puzzled over the fact that my legs didn't seem to be affected. They were numb—perhaps a pinched nerve—but I gave it little thought. There was plenty of pain to go around. Actually, I was thankful that some part of me had survived the crash.

Two orderlies swung me from a gurney to the X-ray table and pain exploded through my body. After moving me two or three times, with each move causing more pain, they finally decided that the best angle was with my head hanging over the end of the table. Once they got me there, they left and I was alone. After a few minutes, my neck began aching from the pressure exerted by my hanging head. I called out three or four times before I finally heard footsteps coming in my direction.

"Hey!" I yelled. "My neck is killing me! Could you lift my head up a bit? It's really hurting!"

I could feel someone's hands gently lifting my head up and then I saw my Samaritan. It was Jeanne.

"Jess, are you okay?" The shock and concern over my physical condition registered sharply on her face.

I tried to smile, but the pain quickly cut it short. "Well, it hurts when I laugh. There's a lot of pain." Exhaustion was beginning to set in, and I was having trouble forming coherent sentences. "No one's talked to me yet. I don't know."

The pain continued to race up and down me, causing everything to turn fuzzy. I found it extremely difficult to concentrate on anything. Some of my friends on the force came through and offered words of encouragement, but I had a hard time making any kind of a response. Another orderly came in and injected some novocaine to ease the pain in my mangled hand.

Some time later Jim Davis arrived, which took some of the pressure off Jeanne. He gave her some moral support and someone to talk with during the next few long hours.

If you've ever driven along a road on which you have to pass through heavily shaded areas, then back into the bright sunlight, and back into the shade again, that's exactly how my mind was functioning. I would catch a phrase or a word that made sense and then there would be nothing but mumbling and distant voices.

During one of those lucid moments, I heard shouting and angry voices coming from the hallway.

"Why wasn't I called immediately?" yelled one voice, obviously angry over something. "As soon as there was the slightest hint of nerve damage, I should have been called. It's been almost four hours! I'll talk to you later!" Then I heard a door slam, ending the one-sided conversation. Stomping feet drew near the X-ray room and then entered.

"Good evening, I'm Dr. John Raaf. I'm the hospital's chief neurosurgeon." Dr. Raaf was probably in his early fifties; he had a slim but athletic build and moved quickly. His voice was gentle yet positive, radiating self-confidence.

His eyes darted quickly from me to Jeanne and back to me. "Jess, I've just gone over your X rays, and there's not an awful lot I can tell at the moment. It looks like a couple of your lower vertebrae took a pretty good whack. But just how much damage, well, I won't know until I take a closer look."

He must have seen the puzzlement as well as the pain on my face. "I mean we're going to have to operate in order to get a closer look. How do you feel?"

"Terrible. The pain never goes away." My voice was soft and weak.

Raaf smiled at Jeanne. "He's all right. We're going to give him something that'll make any pain go away. He's a strong man and has a solid heartbeat, so don't worry. We'll take care of him."

"Doctor," I called out in between pain spasms, "was that you across the hallway a few minutes ago?"

Raaf nodded. "That was me. I get rather testy as the evening wears on."

Jeanne looked down at me and then back to Raaf. "We heard you say something about calling you sooner."

"Well, yes. Any time there is an indication of possible nerve damage, pressure on the nervous system, the quicker that pressure can be relieved the less damage will be done to the nerves. I should have been called immediately. I don't know what happened. Apparently everyone was caught up with whether or not you were going to live. As for contacting me, well I guess that's a moot question now."

"What's going to happen now?" Jeanne asked. It was the same question my mind was pondering, but somehow I couldn't make my mouth work. It seemed as if my tongue were enlarging as I lay there. It felt heavy, as if someone had sneaked in while I was unconscious and painted it with a thick coat of chalk.

"Right now, we're going to take Jess upstairs to the operating room and perform what we in the trade refer to as a laminectomy."

"A what?"

"Laminectomy. Basically, it's a detailed cleaning of the injured areas, removing bone fragments, clotted blood, and foreign objects." Jeanne paled slightly and Raaf smiled. "Aren't you glad you asked?"

I heard myself asking the doctor for something to kill the pain, and seconds later I felt a needle plunge into my hip. As I was wheeled down the hallway, everything became wonderful and the pain had been banished. Then I vaguely recall some bright lights overhead, people in green uniforms and masks peering down at me, there was another needle, and then nothing.

For the next four days there would be only murky ghosts moving quietly in and out of my life. Voices were soft, muffled, and distant. It was difficult to relate to anything except an acute awareness of pain, knife-stabbing bolts of pain that surfaced every time the drugs began to wear off. But before the pain could really establish itself and break through the wall of relief thrown up by the drugs, another needle would arrive and create another period of cloudy, hazy existence.

I was aware of being turned every so often and of the pain that accompanied the turning. It was a means of preventing fluids from collecting in my lungs and increasing the chance of pneumonia. But the turning always caused a need for me to cough, and each time I did, the bolts of pain would lash out in all directions. Even in a semiconscious state, I soon tried to suppress the coughing fits or at least to cough gently, neither of which turned out to be a satisfactory remedy.

Occasionally I recognized Jeanne's voice penetrating the veil that had closed around my mind, and I would attempt to respond, but I'm sure my comments must have been as vague and murky as my mental condition.

Jeanne

As I watched them wheel Jess into the operating room that first night, I knew immediately our lives would never be the same again. Where we would go from here, I couldn't imagine, but I felt the shift. As the doors shut, I said a prayer and left the final result in the hands of God.

It was about eleven o'clock when Jess went in, and by that time Jim Davis and the other policemen had left. For about fifteen minutes I was alone in the waiting room, trying to sort out a suddenly jumbled and complicated life. I was in a total state of shock. One minute my major concern was whether or not the round steak was going to dry out and then suddenly I was faced with the trauma of having a husband who thirty feet away lay shattered on an operating table.

It never occurred to me that Jess might die. I'm not really sure why it didn't. I guess I just assumed God wasn't ready to take him. But other concerns raced through my mind like so many cars on a busy freeway, each frantically trying to reach the same destination. What had the children been told and how were they reacting? What about money? Should I call Jess's relatives? How were our lives going to change? The list of questions went on.

My trance was finally broken by a gruff voice speaking in as soft a voice as possible. "Mrs. Roe?"

"What?"

"Are you Mrs. Roe?"

I found myself staring up at a big, stockily built man with a rather ruddy complexion. His suit, though well fitted, seemed to look out of place on the man, and he seemed to feel out of place in the hospital waiting room. He looked extremely ill at ease as he stood there, not sure whether to sit down next to me or to continue his search for Mrs. Roe.

The man was Captain Bill Hilbruner, Jess's night commander. It took me a few seconds to understand that he wasn't there to check on Jess but rather to keep me company. My mind was still a bit sluggish, still preoccupied with the events of the evening, but he gently led my thoughts away from Jess and guided the conversation toward innocuous subjects, topics I'm sure he hadn't the slightest interest in but cheerfully chatted about for the next two and a half hours. I was surprised that such a big, rough-looking man could be so warm and interesting. A first glance might have led you to believe he was only interested in football or boxing, but he talked enthusiastically about everything from gardening to gourmet cooking.

In between the eradication of aphids and marinated steaks, Jess's brother, J.B., arrived and joined in. Only the appearance of Dr. Raaf around two in the morning broke up the three-way conversation. Raaf, still in his surgical gown, looked almost as tired as I felt.

"How is he?" I asked, wanting to know but not sure I really wanted to hear.

Raaf shrugged his shoulders slightly and exhaled. "I wish I could tell you more right now, Mrs. Roe. I realize that not knowing is probably worse than knowing. But at this point, well, we really can't tell. He's suffered spinal nerve damage. That's the worst part, and it has caused some paralysis in the legs. How much? That's going to take some time to determine. We can't say right now whether or not it's permanent. Sometimes nature does wonderful things that are beyond medical science. But I wouldn't be too hopeful."

Raaf was right. Not knowing is worse. He told me very little. With only hints to go on, my mind could fabricate all kinds of problems based on the fears working deep inside me. "Can I see him now?"

Dr. Raaf thought for a second. "Well," he said with a heavy sigh, "you can look in on him if you want, but he's asleep and, to be honest with you, he's going to be under pretty heavy sedation for the next few days. I doubt very much he'll even know you're here. You look exhausted. Why don't you go home and get some rest. Come back in the morning; you'll feel a lot better. I can tell you that he has a good, strong pulse and is breathing strongly. Go home. It's going to be a couple of long weeks ahead for you."

Everyone agreed with the doctor, and Captain Hilbruner mentioned that he would make sure a policewoman was assigned to watch the children while I was at the hospital. The rest of the evening and much of the next few days still remain a blur. When I got home, I fell into a shallow, nervous sleep and awoke even more exhausted than before.

The phone began ringing at seven-thirty in the morning and continued until I finally left for the hospital. Neighbors were calling to see how Jess was and to offer help. For the next couple of weeks the phone rang constantly as friends volunteered to take care of the children, drive me back and forth to the hospital, or take care of the house. They were all well-meaning in their offers, but the continuous phone calls prevented me from getting any rest at all. The only thing that saved me from a complete collapse was the fact that the children were being cared for. Mike was staying with Jess's brother, and my mother had Chris and Sus.

With little sleep and the uncertainty about Jess's condition, my nerves were completely frayed and reaching the breaking point. Just how close I was to a breakdown was brought to my attention one day after arriving home from my daily visit to the hospital. I suddenly realized I had absolutely no recollection of the trip home even though I had been driving. I couldn't remember stoplights, the streets, or anything else! I was a danger not only to myself but to anyone else out on the highway. I mentally forced myself to calm down and regain control of my life. I told myself I couldn't help Jess if I couldn't first help myself. It took most of the evening, but I finally started functioning like a rational person again. Until then I had been striking out in ten different directions at the same time and accomplishing very little. That one night of self-analysis would prove invaluable in the coming months.

Meanwhile, Jess was mending. As Dr. Raaf predicted, for the first four days he didn't recognize anyone, although there were moments when I thought he responded to my voice, but for the most part he remained unaware of his surroundings. I would sit in that quiet room and listen to him breathe and watch the various liquids drip steadily from bottles hanging over his bed into tubes that were connected to his body. All I could do was offer my moral support and pray. Everything else was in God's hands.

Occasionally Jim or a few of the other policemen would drop by and talk for a few minutes, and their visits boosted my spirits. Regardless of why you're in a hospital, it is one of the most depressing places I can think of to be alone, especially in the late evening. Unknown voices whisper in the night, which somehow makes them ominous, and you notice the sterile, antiseptic atmosphere surrounding you. I always imagined that a hospital was much like a space station with its artificial environment.

For four days I watched over Jess. His complexion slowly shifted from an ash-gray on the first day to a healthy pink by the end of the fourth and finally, on the fifth day, his eyes showed awareness. But it was also obvious that he was in terrible pain.

The veil that had clouded my mind and protected me from the pain finally lifted, but the pain stayed on, giving me a new definition of and respect for the word. Pain is such a relative term, understood only in terms of experience. To one person, it's a pinprick, to another a broken leg. For me, as I came out of that drug-induced fog, pain suddenly reached a degree I had never thought possible. Lightning bolts shot up and down my back, raced up to my shattered hand, then seemed to gather as a loud, excruciating explosion in the small of my back. I did not, at the time, notice those bolts never traveled much lower than my waist.

There was a forest of bottles hanging above my bed, suspended by chrome posts. One set of tubes filled me up with medicine and nourishment, a second set emptied me. I never had to leave the bed. Of course, I couldn't have left it even if I had wanted to. I was totally immobile, strapped tightly to an unyielding board, which must have been made from the world's sturdiest oak.

Finally, as my eyes moved around as much of the room as I could see, I came upon Jeanne sitting there quietly. She smiled when she saw my eyes focus on her.

"Hi," she said quietly.

My mouth was dry, my tongue still coated with chalk. Whoever painted it did a terrific job. "How long have I been here?"

"Four days. How do you feel?"

A few lightning bolts fired off as if to accentuate the question. "Terrible."

"Would you like to be turned?"

"Yeah."

I know in a lot of Hollywood movies the conversations between husband and wife, or lovers, is a lot more exciting or heartwarming, but to be honest with you, there was too much pain to try to be clever, loving, or witty. My mental process was mostly directed at trying to blot out the pain, not at making light conversation.

Those hands that had been turning me during the first four days belonged to a nurse named Mrs. Bones. I never knew her first name, but she was a really warm person, with gentle hands that seemed to understand or sense the presence of pain. Jeanne rang the buzzer and almost instantly I could hear the soft squeaking of rubber soles coming down the hallway.

Mrs. Bones was a large woman. Not especially heavy, but large, big-boned. With a quick flip she put me on my stomach, which eased some of the pressure building in the lower back region. "If you need anything, Mr. Roe, you just call. I'm right down the hall." She smiled at me, then Jeanne, and was gone.

Jeanne talked with me for a couple of hours, but I was still having some difficulty concentrating on the conversation. My mind would doze off, or, as it attempted to fend off another round of lightning bolts, would block out her voice. Finally, around ten in the evening, Jeanne left. It was a routine she would follow for the next four and a half months. In all that time, she was with me during every visiting period from ten in the morning until ten at night. She missed only two days. I always knew that anytime I opened my eyes, she would be there, smiling, offering encouragement. No one could have offered more love.

Early the next morning, Dr. Raaf appeared at the foot of my bed and studied me for a second. Then, with all the warmth of Robert Young, he smiled. "Well, how're we feeling this morning, Jess?"

"Terrible."

Raaf chuckled sympathetically. "I'm not surprised. You've been through a lot over the past week. But you're on the mend now." He glanced at my chart and looked back at me. "I need to make a few tests. You up to it?"

I nodded that I was. I knew I didn't have any dance lessons scheduled for the morning.

"I'm going to be checking your reflexes, Jess." He held up a rather impressive-looking needle. "I'll bet you never thought you'd wind up a pincushion, did you?" That Robert Young smile flashed again as he began prodding my skin. "Can you feel this? How 'bout that? Does this hurt?" The questions continued for about five minutes, before I felt a stabbing sensation around my hip. I was too tired and in too much pain to consider the significance of Dr. Raaf's probing, and he never registered any telltale expressions. He gave the impression of a very methodical professional going about his business.

After the pincushion, he worked on my feet. He had to tell me that, since I couldn't see. He was dragging a thin metal shaft across the bottom of both feet. If the toes curved downward, a normal reflex, things would be considered generally in order. If the toes didn't move, or turned upward, it would be an indication of severe paralysis. Both sets of toes turned upward, but I didn't know it and Dr. Raaf's face was again void of any telltale expression.

"Well, that'll be it for today, Jess. You get some rest and I'll be in tomorrow with another pin. Sometimes I swear I missed my calling! I should have gone into voodoo." He chuckled to himself as he walked out the door. Robert Young couldn't have laid a glove on him that day.

I was alone for a few minutes and there was a voice in the far recesses of my mind whispering softly, "You didn't feel the pin. He poked holes in your legs and you didn't feel it." It was a fleeting voice, off in the distance, and it was gone before I could focus on it. But it would become louder and more demanding as the days passed. Overhead, I noticed the acoustic-tile ceiling and wondered how many holes were up there.

The next three weeks passed quickly, although each day seemed like an eternity. I had been in the hospital twenty-one days before Jeanne brought the children in to see me. I could tell by their reaction they understood I had been seriously injured and was still not very strong.

Both Mike and Chris (Sus was too young to bring to the hospital) walked quietly into the room and spoke in soft whispers. Mike was the first to speak.

"Hi, Dad. Are you going to be all right?"

Children have a way of getting right to the heart of the matter. I tried to laugh. "Sure. Don't you remember? I told you policemen were tough. This is only a scratch. I'll be up and out of here in a couple more weeks." I glanced over at Jeanne. "The doctor said I was getting a lot stronger."

And I thought I was. I was aware of the fact I had lost a lot of weight, but I assumed that was due to the liquid diet I was on. It never occurred to me to ask why I was on that diet and probably no one would have told me at the time that my intestinal tract was paralyzed. Yet I believed I was getting stronger and that I would walk out of that hospital in a few more weeks.

Both Mike and Chris chattered enthusiastically about school and Little League, the new friends they had made, and their both signing up for swimming lessons. Listening to them talk, I felt the first twinge of helplessness, of not being able to contribute to the family, of not being there to watch them grow. But I was sure it was only a matter of two or three weeks and then things would be back to normal.

Jim Davis somehow managed to finagle an assignment at the

hospital. He found out that one of the prisoners needed medical treatment lasting more than a week and convinced his commander he was the man for the guard job. It was fortunate his prisoner was in no shape to escape because Jim spent most of the time down in my room.

Davis was a walking rumor mill. He had the latest information on everything going on in the police department. The most serious rumor was a report originating in Washington, D.C., that a Senate subcommittee on organized crime was gathering its forces for a major investigation of certain Portland political and police officials.

A week after the rumors arrived, so did a young assistant to the U. S. Attorney General. For many Northwesterners, it was the first time they heard the name Bobby Kennedy. Apparently his visit to Portland was not a particularly productive one and he got little cooperation. In exasperation, he told the Attorney General upon his return to the capital that next time he might have to punch a few noses in to get Portland's attention. That remark was immediately printed in the local Portland papers and more than one angered citizen, not amused at the young man's wisecrack, vowed to meet Mr. Kennedy at the airport for the privilege of exchanging punches.

But serious discussions were kept to a minimum. Jim took special delight in passing along the latest antics around the precinct. Veterans were always good for one or two great stories a week. Rookies could always be counted on to bungle themselves into three or four embarrassing situations, and if you could team up a rookie and a veteran in one story, it was considered an epic.

Davis's favorite epic was the torture a green rookie put a gruff veteran through during the midnight watch. Bill Anderson had better than twenty years on the force, which meant he didn't drive. That was the low-seniority man's task, and since Bill was extremely nervous in a car, and wanted to retire in one piece, he always demanded the best driver. The fact that Bill managed to commandeer the best drivers night after night upset more than one of the other senior officers, and they plotted their revenge.

Stanley Adleman was the revenge. Stanley, despite being twenty-five years old, had never driven a car. But since it was a department requirement that every officer have a driver's license, somehow Stanley managed to get his hands on a license the same day he joined the force. But he was the worst driver anyone had ever seen. He couldn't drive a lick. After the shift was over, people would race out into the parking lot and try to get their cars out of the way before Stanley got into his.

Somehow Bill Anderson hadn't heard about Stanley and the web was slowly woven. The other veterans kept Stanley under wraps until one night when drivers were scarce and Anderson needed a driver.

Although Anderson was leery of taking a rookie, everyone kept telling him what a great driver Stanley was and how carefully he drove. Before they had gone two blocks, Stanley had run two red lights, run up over a curb or two, and run another car off the street. Anderson began screaming after one block and after two was begging Stanley to stop the car. Anderson must have seen his entire pension flashing before his eyes as Stanley brought the car to rest up on the curb.

Jim's stories were a great morale booster for me. They got me through some terrible evenings.

In between Jeanne and Davis's visits I had one unscheduled visitor. Just down the hallway from my room was the hospital's ward for mentally unstable patients. Twice during my stay, a patient managed to escape. One made his way into my room, which made for an extremely uncomfortable situation. Apparently I was in no real danger, but as the man stood there with a glazed look on his face I suddenly realized just how vulnerable I was. As he stared at the tubes, I could almost see his hand reaching out and ripping the tubes out of my body. But he did nothing but stare. Finally a nurse came by and escorted him back to his room.

Those are moments that come immediately to mind when I remember those early days.

One of the most inspirational persons I've ever known I met in the hospital. Monica Stuckart. Nurses always brought up her name in conversations with Jeanne and me. All we ever heard was how wonderful and brave this little woman was. Finally, one day while I was asleep, Jeanne walked down the hall and introduced herself to Monica and her husband, John.

Monica and John came from a small farming community just

east of Salem, Oregon. The two owned a modest dairy farm and had two small children. What seemed to be a typical happy life turned frightening when Monica suddenly began to complain of extreme back pains. When she began to lose feeling in both legs, she was brought to Portland for surgery. A seven-inch tumor was removed from her spine, but the operation was too late. She had suffered complete paralysis in both legs. Despite that loss, she was a cheerful, happy young woman, who thanked God each day for giving her another day on earth, another day with her husband and children.

Her husband would come in occasionally and discuss farm business with me because of the time I had spent selling farm equipment before joining the police department. Like Monica, he accepted her misfortune as God's will: a part of life that God intended for them to live. I never heard either of them question why it had happened or express any anger. Monica's only concern was to get back to her family. That was her single goal, and she never lost sight of it. I remember thinking to myself how angry I would be under similar circumstances. I envied her, but was thankful I wasn't faced with such a challenge. I felt I was getting better, but I had been in the hospital for close to a month now and was ready to be released from the torture rack they had strapped me to. All Dr. Raaf would say to me was that I was getting stronger. He always avoided saying when I might be able to go home.

Jeanne

Jess did not know he would never walk again, although I had been told about eight days after the accident. Dr. Raaf had examined Jess a number of times and each time the results were the same, a total paralysis from the waist down. There was no means of correcting the situation. He'd have to be told, of course, but I just couldn't bear to do it immediately.

I convinced myself that he wasn't strong enough yet, that he needed a few more days. Meanwhile he talked about quitting the force and perhaps going back to college. He thought that perhaps he could qualify for some kind of medical benefits because of the accident. I knew he was growing weary of the hospital, and he constantly mentioned the fact that Dr. Raaf seemed vague about his release date. Yet he had never mentioned the possibility that he might never walk again. It was just something that had not occurred to him.

CHAPTER THREE

As the days slowly drifted into weeks, I discovered that I was going through a physical metamorphosis. Hardly a day would go by without a new tube, counterweight, brace, or traction board being added to me somewhere. I accused the doctor of making me his term art project.

As much as I tried to keep my spirits up, I could feel the bitterness creeping more and more into my voice, lashing out like a knife at my family and friends. For a month I had done nothing but count the number of holes in the acoustic-tile ceiling and listen to the hospital noises.

There were 842 holes in the ceiling. For more than a week I had thought there were 843, but one of the black spots I was counting hatched and flew away.

As for the hospital noises, they were getting on my nerves. Throughout the night I could hear the reverent whispers of nurses as they moved softly up and down the halls, their rubber-soled shoes squeaking on the waxed floors. Occasionally there would be a note of alarm in their voices, a sound of urgency in the tempo of the footsteps. You could always tell when someone was dying, and I lay there strapped to that torture rack they called traction and silently waited for my turn.

The mornings were always heralded by the clanking of the breakfast gurneys, the rattle of pans, and the demands of the nurses that everyone rise and shine at 5:30—half an hour before the sun. At 6 A.M. promptly, one of my favorite nurses, Mrs. Nail, would appear with her good-morning smile and give me a light going-over with a washcloth. My face and whatever skin hadn't disappeared under the layers of gauze and plaster got a scrubbing. As she was finishing up, I could hear the squeaky wheels of the food gurney and the rattle of plates and metal signaling that breakfast was being served.

In between breakfast and lunch I waited for the occasional visitor to drop by for a chat and for the doctor to appear on his daily rounds.

It never ceased to amaze me how suddenly he and his nurse would appear at the end of my bed. One moment I would be alone, fighting off the depression that hospitals seem to create if you're there for more than a week, and then, as if by magic, he would be at the end of the bed silently studying my chart. His glasses always seemed to be resting precariously on the bridge of his nose. His eyes would dart questioningly over the top of his glasses at me, then return to his chart.

"Well, Jess, how are we doing today?"

It was always the same question, and after three weeks I was becoming a bit irritable. The pain had diminished slightly but had not gone away, and I was still strapped to a board like some kind of monster who was the subject of experiments all in the name of science.

"I guess one of us is doing all right," I snapped. "At least you have your legs. As for me! Well, that's your department. Tell me, how am I doing?"

Dr. Raaf would smile weakly and bring out his pin and begin poking my feet and legs. "Can you feel that?" was the stock question, followed by my equally stock "No!" Because of the angle at which I was lying, my midsection was forced upward, causing my head to tilt downward. I couldn't see exactly what he was doing, but I understood it was related to my chances of walking again.

I wanted so desperately to feel the pain of that needle plunging into my flesh that I would actually wince, but there was no pain, no feeling. That voice in the far corner of my mind grew a little louder. "You can't feel anything. There should be pain and there's nothing. Will your life be nothing, also?" Then it would disappear as Raaf began talking.

"You're getting stronger, Jess," he said, smiling encouragingly. "Everyone's impressed by your progress."

I was less impressed and felt the doubts begin to grow about ever using my legs again. No one ever gave me a straight answer when I asked. Jeanne would say the doctors were still running tests, the doctors would tell me the tests weren't completed or were inconclusive.

"What about my legs, Doc? I can't feel anything. You come in every morning and stick a needle in me, and I can't feel anything. Am I going to get my legs back?"

"Jess, you're improving every day. Right now, just concentrate on getting stronger, physically and mentally."

"Well, how 'bout getting me out of this torture rack, then. It's killing my back!"

Raaf chewed on the end of his pen for a second and then smiled. "Well, that's a reasonable request. But you still have some mending to do," and with that he would walk away, leaving me there to stare at the holes and wonder why God would do this to me.

I made halfhearted attempts to pray, mostly because Jeanne felt better when I did, but I was sure that if God was listening, He'd see the bitterness in my heart, the growing hatred and resentment I felt for being made to suffer.

I was a corpse up to my waist and the rest of me wasn't in much better shape. My right hand had been shattered and hung there uselessly suspended in midair, each finger individually immobilized to allow the bones and tendons to heal. The bed, as I mentioned, was arched in the middle, forcing my upper torso into a painful, downward angle. Waves of pain rolled up and down my back, but always stopped ominously at my waist.

Later I would hear a song written by Janis Ian about returning soldiers crippled in Vietnam; it expressed some of the frustration I was beginning to feel and the belief that others didn't understand what I was going through.

Yet I still clung to the hope that I would walk again, that everything would, given enough time, return to normal. It wasn't fair, I told myself, that my wife and children should have to suffer. If I couldn't work, they would be deprived of a steady income; without a whole father, my son would lack the proper guidance while growing up. I told myself I wanted to walk again for their sake, but deep down inside I knew my only concern was for me. I didn't want to be a cripple.

During the first couple of weeks I had managed to maintain a stable, optimistic outlook about my future; but as time wore on and my anxieties about walking increased, my emotions became wildly erratic. I was beginning to exhibit all of the classic symptoms of a manic-depressive. My hopes would soar in response to the slightest encouragement and plummet to the deepest depths when I spotted a frown or felt no one understood the suffering I was experiencing.

Each individual, I believe, is allotted only so much time on earth, according to God's wish. He has given us that time in the hope we will seek out, develop, and employ those special skills He has given each of us. It is to be hoped that those skills or abilities will be used to better mankind. But time is a premium commodity and self-pity a ruthless robber of that time. It can become a full-time occupation, consuming entire days, producing nothing but hate and resentment.

I squandered a great deal of time during those trying days on feeling sorry for myself and watching the clear fluids drip steadily into plastic tubes attached to my body. I continually turned my life over and over. What had I done that might have angered God enough to cause Him to put me through this suffering, to take away my legs?

"Why me?" was the recurring question. I had been a good father and a good husband, and as a policeman I put my life on the line every day in order to protect others. Surely, then, I told myself, this pain was only a temporary condition. "All things shall pass," Jeanne had said, and I began grasping at that phrase, giving it a literal interpretation—that the paralysis which bound my legs would pass. It was during these attempts to comprehend the past month of my life that I would pray. I would pray for my legs.

For thirty-two days I stared at that ceiling, counting the holes, recalling the days when I had legs, thinking of those fall hunting trips into the Cascade mountains, remembering when I had played baseball with my son, mentally trying to blot out the fact that I was strapped to a hard slab, enduring stabbing pains that traveled constantly up and down my back.

"Every day just a little stronger, every day just a little closer." I had read the phrase in *Reader's Digest* and had one of the nurses tape it to the metal post that supported those bottles of clear fluid slowly emptying into my body. The philosophy helped me during the desperate black moments when I was ready to give up.

Another support was the nurses. From my position on the bed, the only window I could look out of gave me a view of Portland's

West Hills. During the summer months it would have been an inspirational view, but during the spring it could become extremely depressing. It was over those hills that the black rain clouds from the Pacific Ocean would come rolling in, signaling a daylong deluge.

But no sooner would the clouds begin to gather than there would be a nurse at my side, smiling, laughing, armed with humorous stories to help ward off depression. I always felt their encouragement came from the heart. Only once was a visit obviously forced. That was the day I met Dr. Kimberly.

Mrs. Nail arrived shortly after the first clouds gathered over the West Hills, but she acted nervous. Although we talked at great length about the fight on TV the night before and about Elvis Presley's influence on the younger generation, she never looked directly into my eyes. She busied herself with shuffling papers, arranging flowers, and moving magazines while she talked. I began to feel uncomfortable about it and mentioned it. She apologized and said she wasn't feeling well, but I sensed something else. There was sorrow in her eyes. Before I had an opportunity to pursue the matter, she suddenly left, saying the doctor would be in in a few minutes.

I puzzled over her actions for a moment or two, then dismissed them as unimportant. Everyone has a bad day.

With breakfast over, nothing on television, and a spring downpour about to commence, I was resigned to another gloomy day. As I drifted off into a shallow sleep, I kept thinking, "Every day just a little stronger, every day just a little closer." It continued to give me hope.

I'm not sure how long he had been standing there before I became aware of him, but he had obviously been talking for some time. It was like tuning in mid-sentence on a radio newscast. You find yourself trying to piece things together while trying to keep up with the rest of the story. The picture is never quite clear.

"I'm sorry, I didn't get your name?"

"My name is Dr. A. Gurney Kimberly," the man said rather gruffly. There was a hint of a Scottish accent in his voice and a suggestion of arrogance on his face. "I've done more spinal fusions than anyone else in the world." He didn't actually say that he was the best surgeon in the world, but he left little doubt that he believed it.

I was still a bit confused, since I had come in in the middle of his discussion, and my first reaction was that someone had forgotten to tuck this one into his padded cell. He stood there talking rather rapidly, seemingly enjoying his conversation immensely. He was a rather thin, wiry man, dressed in a green surgical gown and wearing one of those odd-looking green caps. I nodded whenever he stopped talking, but really hadn't the foggiest idea of what he was talking about. A few words did manage to penetrate my confusion, words like "fusion," "operation," and "new life." But I wasn't concentrating on his words as much as on his hands, wondering when this lunatic might start ripping the tubes out of me. I found myself praying for a nurse to arrive and rescue me.

Meanwhile he continued to chatter away. "I'm going to have you up and out of here in a matter of weeks," he said, rubbing his hands together enthusiastically. He paced back and forth in front of the bed as he talked, occasionally glancing at his watch. "You're fortunate to have me here, Jess. You couldn't be in better hands."

There wasn't any one word or gesture that transformed him in my eyes from a raving lunatic into a world-renowned surgeon, but gradually I became convinced he really was who he claimed to be and not someone just playing doctor.

"You hang in there for a couple of days, concentrate on getting stronger, and then I'm going to operate. I'll fuse that back of yours, and, with leg braces, you'll be out of here in no time. Can't have you wasting your time lying around here acting as the hospital pincushion, right?"

Dr. Kimberly laughed at his own joke, slapped me on the shoulder, and walked out the door before I had a chance to say anything. But my mind was racing about, with a hundred different thoughts bouncing into one another. "Going to operate"! "You'll be out of here in no time"! Suddenly the pain didn't matter anymore. I was in a state of euphoria. I was going to walk again! The room seemed to spin as the dark clouds of doubt and worry disappeared. Dr. Kimberly was going to give me back my legs! I was light-headed with joy. For a month I had prayed for recovery but secretly expected the worst. Now it was over. I thanked God for guiding me through this trial.

By the time the nurse had returned, my mind had begun noticing the pain again, but I was still excited by the news. She was obviously surprised by my radiant appearance.

"Has the doctor spoken to you yet?"

"Yes." I beamed. "He was here just a few minutes ago." I laughed nervously, still ecstatic over what I assumed had been a reprieve from a wheelchair. "Everything's going to be fine. Dr. Kimberly said he's going to operate and that I'll be back on my feet and walking again." I couldn't suppress the grin on my face. I felt like a kid who had just hit his first Little League home run or brought home a straight-A report card.

A troubled look swept across her face. "Dr. Kimberly said you'd be walking again? Is that what he said?" The concern and doubt that seeped into her voice were chilling.

"Well, yes—ah—that's what he said." I had meant my response to be emphatic, but I couldn't hide the anxiety that suddenly appeared in my voice. Had I misunderstood? "Why, is there something wrong?"

Mrs. Nail smiled weakly and shook her head. "No, it's nothing, Jess." She glanced at her watch and smiled again. "Time for your pain pill. You've had a busy morning."

I tried to discuss Dr. Kimberly with her, but she gave evasive answers or ignored the questions altogether. She hurried out of the room, leaving me alone. The exhilaration had left me, replaced by a nagging doubt. Once more the stabbing pains made their presence felt.

For the next fifteen minutes I tried to reconstruct the conversation Kimberly had had with me. I was positive he had said he'd have me up and walking again. He was so forceful, so positive, I knew I couldn't have misunderstood him. I convinced myself that the nurse's uneasy actions were the result of something that had nothing to do with me.

Warmth began sweeping over me as the pain pill took effect. I drifted into a pleasant, relaxed state. The tiny knot of anxiety in the pit of my stomach, caused by the nurse, slowly dissipated. I could almost feel the warm waves rolling toward my feet.

I watched as sheets of rain rolled gently across the West Hills.

Every so often the clouds would shift, allowing just enough room for a few fingers of sunlight to knife their way to earth. Everywhere they touched down, a rainbow would blossom into a multitude of colors, then suddenly vanish as the clouds reclaimed the spring skies.

The sun and clouds battled throughout the morning as I slept. When I awoke, Dr. Kimberly was at the foot of my bed again. This time he was wearing a three-piece business suit and a stern expression, the kind that people always associate with impending bad news.

He glanced at the floor momentarily. "How're you feeling?"

"Fine," I responded. The pain pills left my tongue coated with a thin, chalky-tasting film. My tongue was still a bit thick. "Just thinking about that operation. I'm ready anytime you are." I tried to smile.

I saw the uneasiness flash across his face. "Jess," he began, rubbing his face with both hands, "I may have left you with a wrong impression about that operation."

I can still remember feeling the blood drain from my face. I wanted to stop him from going on, from correcting any wrong impression. I knew what he was going to say next, but no words came from my mouth, I just lay there staring at him.

"What I told you was that I'd have you up and out of here. With leg braces and crutches, you'll have a good deal of mobility. The operation is a fusion; it will strengthen your back, give you more leverage. I assumed you'd been told you'll never be able to use your legs again, there's just too much nerve damage. But I can promise you that you won't have to worry about being confined to a bed or wheelchair."

"Never be able to use your legs again." The statement slammed home like a sledgehammer. My throat went dry and a section of my brain began to scream deep inside my head. That voice that I had managed to keep in the distance was now yelling over and over, "Why me? Why me?" All of the fears I had successfully kept in check, under control, burst forth with the force of an avalanche. For a second my mind seemed to flash back to a baseball game, a bicycle ride, the laughter and giggling I engaged in as a child. I recalled racing across a meadow with a friend. Then it all simply evaporated with one phrase uttered by a man I hardly knew.

Dr. Kimberly mumbled something about being sorry about the misunderstanding and that he'd be back for another talk once I had considered the situation. He wandered out the door.

The lunch gurneys were clattering down the hallway, music was being piped into the rooms, voices faded in and out, and the footsteps moved quickly while I lay there staring at the ceiling.

The anger swelled up inside. I'd never walk again! I'd be a cripple strapped with iron leg braces, hobbling around on crutches! The voice kept screaming: "Why me? Why not some drug pusher? Why not some wino or prostitute? Why not some of that scum I've thrown in jail? Why not anyone but me!" Anger, frustration, and bitter resentment took turns raging through my mind. Where the hell was this God that my wife talked so confidently about? What kind of merciful God allowed policemen to be crippled?

I stared sullenly at the maze of plastic tubes that carried life into me and waste out. There was a catheter connected to a bag hung over the edge of the bed, just out of sight. If this was what I had to look forward to for the rest of my life, then life wasn't worthwhile.

Sounds meshed meaninglessly together—a call for a doctor in emergency, the gurneys rattling up and down the hallway—and the nurse came in and I read what I thought was pity in her eyes. She started to say something, but I cut her off angrily.

"Get out of here!" I shouted. "Stop staring at me and just get out! Leave me alone!" The viciousness in my voice surprised me.

I gazed at my shattered hand, my useless body, and laughed bitterly. My life had plummeted to its lowest ebb; I wanted to end it and I couldn't even move. Mentally checking off all possible means of suicide, I just as quickly discarded them as being impractical. Even to take my own life I was going to need help.

It's surprising how many ugly thoughts flash through your mind as your whole life is consumed with self-pity. I pictured my wife waiting patiently for me to die so she would be free of such a burden. My three children would suffer because they had only half a father. Depression enveloped me, and I could feel the frustration welling up inside.

Knifelike pains stabbed into my back, my temples throbbed in tempo with the pounding of my headache, and I was on the verge of screaming when suddenly the pain and tension vanished. The anger and frustration simply melted away, leaving in their place a pleasant, light sensation. Some force was cleansing my mind! If you've ever been in a situation where you thought you heard an unusual sound and immediately stopped everything, even breathing, in order to hear it again, then you can appreciate at least part of the sensation I was experiencing.

It was as if my mind had somehow disconnected itself from my battered body and was floating or drifting in ether. Yet I'm positive I wasn't hallucinating. I hadn't had any pain-killers, and I was in complete control of my faculties. The sensation continued for another thirty seconds or so until I had become accustomed to this increasingly tranquil condition.

As I lay there contemplating what was happening to me, wondering if this perhaps wasn't the afterglow of death, I heard a voice. To this day I couldn't say whether it was an inner voice or came from without, but there was no doubt that I heard it. It was soft, yet commanding; powerful, but not threatening. "You'll be all right," the voice stated. "Don't trouble yourself." There was a pause and the voice returned again. "You'll be all right. Don't trouble yourself," and then it vanished. That was more than two decades ago, and I'll never forget that day.

The pleasant, calming sensation continued for another two or three minutes and then disappeared. The pain returned, but now I knew I could cope with my present situation. I was sure I had been singled out for some kind of miracle, that God was letting me know that He was going to give me my legs back.

Still overwhelmed by the warm afterglow of my experience, I suddenly recalled a passage Jeanne had read to me the night before while trying to cheer me up. "Consider it pure joy, my brothers, whenever you face trials of many kinds, because you know that the testing of your faith develops perseverance." (James 1:2–3; NIV)

Suddenly I felt like a fool. Now I understood what James had been saying. It became so clear. God was testing me. He had taken away my legs in order to gauge my faith in Him. He had issued a challenge, and now it was up to me to respond. I thought God probably wouldn't make it easy for me, that it would be a hard struggle. But that was okay by me. I'd never doubt Him again. I would throw off the weight of self-pity and fight for my legs. He had shown me that I was the only person who could carry on the fight. There was a certain smugness in my heart, however, as I began mentally preparing for the struggle. The Lord had revealed to me that I would be all right. I took that to mean I would walk again.

Later in the afternoon the nurse came back into the room, walking very gingerly, probably hoping I would be asleep. When she discovered I was awake, I could see a certain amount of misgiving in her eyes.

I gave her my best reassuring smile and said teasingly, "Where have you been all day? When I asked you to leave, I didn't mean the state!"

Her eyebrows rose sharply, her eyes flashed. "I don't think 'asked' is the most accurate description of how you put it," Mrs. Nail replied. There was an icy bite in the tone of her voice.

"Look, I apologize about earlier. I had misunderstood what the doctor said and had gotten myself all worked up. I had visions of me hopscotching down the hallway and out of this place. I know there's no apology that can atone for the way I acted, but I really am sorry about that outburst. You've been extremely kind to me over the last few weeks."

The smile came back and she came over to my bed. "Actually, I think you're taking it pretty well. A lot of our patients simply fall to pieces."

"Well, I haven't given up hope of walking. The doctor told me himself they're doing a lot of tremendous things with orthopedic surgery these days. Besides, God will take care of me. I'll walk again."

She smiled faintly and nodded her head. "That's the right attitude," she said. "Don't give up."

We chatted for another fifteen minutes before Jeanne showed up for what I called "her afternoon vigil." It was obvious that she had talked with Dr. Kimberly. Her eyes were red and puffy.

"Oh, Jess, I'm sorry," she said, unable to hold back the tears.

"But it's all right. We can make it together. Things will work out for us. I know they will." She came over and kissed me and ran her hand across my face. Her warmth and love were transmitted through that gentle touch.

"I'm okay, Jeanne. Don't worry about me. I can handle it. I really can. God's going to protect us."

I could sense the puzzlement that gripped her as she studied my face, trying to fathom what I had just said. "This may be hard for you to understand, in fact I'm not sure I understand it, but something wonderful happened to me today, and I know things will work out for us."

"What do you mean?"

I spent the next few minutes describing the sensation I had experienced, finding it extremely difficult to contain the enthusiasm I felt. When I finished, Jeanne just sat there with that puzzled look on her face. "Don't you believe me?"

"Yes, of course I believe you."

"It really happened, Jeanne! I know it sounds farfetched, but it really happened!"

"I believe you, Jess," she said, with little conviction. She sounded like someone trying to appease a child.

"Jeanne, I really experienced this, this—ah—sensation! It happened and it must have been God! There's no other explanation! I'm positive I wasn't dreaming or hallucinating!"

It took a few hours, but gradually Jeanne began to accept my experience as fact. There would never be a way for her to share completely those few exceptional minutes of my life, but she understood that something profound had taken place and that it had helped me over a crucial hurdle in my life. For those reasons alone, she gave thanks to God and prayed that He would be there when the next obstacle arose. She was much more objective and practical about our future, while I had assumed that our greatest challenge had been solved by a promise from God. I smugly thought to myself, "How simple life is when you have faith."

We talked steadily for the next few hours, discussing the problems we were going to face. Jeanne insisted we consider the fact that I might never be totally mobile again, and while I knew that God had assured me that I would be "all right," that I would walk again, I agreed to consider the possibility.

Bolstered by what I considered to be a promise from God, I managed to survive the next few months. As from a savings account, I drew heavily upon what I thought was a guarantee. When pain flooded over my body, I'd concentrate on that brief moment of euphoria when I'd been assured I'd "be all right."

But as I continually drew upon that account, I forgot a basic rule: "You must return as much as you withdraw or your account diminishes." Drawing upon the faith that God offered me, I never offered my faith in return. Without realizing it, I was rapidly dissolving my bond with the Lord. But it happened slowly.

One month from the day my motorcycle skidded under that train I went back into the operating room to have my back fused. The thought of the operation frightened me, but I knew it was the first step back.

Three days before the operation, Dr. Kimberly announced that before he could operate, he'd first have to hyperextend my back. Hyperextension sounded innocent enough, but there's a lot to be said for blissful ignorance. Not realizing how painful it would be, I went more or less jokingly to my own Spanish Inquisition.

Hyperextension is basically stretching, but there was a twist—they were stretching *me!* After extending my spine on what should be considered the rack, Dr. Kimberly put me face up on an operating table that was in three sections. One nurse held my shoulders down, and another my feet. Then Dr. Kimberly cranked the middle section upward, to align the spinal vertebrae so they could be X-rayed before being fused. The pain was so intense that I was on the verge of passing out at least three different times.

The operating room was stifling and everyone's patience was wearing thin. Dr. Kimberly would turn the crank, and I would groan loudly and tell him I didn't think I could take any more, and he'd turn the crank another notch, then study my spine again.

Each time he turned the crank, an X-ray technician would take a picture. I could hear the crank turn, then a pleasant voice telling me to take a deep breath and hold it. During the first part of the session I didn't mind her constant request to take a breath and hold it. But as the tension on my spine grew with intensity and pain, it was becoming increasingly difficult just to breathe, let alone hold it. Dr. Kimberly sensed my agony, but continued to turn the crank.

An unseen hand wiped away the river of perspiration flowing down into my eyes. Occasionally, when it became obvious that I was on the verge of passing out, Kimberly would yell, "Don't let him pass out!" and I'd get hit in the face with an ice-cold towel. He didn't want me to become unconscious because then my muscles would relax, preventing him from observing their normal function along the spinal column.

Someone, not Kimberly, mentioned something about being sorry about the pain. "Don't worry, this beats watching 'Edge of Night,' " I groaned as cheerfully as possible.

"Considering your position, I can't imagine what you'd be laughing about, Jess," Kimberly said in a half-irritated, half-amused voice. He began bending my legs back again, forcing them back and up over my head.

"Take a deep breath and hold it," the technician chimed in.

"You know that old expression, 'kissing someone's feet'? Well, I never thought it would be my own. Besides, you've never had to sit through 'Edge of Night.' "

Kimberly shook his head as he turned the crank. "That's not very funny."

"Funnier than what you're doing to me." I winced as the pain began to build again.

"Take a deep breath and hold it."

After an hour of hyperextension, Kimberly still had not developed the space he wanted between the four vertebrae he was interested in. From my position, all I could see were my feet and an occasional hand darting in and out to wipe the perspiration from my face. Every so often a white-masked face would peer into my eyes, seeming to challenge my right to pass out. If I looked as if I was about to, an icy towel followed immediately. I knew I couldn't take the pain much longer.

"Take a deep breath and hold it."

"Jess," I heard Kimberly call out, "what I'm doing, in case you're interested, is preparing enough space between the vertebrae so that I can perform the spinal fusion.

"Basically, during the fusion, I'll cut away the flesh from the vertebrae and then, using bone slivers taken from your hip, I'll place them vertically in the gaps. They will grow, or fuse, to the spine and establish additional support for the back."

Kimberly sounded as if he were reciting a grocery list as he explained, clinically, what was going to happen. It was almost as if he were talking just to keep himself from getting bored. I'm sure he would have been offended if I'd actually passed out during his impromptu lecture.

I'm not sure how long we had been in the operating room, but the tension, heat, and pain were beginning to show, even on Kimberly as he continued to turn the crank.

"Take a deep breath and hold it." The once pleasant voice had become almost mechanical, and I could hardly breathe now as the pain was reaching my threshold of tolerance.

"Take a deep breath and hold it." The request was repeated.

"If you don't take that blasted picture," came an angry threat from Kimberly, "I'm going to strap you on this table next! Take the picture!"

The doctor's outburst caused a gasp from the offending technician and a few stifled chuckles from the attending nurses, and it managed to break some of the tension building inside me. Kimberly finished the rest of his work in what was probably record time, then pronounced me ready for the fusion operation.

That came three days later, and as they wheeled me into the operating room I had great hopes the operation, despite what everyone told me, would produce a miracle that would somehow restore my legs.

But when I awoke twenty-four hours later, with the nauseating after-odor of ether still in my lungs, I discovered that little had changed. The tubes, the bottles, and the pain, now worse than ever, still dominated my life. Dr. Kimberly didn't seem to notice the crushing blow his words dealt me as he went through the results of the operation.

His voice was cold and clinical, totally detached from any suffering I might be experiencing. "It was a perfect operation, Jess. We fused a section of four vertebrae, and I'd say that within a month you'll be able to get out of here. You can go home and start working with leg and back braces."

"What about my chances of walking without them?"

"Jess," he said impatiently, "we've talked about that before.

You'll never be able to walk without some kind of mechanical assistance." Kimberly gave me a playful slap on the shoulder and turned for the door. "Now you get some rest. It was a long operation. I'll be in to check on you tomorrow."

As he disappeared out the door, I could feel the accusing, frustrating anger return, the façade of faith crumbling like so much dry-rot wood. Self-pity spread like an out-of-control forest fire. I felt that I had been betrayed.

Jeanne arrived in the afternoon and saw the change immediately. Her obvious joy over the success of the operation quickly changed to deep concern.

"Jess, what's wrong?"

"Nothing," I snapped without looking at her, "nothing's the matter. Things couldn't be better; I can't imagine a better way of spending the rest of my life than lying around like a used hassock!" Self-pity dripped from every pore.

"But the doctor said everything is fine. The operation went perfectly. We can return to a normal life again. You'll be able to come home in a couple of weeks. I told the kids this morning that you'd be home soon. You should have seen them, they were ecstatic!"

"Look," I answered, still refusing to look at her, "if I'm going to be coming home, then you better start practicing how to push a wheelchair around! And while you're at it," I yelled, "start reading about catheters and how to move invalids in and out of bed!"

Tears welled up in the corners of her eyes. "I don't understand. A few days ago you were happy, willing to trust God. Now . . . now"—Jeanne paused, at a loss for words—"now you've crawled back into the same hole you were in a few weeks ago."

"Why shouldn't I? Nothing's changed. I'm still here, still in this body cast. All I know for sure is that, maybe, in a couple of months I'll be able to clank around the house like some metallic freak!"

I knew what I was doing to Jeanne, tearing her up inside, but I wanted to strike back at someone and she was the only one I could reach with words. Words were all I had to fight with because I had foolishly abandoned my faith.

That evening was one of the worst in my life. For the next two hours I inflicted all of the hate and venom in my soul upon

Jeanne. I hated each word I uttered, but I couldn't keep them from spewing forth. Never did Jeanne raise her voice to counter my tirade. Although the strain of the past month had affected her as much as it had me, she managed to keep control of her emotions. Tears fell silently as she endured my attacks and my indulgence in self-pity.

Although I managed to tone down my abusive manner, my overall perspective continued to slide, but I made an effort to hide it from Jeanne and the children when they came to visit. While I made no attempt to help myself, I realized that inflicting an additional burden upon them was not fair.

Jeanne

I knew Jess was facing a very traumatic period. The uncertainty was eating away at him. He was consumed by his worry over his and our future, what he could contribute to his family's welfare. Following the fusion operation, his judgment was extremely clouded. He was in a lot of pain, he was simply not the same man. I knew the real Jess was there somewhere, but I wasn't quite sure how to reach him. I prayed to God that Jess would realize that nothing had really changed, that with faith in God everything was still before us, not behind.

His frantic attacks were understandable, but they hurt. He had convinced himself that he was going to walk, and despite the warnings, he had refused to face reality. He was so sure that God would present a simple answer to his problems. When it didn't happen, for a few weeks his view of life was completely distorted.

As May slipped quietly into June, Oregon was caught in the middle of an early, extremely hot summer. Now, in addition to a raging pain, which radiated from the small of my back, and a growing depression, I was fighting a heat wave. On top of that, the hospital's air-conditioning system went into remission. The room was about 92 degrees, but inside my body cast the thermometer registered between 110 and 120 degrees.

To prevent my melting, Dr. Kimberly ordered my cast to be cut lengthwise on each side. That allowed either the top or bottom half to be removed, depending on which way I was lying, during the hottest part of the day. The nurses also packed me in bags of ice. I sometimes felt like an oyster on the half shell.

They had more or less eliminated the heat problem, but I was still left with the pain, and that problem resulted in some violent arguments with Dr. Kimberly. He remained adamant that I be given no pain pills, despite my obvious suffering. He still maintained that pain suppressants relaxed the muscles and slowed the healing process, compounding a patient's recovery time in terms of rebuilding the muscular structure. All he would allow was one sleeping pill each evening. I rarely got more than fifteen or twenty minutes of uninterrupted sleep a night.

The more I demanded something to ease the pain, the more adamant Kimberly became. Finally a young intern who had witnessed these heated shouting matches took pity on me and, without the doctor's knowledge, began giving me something to blot out the pain. I don't know what he was giving me, but it worked. For seven days I was able to sleep at night. I could feel my mind slowly drifting away from my body and those stabbing pains that kept pounding away. My fears and worries evaporated, although there was always a mild feeling of guilt tugging at me from the back of my mind.

I was rapidly becoming dependent upon the intern's magical drug to whisk me away from my problems. After five days, when I knew he was on the floor I'd complain pitifully about my excruciating pain. Within minutes he'd show up with two pills and a glass of water. I suppose it fleetingly crossed my mind that I was becoming addicted, but at that moment the effect far outweighed any possible danger.

Basically it created roughly the same kind of sensation I experienced during that brief encounter with the Lord, although it had neither the calming effect nor the lasting feeling of well-being. After each "trip," to borrow from today's generation, I came back to an ugly reality that drove my depression further and further down. I can see now how people become so easily addicted to narcotics and how frantic they must become during their encounters with the real world.

When Kimberly discovered what had been happening, he was absolutely furious. I could hear him and the intern screaming at each other at the other end of the building. The yelling match went on for several minutes and was finally cut short when the doctor told the intern that if he ever interfered with his treatment of a patient again, he could start looking for a new career.

The intern was transferred to another hospital and I was again left to deal with my personal hell, but without the drugs as a crutch. For two more weeks Kimberly stood guard, making sure I got nothing more than one sleeping pill every twenty-four hours, no matter how much I begged—and I did beg. I begged, cried, swore, and demanded. I told Jeanne to get a new doctor, but she stood her ground; speaking softly, but firmly, she said that Kimberly was the best there was.

Jeanne

I prayed for Jesus to give Jess the willpower to see it through. You could see in his face that he was in deep pain. His eyes pleaded for relief, his skin was drained of any color, and his face was a mask of exhaustion.

There were times when I would waver. After an especially emotional visit, I began to doubt Dr. Kimberly's treatment and went to another specialist. But he assured me that Dr. Kimberly was one of the best anywhere and that Jess was getting the best possible care.

Armed with this reassurance, I spent the next few days giving Jess as much encouragement and comfort as I could. It was as if I personally had committed my husband to the Tower of London and then had to keep telling him that he was being tortured for his own good. Knots seized my stomach as Jess cried out for something to ease the pain. All I could do was keep telling him over and over again to put his trust in the Lord, that God would see him through this trying period. Gradually Jess's agony subsided as he began to mend. The color returned to his face and the deep furrows in his forehead loosened. While he was obviously mending physically, it was just as plain his mental outlook had not changed, even when Dr. Kimberly announced that he was strong enough to go home. Jess had been in the hospital almost five months.

Most of the physical pain had vanished, and after four and a half months I was freed from the body cast. However, I was left with an iron corset, a back brace that cut across my back like thin wire. While I felt better physically, the dark cloud of gloom continued to hover over me. Despite all of the love and understanding shown by Jeanne and the loyalty offered by our friends, I felt cheated by life and abandoned by the Lord. I was now returning to a home where only months before I had mowed the lawn, played catch with my son, pushed my daughters to the sky in their swing. I was coming home all right, but in a wheelchair.

Friends in the Lake Oswego Volunteer Fire Department arranged for my transportation home, chauffeuring me from the hospital to my front door in the town ambulance. I can still graphically remember pulling into the driveway. The August heat clung to me, not like the humid heat of the South, but the kind that lies on you, as if it were dragging the oxygen from your lungs. What little breeze there was only shifted the heat around. Although neatly cut, the grass had turned a parched brown, and the children's swing hung limply from the big oak tree.

Someone asked how it felt to be home and away from the hospital. Without sounding too convincing, I heard myself mumble something about its being terrific and that I was looking forward to being able to relax without having to worry about nurses lurking around every corner, ready to jab me with a thermometer or needle. But deep down inside, I was terrified. From a world where physical disabilities were an everyday occurrence, I had reentered the real world, where wheelchairs and cripples were considered an oddity.

As my friends wheeled me up the sidewalk toward the house, the children came bursting out of the house laughing and shouting. Jeanne was behind them, grinning, watching as the kids hugged and kissed me. They were giggling with excitement.

"Welcome home, Daddy," they yelled. Mike grinned mischievously. "Mom said we had to take it easy on you for a while. I figure 'a while' is about a day."

For a few hours I forgot about my legs and enjoyed the warmth and love of my family. For the rest of the day friends and relatives turned our house into a convention center. It seemed as if everyone we knew came by to say hello and wish me luck. Half the Portland police department patrol cars were in Lake Oswego that day.

For the best part of the day I held up pretty well. Jeanne made sure I took periodic rests and got out of the back brace so the blood could circulate. But as the day wore on, my back began to throb; and the more it hurt, the more vulnerable I became to self-pity. I began to picture myself as some kind of circus freak on display. Voices sounded patronizing, faces seemed to be filled with pity.

Jim Davis, wearing that perpetual grin, came over around seven. "Hey, pard," he yelled as he bounded up the sidewalk, "you finally broke out of that hole they call a hospital, huh? How does it feel to be back in the real world where they use deodorant instead of antiseptic?"

I grinned despite the pain. "Since when did you become an authority on deodorant? I thought you only used it when they elected a new Pope."

"Hey, don't give me a bad time or I'll rust your wheels. Remember, if you're not nice to me, I won't let you watch Elvis on the 'Big Shew' Sunday." Davis grabbed a chair, dragged it over, and plopped himself down next to me. Jeanne came out of the bedroom after putting the kids to bed and smiled when she saw Jim.

"Just in time for a fresh cup of coffee."

"Terrific, at least someone around here has some manners," Jim said as he gave me a sideward glance. "Well, so much for small talk, how does it feel? Glad to be home?"

I twisted my body in an effort to relieve some of the pain building at the base of my back. I glanced nervously toward Jeanne and knew she was listening intently, while trying not to appear concerned. "Of course it's great to be home. Having Jeanne and the kids close by is terrific."

"But—ah—something's not right. Right?"

I took a deep breath and exhaled slowly. Jeanne brought the coffee and then moved behind me and began massaging my neck. "Yeah, something's not right. I'm frightened. I can't shake this feeling of, I don't know, I guess it's a feeling of doom, uselessness. Every time I turn around, something reminds me of the fact that I'm stuck in this wheelchair!"

Both immediately threw themselves into the same arguments I'd heard for days: I'd have a great deal of mobility with the use of braces and crutches, and with hard work there would be little I couldn't accomplish. Realizing that neither was going to allow me to indulge in self-pity, I gave up and moved on to more pleasant topics. Still, there was a twinge of resentment somewhere deep inside me. I resented their stopping me from feeling the depressive monster that was raging within me. I wanted to feel sorry for myself, I wanted them to feel sorry for me, and then I could have become angry because they were patronizing me.

Despite a mounting fear of the future and a growing depression that would soon drive me to a desperate act, for the next few hours I never laughed harder. Jim recounted the latest police "war stories," and the three of us swapped accounts of the trials and tribulations of marriage. But the feeling of well-being was short-lived. After Jim left, I could feel hopelessness again taking control of my mind. It was almost as if I couldn't prevent it, but as I mentioned earlier, you can spend a great amount of time wallowing in self-pity. It becomes a blanket of insulation as you tell yourself others couldn't possibly understand or appreciate the suffering you're enduring.

Jeanne and I talked for an hour or so after Jim left, but the conversation remains vague. I sat there and watched her, trying to penetrate her calm and confident face, trying to detect some sign of weakness or doubt. But there was nothing; she had put her total trust in the Lord that our family would survive, and nothing was going to shake her faith.

"Aren't you afraid?" I asked.

"Afraid of what? The future?"

"Yes. Haven't you worried about how we're going to live, how the children are going to do now that I'm, well, I'm a cripple?" The self-pity was racing.

"Jess, we're better off than a lot of people. You've got to stop thinking about what you've lost and concentrate on what you still have, what we still have! I thank God every night that you weren't killed. I still have you and I love you. I don't care about your wheelchair! You're still the man I married and the Lord didn't take you away from me. We've got enough money and we've got friends, friends who care. No, I'm not frightened, but I am concerned about your attitude. Stop looking backward. Leave the pain behind and let's get on with our lives. We're going to be all right."

My face flushed with embarrassment as I listened to her. There wasn't a trace of bitterness or anxiety in her voice. She was calm. Her concern was only a demonstration of love. Logically, I could deal with what she had said, but I couldn't exorcise the bitterness in my heart. While I knew she was speaking out of love and devotion, that voice that had once screamed "Why me?" was now yelling, "You didn't lose your legs, you can pontificate, but you're not sentenced to a wheelchair for life!"

Despite everything Jeanne did to help me, my spirits continued their downward spiral. The pain in my back was subsiding, but my depression expanded to the point where all I wanted was a way out.

After I left the hospital, Jeanne spent two hours a day applying heat packs to my back and massaging the muscles weakened by the months of being inside the body cast. During these sessions, Jeanne talked excitedly about our future plans, the children, and all our friends who constantly called to see if we needed anything. She meant it as a means of lifting my spirits, but it did just the opposite. I became so depressed I wanted to scream. I wanted to yell at the top of my voice, "Stop talking! Stop trying to make me feel like living! Just leave me alone and let me die!"

A few months before, when I lay in that hospital bed and contemplated suicide, it had been impossible. But now I had some mobility and death could be achieved. It was a Wednesday afternoon, the temperature was in the high nineties, and I was in a black mood. The fact that Jeanne seemed so cheerful only served to antagonize me. If I could have moved quickly, I honestly believe I would have tried to hit her. The frustration had built to a dangerous level, and I wanted to hurt someone. It was only a matter of time before I did something violent to either her or the children.

That particular day, as she massaged my back, the phone rang and she left the room to answer it. From the sound of the conversation, I could tell it was a friend and that Jeanne would be on the phone for a while. Now, alone, I gazed dejectedly at my life. Self-pity is bittersweet. To indulge in it you must first acknowledge that you are less than you once were. That is the bitter, but, if carefully nurtured, bitter can be blended into a dangerous sweetness.

Once I admitted that what had been could be no more, I sank into sophomoric remembrances of how wonderful things used to be. I recalled forgotten walks along Cascade streams, those Sunday three-legged races, even running for cover during a sudden downpour. And then, when I had become addicted to self-pity, I reveled in how life had so harshly mistreated me. From this point, suicide is just a short step. Consciously, I thought life was no longer tolerable, but my subconscious was saying, "They'll be sorry when I'm gone, I'll teach them to turn me into an albatross."

All of the anger, the frustration, and the self-pity now came crashing down upon me like a tidal wave. I stared intently at the closet door and gauged the drop from the table I was on to the floor. Two, maybe three feet. I could roll off the table and cushion the fall with my forearms. From there it would be a simple matter to pull myself across the floor to the closet door and, by propping myself up, swing it open.

Beads of sweat formed on my lips as my mind moved me toward the door. Behind it hung my loaded service revolver and freedom from this useless life! I knew I wouldn't be able to reach the gun from the floor but hoped there'd be a coat hanger on the floor. It would take some hard work and a little luck, but with the hanger, I could jab at the bottom of the holster until I knocked it off the hook. I could hear it clang to the floor and I'd hold my breath and pray that Jeanne didn't hear it. I could almost feel the coolness of the dull metal against my forehead. A river of perspiration flowed down my shoulders and across my ribs and formed a small pool under my stomach. I could hear the metallic click as the hammer moved into striking position. . . .

At that moment Jeanne reentered the room. For a moment I didn't realize she was standing there. The vision of the hammer falling toward the cylinder in slow motion consumed my entire attention.

Jeanne

For what seemed like an eternity, but probably was no more than a few seconds, I'm sure I could read his mind. I could feel the coldness of his vision, his desperate need to strike out at someone.

> It was almost as if he were in a catatonic state, he was hardly breathing, there was no movement. His eyes were trained on the closet door and were glazed. I knew what was behind the door and in his heart.

"Jess, are you all right?"

Jeanne's voice was soft, as if it were coming out of a fog. It took a moment or two before my conscious mind regained control and allowed me to respond.

"What?"

"I said, are you all right?"

"Yeah, I'm okay. Just thinking about going for a walk or something." My voice was cold and distant.

"You were thinking of committing suicide, weren't you?"

For the first time, I looked at her. Tears streamed down her face. "No, no, I wasn't."

"Jess, please don't lie to me. I don't know how to explain it, but I know what you were thinking." She came over and caressed my cheek. "Do you hate me that much?" Staring down at me, she paused for a second and swallowed. "Isn't there any love left in your heart, if not for me, at least for the children?"

The intensity of her question made me turn away. "With me dead, it would be easier for everyone."

"That's not the reason," Jeanne said softly. "You want to get even with everyone. You want to hurt us. Death is your way of punishing us because we can walk." She sat down next to me and ran her fingers through her hair. "Jess, I love you, I always will, so will the children. They look at you as their father, a man who loves them. They look up to you."

"How can they look up to a cripple?" I answered in frustration.

I heard her take a deep breath and let the air escape slowly. "That's up to you. It's easier to look up to someone with a handicap than it is to someone who's dead, to someone who didn't want to be near the ones who love him."

Everything Jeanne said was true and it hurt to admit it. I did want to get even, to hurt them by killing myself. I was angered by a God who seemed so insensitive.

"You keep throwing this wonderful All-knowing at me. Well,

what's He done for me? Does He think this world needs more pencil vendors?"

"Jess, I don't pretend to know what He has in mind for you or me. I just know I believe in Him. Jess, Roosevelt couldn't walk and he became President. Look at Helen Keller! Maybe He wants you to do something else with your life. I don't know, but I do know that neither of us will find out if you're dead! If God had wanted you dead, He had plenty of opportunities to arrange it. But you're alive, and you have to believe that by responding to the trials He sets before you, you'll be a better man. You have my love and the strength of God if you want it. But it's up to you to reach out. No one else can do it for you."

It took a few minutes, but slowly what Jeanne said began to take hold. It's very easy not to challenge your life; it's easy to accept everything as beyond your control. I know there are people who say to themselves every day, "I'm unhappy, frustrated, I want to change my life." Yet seldom does change occur, because life is comfortable. Nothing forces us to challenge our ability, question our way of living. We don't change what we don't like because changing demands too much of us.

The necessary changes come only when we face the problem honestly. It took my wife's love and her belief in God to make me stop searching for an easy way out and begin developing a new life. God was beginning to reveal Himself to me. Insight is almost a miracle by itself. That sudden moment when what has seemed so murky becomes clear produces a warmth, a sense of accomplishment. Suffering and challenges—I suddenly discovered they can be one and the same, depending on how you and God approach them.

CHAPTER FOUR

> This is the message we have heard from him and declare to you: God is light; in him there is no darkness at all. If we claim to have fellowship with him yet walk in the darkness, we lie and do not put the truth into practice.
>
> I John 1:5–6; NIV

Knowing the answer to a problem does not, however, necessarily mean the problem is then easy to solve. Insight is God's gift. It is that moment when the mind suddenly focuses on an issue that until then seemed unsolvable or incomprehensible. But unless you seize the insight and grip it with all your faith, the sharp image has a tendency to soften, to go slightly out of focus, and then you run the risk of losing your direction.

Some call it willpower, self-determination, or perhaps personal character. For me, I would define it as concentration: the ability to keep the mind riveted on what it is that you, and God, want for you. In geometry, there is an axiom which simply states that the shortest distance between points A and B is a straight line. Simple, if from point A you keep point B firmly in sight. If you lose your concentration, if you lose your grip on the insight God allowed you, getting to point B, even when you know the theory, can be a difficult and taxing trip.

I understood where I was starting from and where I wanted to go, but my concentration drifted like the oncoming clouds of fall. At times I lost my grip and allowed my emotions to take me on a long roller-coaster ride, rising over the crests of happiness, then plunging wildly into deep valleys of depression. I wanted to be at point B, but I expected to arrive without sacrifices.

The high points of my emotional trip were moments I'll never forget. Concern and love were showered upon us by friends, neighbors, and people we had never met before. Jeanne and I still reflect on those trying days and enjoy the warmth people shared with us.

People dropped in at various times throughout the day offering help and encouragement. The teenaged daughter of a couple who had just moved into the area dropped in two or three times a week just to visit with me. I know that when I was sixteen visiting someone like me would have been the last thing I would have thought of doing. But there she was like clockwork, smiling and talking excitedly about high school, the new friends she had met, how the football team was doing, and how interesting her classes were. I'll always remember her bright smile and how thoughtful she was. I find myself thinking every so often about her and I pray the Lord was kind to her.

Of course, there were others. The local butcher would drop by unannounced and leave a couple of steaks, the poultry delivery man would follow a day or so later and drop off a half-dozen fryers. Someone was always stopping by and offering to mow the lawn, wash the car, or weed the garden. The house was in a constant state of motion. As a policeman, I had always seen the worst side of society. After all, we were never called unless there was an emergency. I had begun to believe that there wasn't a good side, that mankind was lost, all of us condemned to murder, rob, and maim our neighbor. The outpouring of love and concern we experienced made me realize that my view of society had been confined to an extremely narrow spectrum.

Portland police cars were constantly parked in front of our house, and officers stretched credibility to the breaking point to explain why they were twenty miles off their normal patrol routes. East Precinct officials had to look the other way to ignore the growing number of "hot pursuit" reports that so often ended with the suspect eluding the pursuing patrol car within a block or two of our house. Of course, since they were now in the area, no one could object to their paying a quick visit to a fellow officer.

Larry Plaisance and John Hoffnagle, two good friends of mine, dropped by one day while "testing out a car that had just been overhauled" (the third time that month) and noticed I had to negotiate two sets of steps and a ninety-degree turn in order to get from the kitchen to the patio.

Larry turned to Hoffnagle and shook his head. "That won't do at all, will it, John?" John stared at the hallway for a moment, then shook his head slowly. "Nope. Won't do at all," he said solemnly.

That Saturday, at six in the morning, Jeanne and I were awakened by the sounds of hammers pounding and saws rasping. By the time we reached the kitchen, there was a rather large hole in the outside wall. By noon we had a new doorway leading directly to the patio. When the last nail was pounded into place, John and Larry just stood there with grins on their faces, obviously proud of their handiwork. Smiles of friendship can never be forgotten.

Meanwhile, Lake Oswego residents had never had so many warrants served for parking violations. Normally, when out-of-Portland residents got parking tickets, they just threw them away, correctly assuming the city wouldn't expend too much time or money on collecting an overdue parking ticket. Officers avoided serving warrants like the plague, since it was extremely boring and time-consuming. Therefore, warrant serving, at best, was done infrequently and a bit haphazardly.

But after I returned home, Jim Davis would collect all the warrants to be served in the Lake Oswego area and make a special effort to deliver them. To the old saying "The only thing certain is death and taxes" Lake Oswego residents added: "and parking violation warrants." More than one resident was startled to discover a big, rather gruff-looking Portland police officer camped on his doorstep in the morning. Jim would deliver three or four, then drop by for coffee and chat for a while before returning to his warrant-serving rounds. I suspect that Portland city officials must have been a bit puzzled over the sudden increase in voluntary payments for overdue parking tickets from the Lake Oswego area; I know Jim enjoyed describing the looks of consternation on people's faces when he pulled up in front of their homes.

In between visits, Jeanne made sure I kept busy, trying to occupy my mind. During the first four months I must have built every model airplane ever produced. I also exhausted the entire inventory of paint-by-number pictures. Somewhere out there is a hobby shop owner who was able to retire early because of me.

Just about the time I was beginning to think people, animals, and landscapes weren't normal unless they had numbers and lines printed on them, Louie rescued me.

Louie was Leo Critchfield, an old high school buddy I hadn't seen for a couple of years. One day, in between the delivery of chicken, steak, a visit from Jim Davis, and a numbered painting of a mustang rearing high into the air, Louie came to the door armed with a chessboard and a silly grin on his face.

"You know how to play chess?" he asked. No "How are you, long time no see" just "You know how to play chess?"

"Heck, no," I said in amazement. To me, chess was only for those with high IQ's who possessed an analytic mind and could think in terms of abstract concepts. I was wrong, of course. Actually, millions of people play chess. However, the best are those with high IQ's, an analytic mind, and an ability to think in abstract concepts. Neither Louie nor I fit that category.

Louie smiled again. "That's great, because I know just enough to be able to thrash you. So you better be a fast learner or enjoy losing." He laughed as he walked in and began setting up the pieces.

That launched the little-known Lake Oswego Amateur Chess Club. Louie was a constant caller, arriving almost daily, his face unable to mask the expression of total confidence in the outcome of the match. It wasn't so much the losing that galled me as the triumphant laugh Louie used when he called out "Checkmate!" After about three weeks of solid trouncing, I came to the conclusion that my game was not going to improve without help. In self-defense, I began rummaging around in our encyclopedia, picking up a few pointers, and Jeanne bought me a book entitled *Chess for the Uninformed.*

Interest in the game expanded rapidly as visitors first became curious onlookers, then amateur kibitzers, and finally full-fledged chess players. Within a month, more than a dozen players were mapping out strategy. During the early stages there were smiles as players blundered through the games, making ridiculous mistakes. But as everyone became more competent, the innocent smiles of the novice slowly gave way to the more concerned frowns of a concentrating competitor bent on winning. There were never any hard feelings, but a game introduced to pass the time had mysteriously evolved into a war of the minds—with absolutely no quarter given.

Perhaps the best example was McMullin. In the beginning, Moon and I were pretty evenly matched, but after consulting the encyclopedia and picking up a few tips, I started beating him on a regular basis. Moon was not what you might call either a good or a graceful loser. After I took three straight, hard-fought matches one night, Moon, without saying a word, jumped up and stomped out the door, slamming it behind him.

I didn't see or hear from him again for three weeks. Then suddenly, one night, he walked through the door, chessboard under one arm and a smile on his lips. "Let's play," he said. He never uttered another word for the next three hours. He just sat there and destroyed me. Maybe he was a poor loser, but he was certainly a great winner. He grinned so much I thought his face would fall off.

It took more than a week, but I finally discovered the source of Moon's newfound ability. He had been taking lessons from a local expert. That touched off what we referred to as the "Great Lake Oswego Chess War." Once it was discovered that Moon had turned "pro," everyone else began seeking outside advice. It was, perhaps, the most basic example of escalation. Throughout the rest of the fall and winter, players skulked about seeking clandestine aid in preparation for the next chess confrontation. No one would admit outright they were boning up, but it was common knowledge that it was every chess player for himself.

Those were a few of the high, happy peaks during the early months, but they were always accompanied by equally deep valleys of depression. Instead of reaching out for God when I felt the fits of self-pity seizing control, I withdrew into a self-imposed world of darkness and spite. God's love and encouragement, like Jeanne's and our friends', was always there. All I had to do was reach out.

Reaching out for help may seem such a simple act, but it forces a number of unpleasant admissions. By reaching out, by saying "Help me," you are admitting to inadequacies, that you do not always have control of your life. There are many in our society who feel that if they cannot, by themselves, solve their problems, they are failures, that society will judge them weak. Given that philosophy, it is easier to withdraw, to look upon expressions of love or offers of help as charity or to believe you are being patronized.

I truly believe that asking for help, either spiritually or physically, is a sign of courage, an indication you have decided life is worth continuing. But as 1956 vanished in the northwest snows and 1957 began, I was too weak to reach out. I was angry, and frustrated, and at times I wanted to punish those enjoying normal lives. I returned to the same desperate state of mind I had experienced in the hospital. I no longer thought of taking my life, but I waited patiently for it to end. Sometimes the distinction between suicide and death is an extremely thin line. Saying "What's the use?" can be just as lethal as saying "I choose not to live any longer."

I couldn't control my bladder. It's a problem that plagues all paraplegics and quadriplegics. When accidents occurred, the rage rose inside. I felt so helpless and degraded. Not being able to control bodily functions is a humiliating experience. To have it happen in front of friends, or, even worse, total strangers, can be devastating.

Before my motorcycle accident, conversations were carefree and free-flowing. But afterward I could sense everyone picking their way through conversations, making sure they didn't raise a subject that might remind me of my condition. It's the same kind of reaction people have when talking with a blind person—they cringe if they use the phrase "Have you seen?" or "Isn't it a beautiful day?" It's a natural reaction, but the awkward pause only underscores the situation, as does cautiously trying to skirt possible sensitive topics.

And there was my physical appearance. Every time I looked into a mirror, I found an unfamiliar image staring back at me. I had lost a tremendous amount of weight. My eyes and cheeks were slightly hollow, my face gaunt. My physical strength was eroding at a frightening pace.

And if I felt the frustration and tension, Jeanne must have experienced the same force. But if she did, she managed to mask her anxieties better than I did. The pressure of taking care of the children, overseeing our finances, and trying to cope with a volatile husband must have been a heavy burden.

Jeanne

It was difficult trying to gauge Jess's emotions from day to day. One moment you saw a genuine smile of happiness, and then a dark cloud of doubt, anger, or frustration would thunder across him like an angry storm.

The children never seemed aware of his feelings, and he struggled to keep his bitterness from them. He spent hours building model airplanes with Mike and Chris (Susan was still too young), partly to pass the time, but also because it was one of the few activities that allowed him to be close to his children. They would talk about school, friends, Little League, and their other activities for hours and I would feel reassured by the warmth that was generated. But when his mind wasn't totally occupied, when Jess had the opportunity, his determination would vanish.

I constantly worried about saying the wrong things around him. Money was not a problem since he was receiving full medical coverage and full disability, but if I showed some concern about the car or business dealings, the anxiety and sense of uselessness emerged. He had been an excellent golfer before the accident. Afterward, once he came home, I always checked the television schedule on Sunday before turning the set on. I was afraid of tuning in on a golf tournament that might send him plunging into a depressive state.

Thoughts of suicide had vanished, but another factor had emerged that was just as frightening and more difficult to combat. Jess was giving up. I saw that those emotional slides into depression were slowly draining his resolution to fight, to stay alive. He was making no effort to overcome his physical limitations and refused to discuss the situation. He never said it, but you could easily read it. It flashed across his face, speaking as loudly as if he had shouted: "What's the use! I'll always be a physical freak, condemned to a wheelchair for the rest of my life! Forced to watch the world pass me."

The battle to save his life while on the operating table and during those unsure days afterward was something I could deal with. It was a tangible, physical situation. X rays, charts, and doctors could be touched, they could be seen and explained. But now I was faced with something just as significant in terms of Jess's life, only it was no longer something I could touch, physically. How do you reach someone's will? I watched as he steadily lost weight, his muscles hung loosely on his arms, his face was drawn; he seldom bothered to dress or shave and would lapse into long periods of silence.

Jess controlled the eventual outcome. He and God. I offered my love and understanding, but I could do no more than that. I became his cheerleader, along with our close friends and the children, but it was Jess's game. Somewhere inside, he would either have to accept the challenge, to reach out and try, or quite literally wither and die. I prayed and waited for Jess to make his decision.

CHAPTER FIVE

That decision was not long in coming. It was pushed nearer by yet another operation, but this time it was Jeanne who went under the surgeon's knife. A small tumor had developed at the base of her right thumb, causing extremely uncomfortable pressure and pain on a nerve junction.

Although the operation was minor, Jeanne was unable to use her right hand for almost a month. Until then, Jeanne had lifted me in and out of bed, helped me in and out of the wheelchair and in and out of chairs. In fact, Jeanne and our friends had unwittingly helped convince me there was little I could do for myself. So eager were they to help, to eliminate frustrations and make sure everything was immediately at hand anytime I wanted it, that I never had to lift a finger. I forgot the elation a person feels when he's forced to struggle on his own and overcome a problem. It's a feeling that creates self-respect. But I had forgotten what it was like to be independent. The more they did for me, the more I became convinced there was little I could do for myself.

Now, with Jeanne out of commission, I had to come to grips with everyday problems such as getting out of bed, and solve them. I quickly discovered I had lost most of my strength. Even the slightest struggle left me tired, but with the help of Mike and some sideline coaching from Jeanne, I managed to get in and out of bed, wash the dishes, and cook dinner. They were small triumphs, but they were the first positive steps I had taken in trying to survive in my new life as a paraplegic.

Another situation which was about to force that important decision from me came late in February. As usual, the Oregon weather was foul. Rain fell in heavy sheets and the wind drove the drops hard against the house, pounding the roof like thousands of drumming fingers. It was a Sunday afternoon and the family was at the dinner table playing Monopoly when, without warning, Dr. A. Gurney Kimberly showed up at our front door with the same expression that sent nurses scurrying for cover.

"How're you doing, Jess?"

"Okay, I guess. Little bored, but I'm alive."

Kimberly looked at me critically, as if he challenged my last remark. "You've lost a lot of weight. Actually, you don't look much better than you did when you left the hospital." The words were spoken with icy coldness. I glanced nervously over at Jeanne, whose eyes had narrowed with anxiety. "Maybe I didn't mention this before, Jess, but the average life expectancy for a paraplegic following the accident is only about five or six years."

I could feel his eyes boring in on me as he paused long enough to let his comment sink in. "You know why?"

Shaking my head, I attempted to avoid those piercing, condemning eyes. There's nothing worse than having someone point out a terrible fault of yours and knowing, if you'll pardon the pun, you haven't a leg to stand on.

"They die, Jess, because they become inactive. They just sit around on their butts and die. They give up. Pretty soon the kidneys stop functioning, the liver deteriorates, then the whole pumping system goes to hell. Now, for the most part, I really don't care—except when they're my patients. I put a lot of hours in on you, and I get a bit annoyed when you just sit around waiting to die."

As Dr. Kimberly talked, he was slowly drawing closer to me, making sure I didn't miss a word he was saying. Jeanne went over and sat down next to Mike and Susan and watched wordlessly, wondering what was going to happen next. Everyone had tried so hard to coax me lightly into doing things for myself. This, I knew right away, was not going to be one of those light coaxing sessions. Dr. Kimberly was not known for his subtle approach to problems.

"You see, you got the best surgeon around. Now, I worked in that operating room for hours. I gave you the best my skills could offer. My neck ached for hours afterward, I had a headache from concentrating so hard, and I pushed myself to utter exhaustion just so you could live! So you might have an opportunity to lead a productive life! Yet, from all indications, you've just been sitting around here dying. I didn't go through all of that so you could sit in this wheelchair and feel sorry for yourself!"

"Well, what am I supposed to do?" I shot back angrily.

"By God, you're not supposed to sit around here!" he said just as angrily. He didn't yell, but he didn't need to. I knew he was steaming mad. "Have you started your rehabilitation program?"

"No," I said defensively, "there's been too many things to take care of around the house."

"Yes," he responded sarcastically, "I can see you've been very busy." He studied me for a moment. "Five or six years, Jess. That's the average life-span for most people in your condition. It doesn't have to be that way. There are a lot of people who live a normal, long life. But I guarantee you they are the ones who refuse to look upon that wheelchair as an anchor. They refuse to dry up slowly and die."

Dr. Kimberly got up and walked over to the telephone. "I'm going to make an appointment for you tomorrow at the rehabilitation center. They'll give you an examination and set up a program for you. They can help you, Jess, but only if you want help. No one else can do that for you. If you haven't the guts to find out what you're made of, then you'll die! Maybe you'll get lucky and hang on for seven or even eight years, but that'll be it. Here's another thing to remember: if you do go to the center, you'll have to work. They won't have time to coax you. If you won't try, they'll send you back home where you can die at your leisure."

I would hear another lecture much like the one Dr. Kimberly gave me, only it was delivered with even more fierceness and determination. There was a long road ahead of me, but I had now taken a few steps down it.

If that Monday was to symbolize the beginning of my physical, as well as mental, rehabilitation, there was nothing immediately apparent to serve as an omen of good fortune.

It was a dark, dreary day. The sun hardly made a dent in the thick cloud cover. Rain had fallen earlier in the morning, a blanket of wetness covered everything, and you could smell more rain in the air. As Jeanne pulled the car up in front of a tired-looking two-story brick building, I thought to myself, "I don't want to go inside. I don't want them to demand things of me. I'm not ready yet." What I was really saying was "I'm not sure I can meet the challenges, and if I fail, where does that leave my life? What will be left for me if they can't help?"

And yet, as these questions raced through my mind, Jeanne was helping me into my wheelchair and talking excitedly about the rehabilitation center and the freedom the programs could offer me. I didn't want to go, but I was moving toward the huge double doors. I didn't yell out, "Take me home! Please take me home!" but, Lord, I wanted to!

The only other time I felt so helpless, that my life was out of control, was when I enlisted in the Army. As I raised my hand for the oath and the officer told us that if we wanted to change our minds, this was the time, I suddenly realized I was leaving a world I knew and was comfortable with, a secure world, for one that would make demands and challenges. Both would undoubtedly change me. But I couldn't be sure what those changes would be. I wanted to say, "Maybe I'll change my mind," but I didn't because of what others might think.

Now I was rolling toward the rehabilitation building and a feeling of total inadequacy swept over me. People were going to force me to attempt things I would be unable to do. Despite the dismal picture Dr. Kimberly had painted, the last thing I wanted was to perform for people so they could gauge just how much my body had deteriorated and how little I could do for myself.

During a brief conference with the center's director, Dr. Arthur Jones, we were told that the center would arrange transportation back and forth so that Jeanne would not be tied to my schedule. As it turned out, this was also the first step in a process of stopping me from depending upon Jeanne and letting Jeanne discover that I could exist without her being by my side every minute. Before that day Jeanne felt, as did I, that she couldn't leave me for more than a few minutes. Even if she was just going to be gone for ten minutes, she would place anything I might possibly want within arm's length. If possible, one of the children would stay with me, or perhaps a neighbor would keep a close eye on me. I never had to do anything for myself. That was about to change.

From the moment Jeanne pushed me through the doorway and into the center, she was encouraged to leave. They wanted to restore as much of my self-reliance as possible, and they wanted Jeanne to rediscover her own life. It would be revelation for both of us.

Jeanne constantly encouraged me to reach out and establish a new life, but at the same time part of her served as a link with the past, a past in which I could walk. Neither of us realized it at the moment, but my new life began and that link with the past was broken the second she walked out the door. The instant the door shut, I was forced to start facing reality. No longer would there be someone at my side asking if I needed something. Now I would be encouraged to help myself, and at times the encouragement would be none too gentle.

The center's rehabilitation program rivaled any Olympic training plan. Most of the patients worked as hard as or harder than any athletes preparing for the games, although their goals were different. For the athlete there was the big game or event and the glory for being successful. Hard work and success meant to the patients that they might survive in a world designed for people who could walk and reach out with their hands.

Before actually entering the rehabilitation program, I was given a physical examination that would rival any given to a used car prior to purchase. Drs. Adams and Moore pushed, shoved, and pulled my muscles in every direction imaginable. The two stretched and twisted my legs until the pain became unbearable.

My frustration level rose rapidly as they continued to probe and prod my body. "Why are you spending so much time with my legs? They're dead!" I snapped angrily.

Dr. Moore smiled and responded with an answer I'm sure he must have delivered a thousand times before. "Jess, first we need to know the condition of your muscles, which ones can still be controlled and therefore contribute to the body; and second, if you don't exercise these muscles, you could have some serious complications set in later on."

I didn't understand. "But I'll never be able to use my legs again, right? So what difference does it make?"

Moore gave me another of those patient smiles. "We have to develop every muscle showing the slightest sign of life, and you"—he paused to emphasize the word "you"—"you have to exercise in order to prevent the muscles and joints from stiffening up and cutting off the circulation. Without exercise, Jess, the circulation stops and it begins to affect the kidneys, the liver, the whole—"

"Stop, please stop," I sighed in resignation. "Don't tell me. The pumping goes next and then I'm done for, right?"

The patient smile broke into a grin. "Ah, I see you've had a talk with the good Dr. Kimberly. Well," Dr. Moore said, taking a deep breath, "that's exactly what happens. After this examination we'll lay out a program for your physical therapist and then we, or rather you, can get to work."

After two days the doctors came up with a conclusion I was already sadly aware of: my body was in a horrid state of disrepair, and at the moment there was little I could accomplish by myself.

The next step was a two-hour conversation with the staff psychologist, Herbert Snare. Herbert was a soft-spoken, gentle-looking man that everyone seemed to like. He seemed to take a genuine interest in each person's problems and devoted a great deal of energy trying to solve them.

"Jess, one of the first things you have to realize," he said as he scanned my chart, "is that your emotional state will continue to fluctuate wildly as long as your body continues to deteriorate. It's a matter of self-esteem, Jess. The more you learn to do for yourself, the better you feel about yourself. The same holds true for your body. The better physical shape you're in, the better you'll feel about things emotionally."

I mumbled something about that making sense and continued to listen quietly.

"Look, Jess, it's not going to be easy. It can be a very humiliating experience at the start. Your victories will be few and far between, and they'll probably be small to start with, but I promise you that with each victory you'll gain a little more willpower to push on with." I nodded my head and he smiled. "Anytime you've got a problem, come on in and we'll talk, okay? That's what I'm here for."

Herbert Snare was there to talk with, and Clara Brenner was there to get me started. She was all smiles as I was introduced to her. She was a young, pretty woman and she would be my therapist for the next few months. She was slender, with dark hair, sparkling eyes, and a genuinely warm smile. Her voice was bright and cheerful, full of confidence and eagerness. I took an instant liking to her, knowing instinctively I could talk her out of anything. If I had learned one thing during my years on the force, it was how to spot a soft-hearted person. They were usually the ones who easily fell prey to the con man's line.

The first day was more or less an orientation visit. With Clara acting as guide, I was given the grand tour of the center. Physical therapy was downstairs and looked like something out of the Spanish Inquisition. There were all kinds of odd-looking machines designed to stretch and pull the body in any direction the therapist desired. There were four sets of parallel bars and a set of weights, and the floor was almost completely covered with mats to soften the many falls everyone took during training. To make things even gloomier, the ceilings were high and the room was poorly lit. The dullish green light given off by the fluorescent bulbs served to accentuate the institutional green paint, which covered just about everything but the windows.

Upstairs in occupational therapy there were more machines connected to wires which in turn were connected to weights, and again there was no shortage of green paint. It was in OT that I would spend my first few weeks. During that time I would learn how to get from my wheelchair into bed, from the wheelchair into a car, and vice versa. It was the first step in gaining independence.

In between tours, I had an opportunity to look around the center and watch the other patients. There were about thirty busily trying to restore some kind of normality to their lives. That included nine children. The oldest couldn't have been more than eight. They were victims of polio, birth defects, or freak accidents that left them quadriplegics or paraplegics like myself. What struck me as odd was the fact that they were laughing and giggling like any other children their age.

I watched for about five minutes. Kids with leg and body braces up to their chins (some wore skull caps because of their constant falling) racing around the room as if everything were normal. I thought to myself, "How, in this dismal room, with all these patched-up bodies, can anyone smile?" I began to feel the fear seize up inside me again and that desperate urge to scream for Jeanne to take me back to the safe confines of our home almost overcame me.

Clara seemed to sense my despair. "It's an amazing thing about these youngsters," she said, smiling, as she pushed me toward them, "they understand they're not like other children, but they want to live. I mean, it's never occurred to them there was any other choice, so they're determined to make the best of it. They work very hard. I think everyone can learn from watching them."

Clara's comments worked on me for the rest of the day, as we went from area to area. As much as possible, the staff tried to run the center on a "large family" basis. I suppose the theory was that if everyone knew one another, there would be less embarrassment over failure and more of an inclination on each one's part to offer encouragement and praise, or to gain inspiration from others' triumphs. If that was the strategy, it seemed to work admirably. As I later discovered, the therapists and their aides were probably better psychologists than the psychologists. They worked so closely with us, living through our suffering and triumphs, that they seemed to know intuitively what to say or when to say nothing. They were always there when you needed them.

On Wednesday I began my first full rehabilitation session at the center, and at the same time the names I had been given in introductions the previous day were slowly taking on faces and histories. Like many, I suppose, when introduced to a number of people all at one time, it's difficult for me to put names and faces together for the first few days, but Clara helped by explaining some of each patient's history and progress at the center.

One name I immediately fitted to the face was Monica Stuckart. I hadn't seen her since she left the hospital, but I was delighted to discover she was at the center. Her smiling face and complete faith in God and her future bolstered my flagging spirits. There was absolutely no way anything was going to keep her down. To accept confinement to a wheelchair meant she would have to give up some of her duties as a mother and wife, and Monica had no intention of letting that happen. "With three youngsters running around the house," she said, laughing, during a break, "there's no way in heaven I can afford to sit in a wheelchair and try to keep up!"

Another face that was easily placed to a name was that of Ronnie Anderson. Ronnie was a volatile twenty-one-year-old Swedish seaman. While he had been off-loading cargo in Coos Bay, Oregon, a cable had snapped and severed his right leg just below the knee. For a robust man just beginning his life, the loss of his leg was traumatic, and for a few days he brooded and was totally inconsolable. The first time I saw him, he was yelling angrily at Loraine, his nurse, and she was yelling back in an equally angry voice. An outsider might have been under the impression that Ronnie was complaining about having to work too hard. It was difficult to tell, since Ronnie had a very strong Swedish accent. But that wasn't the problem at all. In fact, it was just the opposite. Ronnie was upset because staff members wouldn't let him work as much as he wanted! Still angry over the loss of his leg, Ronnie took that anger and channeled it: instead of letting it consume him, he converted the emotional energy into an almost insatiable drive to walk with an artificial leg. He would not tolerate any delays in his progress, which resulted in what today's politicians would refer to as a heated but meaningful dialogue.

Arnold Erickson was another patient I quickly became acquainted with. You didn't have to be a psychologist to feel the resentment radiating from Arnold, but it was a bitterness which, like Ronnie's, was controlled. Arnold was a near-quadriplegic, having no muscle control from just below his shoulders on down. Unlike most of us, who suffered from the results of an accident or disease, Arnold's condition was the result of a bungled operation. He had gone into the hospital for minor surgery, but someone had been sloppy about monitoring his blood pressure. His pressure dropped alarmingly, but before it was noticed and corrected, an aneurysm formed in the wall of an artery, causing a total and permanent paralysis from his shoulders down. It amazed me how he was able to reserve his bitterness for only those responsible for his condition. Never did I ever see that anger inflicted upon others. I wished I could have been that strong during the early days following my accident.

And finally, there was Magda. Magda Goergeny had one of those stern, square faces that people might immediately interpret as meaning she was a harsh woman. She was never harsh, but she was demanding and uncompromising. She was muscular but not stocky and always walked in a brisk, positive manner. She had been in the United States only a year when I arrived at the center, and spoke with a strong Hungarian accent. She and her husband, Emil, had fled Hungary during the final days of World War II. At the border they were challenged by the invading Russian troops, and during their escape Emil was hit in the face by a flamethrower and blinded. Yet the two managed to make their way to Oslo, Norway. From there they finally received sponsorship to Portland, Oregon.

Although only on the center's staff for a short while, Magda had already established herself as one of the best physical therapists there—certainly the most demanding. She constantly urged her patients to push themselves to their limits. But for Magda there were never limits, only plateaus. If you reached a personal goal, she would immediately set a new one and the work began once more. As I went through my paces at a much more relaxed tempo under the supervision of Clara, I would watch Magda push her patients to exhaustion and thank God I was not in her charge.

Where Magda demanded, Clara encouraged. She reasoned with you and tried to point out logically that everything you did was for your own good. For many patients her approach was excellent, but not for a policeman who learned in the streets how to handle people. Clara was such a sweet person, I doubt it ever occurred to her that I was goldbricking.

After the first two weeks of therapy, I was appalled at my physical condition. During my first session I worked on a weaving loom. But instead of weaving, the loom pulleys were attached to weights. The idea was to develop the muscles in the arms in order to prepare the patient for the strenuous crutch-walking sessions. For my first effort, Clara put two and a half pounds on the pulleys. After only three pulls I was completely exhausted. Obviously the dejection must have shown on my face.

"Jess, there are people who come here who can't even pull the loom once. You're not here to prove to anyone how strong you are," she said in that soft, reassuring voice. "You're here to get stronger. This is a start. Don't let it get you down! In two weeks you'll be up to five or eight pounds. I promise!"

A year earlier, I had been a six-foot, 165-pound policeman who could wade into the middle of a wild donnybrook and bring things under control. Now someone was telling me that, with some hard work, in a week or two I would be able to pull five or eight pounds with my arms. All of those fears suddenly came home again.

Jeanne

There was an immediate change in Jess during the first week at the center. He was enthusiastic about having something to do, having some kind of a schedule to adhere to. He talked about getting back in shape, becoming active again. But that lasted only a week. Then suddenly the enthusiasm disappeared and in its place returned the familiar apathy and attitude of "What's the use?"

Jess wanted to overcome his handicap and he wanted to become independent, but he had to struggle to overcome the depression that bound his willpower just as much as the paralysis bound his legs. When we talked about it, he would smile and insist that things were going well, but he was a terrible liar. It was the same pattern I had seen before. One day he was happy, the next depressed. It was obvious that emotionally he was still living in the past, still remembering a body that instantly responded to his commands. Trying to put those memories away was difficult for him. When the pressures of the day or the exercises reminded him of how far he had fallen and how far he had to go, it was easier to slip back into the past and stay there, secure with his memories. It was as if he believed that by holding on to those memories he'd never have to face the present.

We had been told that after the first two weeks the center would arrange transportation, so that Jeanne would not have to be tied to my schedule.

I spent the following Monday morning at home (the start of the third week of therapy) waiting for my ride to show up. As I sat there in my wheelchair, I gloomily counted off all the things I couldn't do for myself. It never occurred to me to take an inventory of the things I could do. I know Jeanne was able to read my emotions, even though I kept telling her that things were improving. I just couldn't exorcise the deep-seated anger that continued to remind me I was a cripple and could no longer do things for myself. I was still angry with God for taking away my legs. The voice kept saying, "Without legs you're not a man! Without legs you'll never be able to move freely again."

As the voice continued to enforce my depression, Jeanne told me my ride had arrived. With as much enthusiasm as I could summon to mask my real attitude, I smiled and made some comment about how Jeanne could go out and enjoy shopping while her husband was slaving away in the torture chamber.

I think God was trying to tell me something that day. Here I was bemoaning my plight and how my freedom had been taken away, but as I rolled myself toward the waiting car I discovered a shocking thing. Arnold Erickson was the driver! Arnold was more seriously disabled than I was—almost a quadriplegic. Yet there he was sitting behind the steering wheel grinning at me.

"Jess"—he laughed—"your mouth just fell on the ground. There's a big enough gap there to park a new Buick."

I sat there trying to recover from my surprise. "Well, Arnold, I . . . I mean, I wasn't. Ah, I'm sort of surprised!"

"Let me guess. The police department didn't hire you for your ability to think on your feet, right?" Arnold glanced at the wheelchair. "Of course, you're not exactly thinking on your feet, are you?" He smiled.

"No," I said, shaking my head slowly. "Are you sure you drove here?" I asked suspiciously.

Arnold glanced around in the car. "All right, you got me. Actually, Claude Rains drove. I just came along to confuse people."

"I mean, how can you drive?"

"Jess, I can't believe you've never heard of hand controls. I can do anything any normal person can do in a car as long as I've got these hand controls. Everything but dance, but then, who dances in a car? Know what I mean?" Arnold was certainly enjoying himself as he explained how the hand controls worked.

As we took off for the center, Arnold gave me a quick demonstration of the controls and explained that having the use of a car was extremely important. "With this car, Jess, I'm not tied to a wheelchair and I'm not dependent upon others. I can do things for myself. Of course, I don't have as much movement as you do, but I've done all right so far."

Arnold went chatting happily along, obviously pleased to have the company and delighted to be able to show off. It seemed a bit ludicrous that two men who together couldn't walk two feet were racing down the road at forty miles an hour. As Arnold drove, I couldn't help wondering what other drivers might have thought if they knew we were on the loose. I also couldn't help but think of what an idiot I had been. I had all but given up any real hope of creating a normal life for myself. I had convinced myself I wouldn't be able to get back into society's mainstream, that I would always be an outsider looking in. After all, how much could a man without legs accomplish? Yet there I was sitting next to Arnold, who had less mobility than I, and he was driving! I began to reevaluate my situation. Obviously I could do a lot more than I gave myself credit for, but someone was going to have to push me.

By mid-June the next year I had made some notable improvement in my overall muscle development and had put back a few of the pounds that had melted away over the past fourteen months. I had also been fitted for leg braces, fifteen pounds of clunking metal that at times made me feel like some kind of robot. Once the leg braces had been properly fitted, I began crutch walking, a rather strenuous procedure, especially if you're not in top physical shape. With the braces in a locked position, you use the crutches as a kind of fulcrum and then swing through the crutches with your body acting much like a pendulum. The secret is to make your body follow through and plant your braces solidly to act as a support platform so the crutches can be swung forward to begin the movement again. Crutch walking demands a great deal of upper-torso strength, especially in the arms and shoulders. Being a good crutch walker requires a total devotion to physical exercise.

Clara, through her constant encouragement and gentle jabbing, brought me to a plateau I was comfortable with, and that's where I stayed. I could do about fifteen push-ups and five or six chin-ups and could move across about half the distance of the twenty-foot-long parallel bars before giving up. When she pressed me to do more, I always managed to talk her out of it.

"Clara," I groaned, "my arms are killing me. We've been at it for more than an hour! Tell you what. Let's take a quick coffee break, and I can rest. You've really been pushing me all morning," I lied. "You keep this up and I'll report you for picking on cripples."

"Pushing you!" She laughed. "You've been ducking any hard work all week. Jess, you're just lucky Magda doesn't get her hands on you. She's been watching you, and there's no way you could talk her into a coffee break."

I glanced over at Magda, who was working with one of her patients and putting him through a really tough workout. "Yeah, her idea of a break is a compound fracture. But you're not like that, are you? Come on. I'll buy the coffee."

"Big deal! The coffee's free!"

"Yes," I countered emphatically, "but it's the thought that counts." Clara sighed, knowing she was in a losing battle, and pushed me over to the small coffee room at the far end of the first floor. Once there, we sat back, enjoyed a couple of cigarettes and two or three cups of coffee, and gossiped. I talked about baseball, and she pretended to be interested. She talked about roses, and I pretended to be bored.

Elvis Presley was taking the country by storm; the upstart Milwaukee Braves, behind the pitching of Warren Spahn and Lew Burdette and the slugging of Eddie Mathews, were on their way to the World Series against the New York Yankees; there were rumors that the Dodgers and Giants were about to abandon New York in favor of Los Angeles and San Francisco; and President Eisenhower had issued something called the "Eisenhower Doctrine," which was a warning to the Communists to keep out of the Middle East. Apparently they didn't take it too seriously. Meanwhile, it was an excellent year for roses.

In between green thumbs, home runs, and world affairs, we watched Ronnie Anderson battle with Loraine. This particular day he was storming around the room, hopping on one leg, yelling back at Loraine, who returned his fire with equally enraged volleys. Ronnie was upset because Loraine wouldn't let him wear his artificial leg. The fact that the leg stump had become infected by wearing the artificial leg too soon after the operation didn't seem to bother Ronnie. Loraine, on the other hand, was letting him have it with both barrels, implying that if he didn't calm down and start acting reasonably she was going to start hitting him over the head with his artificial leg in an effort to pound some sense into him. Loraine was not your basic shrinking violet. The two moved around the room shouting at one another: Ronnie hopping on one leg, letting forth with a volley of Swedish oaths; Loraine in hot pursuit, threatening to smack him over the head with his leg. I'm not sure Groucho Marx could have written a funnier scene.

As we enjoyed the Ronnie and Loraine show, Magda walked in and smiled at me and said in a quiet, threatening tone, "Jess, someday you're going to be my patient and you're not going to have time for this nonsense."

I laughed and told her I was Clara's patient and had no plans for changing. I had no intention of falling into Magda's hands.

Lake Oswego motorists, meanwhile, were enjoying a reprieve from the relentless warrant server Jim Davis. Davis had now shifted his attention to the rehabilitation center, much to everyone's relief. Jim would show up just about every day. He took it upon himself to act as my official tormentor. When he was there, a moment wouldn't go by without some kind of caustic remark being offered.

Watching me work on the loom, Jim would snort and giggle, then sort of lean over my shoulder and whistle, "Hey, pard, make me an oriental rug, okay?" Davis was always harassing me, trying to get me to push myself a little harder. He had to try everything I did. Push-ups, parallel bars, crutch walking, the works.

He also partook of the coffee breaks and never failed to add to the round of gossip. Gossip was especially rampant during 1957. Both the city and Multnomah County had come under heavy criticism, as public officials and law enforcement officers were being linked to organized crime. Jim was constantly relaying the latest news about fellow policemen now under an investigative cloud. He also recounted the latest exploits of fellow police officer "Tiger" Loose, so named because of his unpredictability and his tigerlike determination to see things through to the end.

Tiger was one of the greatest human beings I've ever known. He was the kind of man who would give you his last dime, the shirt off his back. Tiger was always ready to help, which on a number of occasions proved to be his downfall. Tiger had a Christian attitude, but at times he lacked discretion.

Jim always brought his own coffee mug. It was a huge beer stein that devoured half a pot of coffee at a sitting. He reminded me of Uncle Remus as he took a sip of coffee, then leaned in and smiled mischievously. "Tiger struck again."

I shook my head knowingly. "What happened this time?"

"He was parking cars up at Bart's Place, you know, the restaurant up on Eighteenth and Burnside." (One of Tiger's moonlighting jobs was parking cars at a local nightclub.)

I acknowledged I knew where it was.

"Well, Tiger is parking cars and he spots this wanted felon driving up in a Cadillac. This guy's about six-three and two hundred ten pounds." Davis glanced at both Clara and me and started laughing uncontrollably.

"Clara," I said, sensing what Jim was about to describe, "Tiger's about five-six and maybe one hundred forty-five pounds." I looked over at Jim. "You going to be okay?"

"Yeah," Davis wheezed, trying to wipe the tears from his eyes. "Yeah, I'll be okay," and he started laughing again. Soon both Clara and I were swept up by Jim's laughter and neither knew why. As we struggled to regain our composure, I spotted Magda walking by the room. She was not smiling.

This went on for another two minutes before Jim finally gained control of himself. He took a deep breath and then went on as if nothing happened. "Now, where was I?"

"Tiger spotted this rather large wanted felon driving a Cadillac."

"Right. So anyway, Tiger waits till this dude steps out of the car and tells him, 'You're under arrest. I'm a police officer.' The guy takes a look at Tiger's parking attendant suit and just walks away. Tiger starts screaming that he's under arrest and jumps the guy. By now the guy figures that either Tiger really is a cop or a lunatic. So he pounds the heck out of Tiger, jumps in his car, and drives away."

Clara sat there spellbound by Jim's description and I laughed so hard I almost fell out of my wheelchair. "Don't tell me Tiger chased him!"

"Yeah, Tiger jumps up and chases the guy on foot. He catches up with him at the next stoplight and yells at him to get out of the car, that he's under arrest again. Well, the felon gets out of the car, which is unfortunate for Tiger," Jim gasped, trying to stifle another laugh seizure. "Tiger takes another beating, the guy hops back into his car and roars off down Burnside. Tiger gets up, brushes himself off, and takes off after the car. All the time he's trying to flag down passing cars to call the police for help. This goes on for fourteen blocks! By the time the dude and Tiger reach

First and Burnside, they've had seven fights, Tiger's lost them all and has been beaten silly. But I'll give him credit"—Jim laughed again—"he never gave up. Finally a patrol car intercepted them and arrested the guy."

"I don't believe it!"

Jim wiped the tears from his eyes. "But the greatest line of the whole night comes from the guy. He's beaten Tiger up so many times, he thinks he's about to have a heart attack! He told the arresting officer he couldn't have thrown another punch, he was too exhausted!"

Of course, it wasn't always a one-way street in terms of anecdotes. One of my favorites was about Dr. Moore. Dr. Moore was a great believer in physical fitness and always encouraged patients and staff members to develop their bodies through exercise and weight lifting. His biggest measuring stick was the bench press. It was his opinion that everyone should be able to bench-press his own weight.

One day, during the course of a heated discussion over the merits of weight lifting and one's ability to press one's own weight, Dr. Moore ripped off his smock and sports jacket and headed for the weights, with everyone following closely behind. Moore took his weight lifting seriously and angrily threw weights on the barbell.

For those of you not familiar with weight lifting, to perform a bench press the lifter must lie flat on his back on a bench. The weights are held by two supports directly above the lifter's chin. When the lifter's ready, he pushes the weights up and off the supports and brings them down to his chest to begin the bench presses.

With everyone crowded around, Dr. Moore, all 135 pounds of him, was ready for the demonstration. He pushed the barbell off the supports and brought them down to his chest. That was the first indication that perhaps things were not going exactly as planned. Everyone noticed how quickly the barbell dropped to his chest and how oddly his eyes seemed to bulge.

The bulging eyes were quickly followed by a red face that turned a deep shade of maroon as Dr. Moore tried to push the weights up and off his chest. The blood vessels in his temples and forehead rose to the surface and his cheeks expanded as he struggled to move the weight, which seemed totally oblivious to his effort. It seems the good doctor, in his haste to prove a point, had inadvertently put 190 pounds on the barbell, not 135 pounds. Probably, at any other time, Dr. Moore would have called out for help, but he was center stage this particular day. Pride demanded he overcome his predicament, which he did, and without developing a hernia or a broken blood vessel.

As nonchalantly as possible, Dr. Moore smiled. "See, everyone should be able to bench-press his own weight; just make sure you know your weight and the weight of the barbell!"

We spent a lot of time swapping stories during those five-minute coffee breaks that somehow magically extended into an hour. Magda did not approve, that was evident by the numerous scowls she shot toward the coffee room, but we ignored her accusing looks as much as possible.

Then one day, as I wheeled myself into the physical therapy room, Magda came up to me all smiles. "Why, Jess, how are you feeling today?"

"Just great, Magda. Yourself?"

"Fine. Just fine."

I was beginning to feel a bit uncomfortable. "Well, I've got to be going. I'll see you later."

"Going to the coffee room?"

I nodded confidently. "Yep. Gotta relax a bit before we get under way."

"No, I don't think so, Jess. You're not going to have the time. You're my patient now."

"Sorry, I'm with Clara."

Magda smiled warmly. "No. I had a talk with Dr. Jones. From now on, you'll be working with me. We'll be taking coffee breaks when you've worked hard enough to have one. Come on, Jess," she said, pushing the wheelchair toward the parallel bars, "we've got a lot of work to do."

It was like joining the Boy Scouts and then discovering that the Marines were running the program. Magda got hold of me and wouldn't let loose. She was convinced I was loafing and would never get any better until someone pushed and shoved me into it. She was absolutely right. Clara had a soft heart for everyone; Magda, on the other hand, had a soft heart only for those who earned it. For the slackers, it was a heart of stone and a will to match.

"Jess, you may hate me now, but you'll love me when it's over." Those were Magda's words, but I swear John Wayne used the same ones when talking to Marine recruits in *Sands of Iwo Jima.* She was true to her word. For the next three weeks she pushed me as hard as any Marine drill instructor. Immediately she demanded that I begin doing twenty instead of fifteen push-ups a day, she increased my chin-ups from five or six to ten, and then raised the number of repetitions for both exercises by five the following week. Before, I had been spending ten or fifteen minutes on the parallel bars; now it seemed as if I was spending my whole life there. And all the time, Magda was there with words of encouragement: "Jess, you're not working hard enough!"

I devoted a good deal of time to trying to talk her into slowing down, to take a break now and then, but she was adamant. No breaks unless I earned them. We got into some rather heated and loud discussions concerning her ideas about physical therapy.

"Magda," I snapped, "the whole idea is to improve the patient's health, not kill him!"

Magda's stern face remained unchanged. "Jess, you're not working hard enough! Unless you try to discover your absolute limits, unless you're willing to work hard enough so you don't have to depend on Jeanne to do everything for you, you might as well be dead."

"Great, but you've still got to have a little sympathy for your patients."

For the first time I saw a flash of anger in her eyes, but she managed to check it. "I've got sympathy for anyone who has to struggle to have a normal life. Sympathy, Jess, but I won't feel sorry for them. Feeling sorry is only for people who don't try. I'm trying to restore dignity. The more you can do for yourself, the more dignity you'll have."

"You call this dignity," I complained, pointing to my leg braces and crutches. "I'm nothing more than a metallic freak. A clanging amusement park for people to stare at. Tell me, Magda, what's the use?"

The anger flashed in her eyes again and this time she didn't bother checking it. "You've been complaining ever since you became my patient! Well, Jess Roe, see those children over there? Look at them! Some of those children will never have half the life you did. They were born unable to use their legs, their arms. Some of them are never going to get any better and they probably know it. But they don't complain. They work hard and they laugh. They want to live and they enjoy as much of life as God will let them. But you, a big, strong man, you sit here and complain about a little work and how it doesn't do any good. Well, Jess, if it doesn't do any good, then go home. Go home and let Jeanne wait on you hand and foot. Let your friends feel sorry for you, and then you can die in comfort. Go home if you don't want to work! But if you want to find yourself, then stop complaining and start working! But I don't have time to listen to you whine about how unfair things are. No one ever said life was fair!"

Before I could react to Magda's outburst, she brought my wheelchair over, got me into it, and pushed me over to the coffee room. "If this is where you want to be, then stay here! Anywhere else and you'll be in the way. If you get bored and are ready to work, I'll be with the children. They enjoy the attention!"

Then suddenly I was alone to mull over what Magda had said. I don't think even John Wayne would have talked to his troops that way! For the first time in almost a year, I remembered the afternoon in the hospital when that voice came to me and told me I would be all right. It suddenly occurred to me that perhaps Magda was a partial fulfillment of that promise. She offered the hardest, most difficult road to travel. There would be no shortcuts, no easy way to get from point A to point B, but it was a straight line, the shortest route: hard work and determination. She also held out the promise of something else: dignity, a true gift from God. If a person has dignity, everything else follows. The dictionary defines dignity as "a state of being worthy, honored, or esteemed." I think a more simple definition would be: "Christian attitude."

I sat in the coffee room for about ten minutes; then, as unobtrusively as possible, I wheeled myself back out onto the floor and over to where Magda was working with a five-year-old quadriplegic.

I watched her working with that youngster and for the first time saw the compassion I had thought absent. It was there, I just hadn't taken the time to look. After ignoring me for a couple of minutes, she glanced over her shoulder and smiled. "What took you so long?"

She had known I would come back. "I was trying to figure out which would kill me first, coffee and cigarettes or you."

"I will," she said, grinning, "but you'll be a lot healthier when you go, I promise. I will also promise that you're going to be very tired at the end of the day."

She was absolutely right. For the rest of that day and for the next five months, Magda poured it on. Chin-ups, push-ups, muscle massages, stretching exercises; I spent as much time on the parallel bars as any Olympic gymnastic hopeful, crutch walking would go for what seemed like hours, and always Magda kept yelling encouragement.

"More, Jess, do more. You're not working hard enough, you've got to work harder."

After one particularly hard day, Magda had me doing push-ups to finish the session. After forty I was starting to fade a bit. "Magda, that's it. I'm too tired to go any further."

"Tired! You've only started. You've got thirty more push-ups to do."

"I can't make it," I argued. "Ten more. I'll go to fifty and that's it."

Magda nodded. "Okay, you do just ten more. But you get a handicap."

"That's a cruel pun, Magda."

"Maybe, but it's a handicap or thirty more." With that she grabbed a five-year-old with leg braces and put him on my back. The youngster probably weighed about forty pounds, but the braces were another twenty pounds! I had already done forty push-ups and now Magda expected me to do another ten with an extra sixty pounds on my back.

If that weren't bad enough, Jim Davis arrived on the scene. "Hey, Magda." He waved cheerfully. "How come you're letting Jess slack off? Giving piggyback rides to the kids. I thought this was supposed to be a rehabilitation center, not a carnival. Come on, Magda, you starting to turn into a softy?"

Magda grinned and I groaned under the strain.

"Hey, pard, when the kid's through can I have a ride?"

I made it, no thanks to Davis, but afterward I could hardly move. Magda and Jim had to help me back into the wheelchair.

"Okay, Jess." Magda smiled. "Let's take a break."

"A break!" I gasped. "The session is over!"

"Yes, but it's the thought that counts."

That was how I spent the next five months: under the uncompromising eye of Magda and the barbs of Davis. During that time, Monica completed her training and was ready to tackle her family once again. And somewhere, in between all the shouting and yelling, Ronnie Anderson and Loraine fell in love. Soon after I completed my rehabilitation program, they got married and bought a dairy farm south of Oregon City.

As for me, I was now ready to take charge of my life again. I was sure that nothing could ever be as terrible as first losing your legs and then having to go through therapy with Magda.

PART TWO

Come unto me, all ye that labour and are heavy laden, and I will give you rest.

Take my yoke upon you, and learn of me; for I am meek and lowly in heart: and ye shall find rest unto your souls.

For my yoke is easy, and my burden is light.

Matt. 11:28–30;
King James Version

CHAPTER SIX

Therapy sessions are designed to strengthen the will as well as the body. The purpose is to demonstrate to the patient that the body can do many things if asked. The key is the mental attitude of the owner of the body.

I still perceived myself as handicapped, even though Magda had physically prepared me for my return to society. Consciously I had proved that physically I could do just about anything I wanted, but subconsciously I still retained that prejudice against the handicapped. Mentally I was still restricting my life because of a deep-seated belief that handicapped people shouldn't be active.

Magda had forced me to realize that, physically, I could accomplish a great deal, but it was Jeanne and Jim Davis who insisted that I apply that ability. They demanded I start thinking like a person with legs.

Before, if I needed something, I only had to suggest and someone would see to it that I got it. Suddenly things had changed. If I wanted a cup of coffee and it was convenient for Jeanne, she would get it. If it was obvious that I could do it myself, that's what I was told. There were no more free rides.

At home, I was being "encouraged" to become independent and Jim Davis was pushing me to get out, to reestablish myself with the old routines. One of those routines was fishing. Before the accident, Jim and I would go fishing two or three times a week, and now Jim was pressing me to start again. From the moment I began therapy, Jim kept insisting we go fishing and I kept insisting that it wasn't possible. The badgering continued until Jim decided to resolve the matter once and for all. After enticing me into an afternoon drive, he announced that we were either going fishing or I could walk home.

"What do you mean, we're going fishing?" I demanded.

"You've been givin' me every excuse in the world as to why you can't go fishin', and none of them make any sense to me. You just don't want to try it!"

"Don't make any sense!" I thumped my leg braces. "These things weigh better than twenty pounds apiece! What happens if I fall into the water?"

Jim thought about that for a second and then smiled. "Well, if we tie a rope around you, you'll make a terrific anchor!"

"Very funny," I said, trying to stifle a laugh.

"What are you complaining about anyway, Jess? You were a terrible swimmer before you got those braces. At least now you'll have an excuse."

We argued back and forth for a few minutes, but it was obvious that I was going fishing whether I wanted to or not. Actually, I did want to, but I had convinced myself that people in wheelchairs didn't go fishing. After I took a look at the ramp leading to the marina where Jim kept his boat, I was certain that people in wheelchairs didn't, or at least shouldn't, go fishing.

"Okay, Mr. Tour Guide, how do you propose we get around that?" I said triumphantly, pointing to the long ramp. The walkway leading to the marina was almost two hundred yards long, with about a thirty-degree decline, which was too steep for crutch walking. It was just barely wide enough for the wheelchair, but wood strips had been nailed across the ramp about every foot in order to give walkers a better footing during the rainy weather. The builders, of course, like me, had not considered the possibility that anyone would attempt to navigate a wheelchair down the walkway.

Jim studied the ramp for a second, then shrugged his shoulders. "No problem. Get in the wheelchair and I'll push you down."

"Down that! You're kidding. Those bumps would rattle my brain to pieces!"

"Fishing demands certain sacrifices, Jess. Besides, Jeanne showed me your grades from high school. I don't think the rattle would hurt much." He laughed.

I pointed to the narrow walkway. "There's hardly enough room for the wheelchair," I complained. "One bad bounce and I'd be in the water."

Jim studied the water for a moment. "I don't know, seems like a silly place for an anchor. If I drop you over, pard, I'll do it someplace useful. Quit stalling, we're going fishing! And, since you're not carrying anything, you get to hold all the gear."

He immediately unloaded his pickup and transferred everything to my lap. I looked like a vandalized float in a fishing derby parade. Then we were off, and for the next few minutes I lived in terror as Jim pushed me down that long ramp. The constant thumping created by the strips of wood bounced me around like a runaway "Magic Fingers" bed. The tackle boxes were clanking against the metal wheelchair, the fishing poles were swooshing up and down, and the tires pounded out a constant beat against the wood strips. We must have sounded like a Wagnerian opera arranged by Spike Jones.

There was about a ten-foot drop into some very deep water, and the wheels were perilously close to the edge. Jim must have noticed my knuckles, which were turning an unusual shade of white, and tried to ease the tension with small talk.

"Boy, if I lost my grip, you'd really be in for a fast, bumpy ride. Probably get wet, too."

"Thanks! That makes me feel a lot better."

"Thought it would," Jim said cheerfully.

The thumping continued and rattled me around in the chair. I expected at any moment to be bounced right out of my wheelchair and into the Columbia River. If it had happened, I was prepared. I was going to yell "I told you so" as loud as I could before I hit the water.

After what seemed a lifetime, or at least a summer of television reruns, plus some additional cheery comments from Jim, we arrived at the boat, the *Little Jewel.*

Jim wiped the sweat from his forehead, rubbed the top of his crew cut, and smiled. "She's in great shape, ain't she. I even plugged up most of the leaks in honor of our fishing trip."

"*Most* of the leaks?"

"Well, you're never sure if you got them all until you take her out on a shakedown cruise. That's why you're along." He grinned.

"To help on the cruise?"

"Un unh. You get to bail. I figure terror makes people bail faster."

"I'll remember that as the *Little Jewel* slowly slips beneath the waves."

I sat there for a second studying the boat, then asked what I thought was a penetrating question. "Say, Jim, how are you planning to get me aboard? I can't climb in and I'm going to need something to sit in while we're fishing."

Jim rubbed his chin for a second. Obviously he had not thought about that problem, but it didn't take him long to find a solution. With one quick motion, he picked me and the wheelchair up and gently put us down in the boat.

"There, that wasn't so tough, was it?"

The ease with which Davis picked me and the wheelchair up amazed me. It was a combined weight of about two hundred pounds, and he made it appear as if I were a small sack of potatoes.

A few minutes later, the lines had been cast free and we were drifting quietly down the Columbia. I felt the late July winds as they rushed toward the Pacific, carrying with them a hint of an early autumn. You could smell the crispness in the air. The tranquil sound of the water lapping against the boat gave me, for the first time in many months, a sense of freedom. As the current swept us downstream and the wind rippled through my hair, I felt the confidence building in me.

At the time I defined it as confidence, but now I believe it was the Lord. After months of turning my back on Him, of refusing to accept the new direction my life was taking, I was finally reaching out to Him. I had taken a few steps down the path. There was still quite a distance to go, but the apprehension of my journey was being melted away by one of God's miracles, nature.

It was a beautiful, clear day. The sun's shimmer danced across the river's surface. Neither of us said much. We let the time slip away, enjoying the solitude of the river and the closeness of our friendship. The *Little Jewel* drifted on toward Shell Island, where the steelhead gather before heading upstream to their spawning grounds.

Jim and I never interrupted their journey. Before you can fish you have to anchor, and we never quite got the hang of anchoring. We'd drop the anchor over the side and, once we were sure it was solid, we'd start fishing. No sooner did we get our lines in the water than we noticed we were drifting downstream. We would have to reel in the lines, spend another ten minutes trying to get the anchor to set, and then reset our lines. This little comic opera was repeated about every twenty minutes, much to the amusement of the veteran fishermen, who didn't bother to conceal their laughter. Occasionally someone would shout advice about how to make the anchor stick, but each suggestion was usually countered by another as we slowly drifted away.

We laughed and complained that, instead of an albatross, we were condemned to life with an anchor around our necks. Jim hinted darkly that if I didn't learn to anchor the boat soon, I might become the anchor, and I pointed out that it was not so much the anchor as it was a skipper who didn't know how to position his boat. Finally we came to the conclusion that our anchoring problems must have been tied to sunspots and obviously had nothing to do with our boating ability, which of course left both of us off the hook.

The same could be said for the fish. We fished that entire summer, many times with Mike along with us. We came armed with the latest fishing tackle, the hottest bait, the best techniques, and never once had to argue about who would clean the fish. Not once did we get a strike. We were certain it was not a reflection on our fishing skills, but Mike kept counting aloud the number of fish being pulled in by the other fishermen. Mike suggested that perhaps they knew something we didn't, and Davis suggested Mike walk home.

Veteran fishermen are not inclined to share fishing secrets with anyone. They conceal the way they rig up and the type of bait or lure they are using. But finally, one day near the end of the season, an old-timer who often anchored near us took pity on our plight. We must have looked like a couple of kids with our noses pressed up against the window of a candy store as we watched fishermen hauling in big catches while we passed the time reanchoring and thrashing the water with our lines.

I looked over at the old-timer and sighed. "We've tried everything but Jimmy Durante imitations."

The old-timer, who wore a fishing hat that looked as if it had been condemned by the Board of Health and smoked a pipe that had survived the Crash of '29, smiled and nodded, saying nothing.

The mere fact that he acknowledged our presence was, for an old-time fisherman, as if he had suddenly discovered that we were long-lost cousins. Encouraged by this outpouring of emotion, I decided to press my luck. "What do you think we ought to try?"

There was a bit of a pause and then he sort of quietly cleared his throat while considering the question. "Dynamite." It was delivered with a perfectly calm, straight face.

Jim almost fell out of the boat laughing. "Dynamite?" I laughed.

"'Bout the only way you're going to catch anything the way you're fishin'. You're fishin' too high off the bottom. Fish are going under your bait. Everyone knows that."

He then went into a lengthy discussion of how you have to find bottom, locate depressions in the sandy bottom, and then rig your line so that your bait hangs just over the lip of the depression. With that setup, the steelhead, which tend to swim in a line conforming to the contours of the riverbed, will spot the bait as they come out of the depression.

"The way you guys have been rigging up, 'bout the only thing you'd catch is a deadhead log."

It had never occurred to us that the fish were swimming under our lines, but after we rerigged, both of us immediately got strikes and just as quickly lost them. But a short time later I hooked a jack salmon and, after some trying moments, finally landed him. It was probably one of the ugliest fish I have ever seen, but that day it was a beautiful sight. The string had been broken, we had officially become fishermen. We even got a good-natured round of applause from the old-timers who had suffered through our summer with us.

The trips up and down that long ramp were numerous that summer, and by the time the season closed, my wheelchair was a shambles. It had been thumped and rattled to pieces. But if it had fallen apart, I had picked up the pieces of my life. Fishing is a leisurely pastime, but it helped me realize that everything was now up to me. There was no longer an excuse to feel sorry for myself. I could do things if I was willing to admit that occasionally I needed some help. It was a major hurdle, and although it would still be years before I stopped avoiding restaurants because I felt everyone was staring at me, I had met and overcome an important challenge: moving out into public and functioning with a degree of self-respect that allowed me to retain my pride.

Jeanne

It was a good summer for the whole family. Jess began to find himself during those afternoon fishing trips with Jim. There was no miraculous change in his attitude, but you could sense the confidence returning. His voice lost its heaviness. In its place, the warmth I remembered and loved reappeared.

The smiles, which a month or two earlier had been forced, now came naturally and his laugh was strong. And fortunately I wasn't fond of fish.

It was one of the most beautiful summers of my life. The fears and doubts about our future were melting away as quickly as Jess's doubts about himself. God had been kind to us. He could have taken Jess that day; He could have let Jess give up. He could have let Jess's family and friends give up, but He didn't.

I remember seeing a quotation hanging in a child's room one time which explained that "a baby is God's way of saying life is still worth living." So are a genuine smile and a strong laugh.

John F. Kennedy, when questioned about his act of heroism during World War II, noted dryly, "It was an inadvertent act. They sank my boat."

My reemergence into society was much the same. Once Davis had forced the issue, there was no turning back. Even if I had wanted to sit back and relax, the Lord seemed to have other plans for me.

That fall we received a settlement from the railroad company. Although it was not a large sum, it allowed Jeanne and me some financial freedom, or at least that was our first reaction. But before we could enjoy the first savings account statement, a friend of mine came up with a business proposition.

"A housing development!"

"That's right. Have you ever thought about developing some property?"

The man making the suggestion was Bill Holden, an old school chum and a developer in the Lake Oswego area. He had just completed a development and was looking for a new project. He was now looking directly at me.

"I haven't the foggiest idea about developments."

"Jess," Bill said, laughing, "if people really understood developments, I mean, understood the risks, no one would ever develop anything."

"Well, that's certainly reassuring."

Jeanne and I talked about the risks and, of course, the possible returns. We knew absolutely nothing about developing property but knew that Bill had been successful. So, instead of leaving the money in the bank, we put it in the ground—literally.

That spring, Cherry Crest was launched. For a novice, putting together a development seemed like a simple matter. Pour a bunch of foundations, hire someone to frame and put up the subwalls and then the sides. Someone else does the interior and finish work, and, like magic, everything is done.

I hadn't considered sidewalks, curbing, sewer systems, paved streets, not to mention city and county planning regulations and utility hookups. Bear in mind, this was prior to comprehensive plans, the Environmental Protection Agency, and various other governing bodies formed to protect the consumer.

As bills began to mount, although Bill assured us that the cash flow situation was stable, I began to worry. Everything was right on schedule, but I noticed that we were spending a lot of money hiring other people to do a lot of jobs I knew I could do, given the proper equipment.

The challenge finally came when we received a low bid of twenty-five cents a foot to cover the sewer and water lines that had to be laid. This was in 1958, and twenty-five cents would still buy a lot of things. After looking at the available tractors or backhoes, and researching the possibility of having the tractor rigged with hand controls, I decided I could do the same job for considerably less.

After buying a used tractor, outfitting it with hand controls, and taking a few quick lessons, I discovered that I could do the same job for eight cents a foot, and when the job was over I would still own the tractor.

The first few days, I have to admit, were a bit scary. I sat on that tractor and pushed dirt into the ditches and considered the possibility of accidentally moving too close to the ditch and dropping a track into it. The tractor would have rolled over and I would have gone with it. There was no possible way for me to jump off that machine. I had to have help getting on it, and then I was on my own. If it went over, I went with it. There was no safety roll bar or roll cage. Today, our operation would have been shut down. But we were working at a time when no one really thought much about safety precautions. You just got the job done, on the basis of how fast you could complete it, and didn't worry about the safe way of doing things.

Today I realize how foolish I was, but at the time it seemed like the thing to do.

The tractor proved an immediate success and soon contractors building homes in our development hired me to do landscaping work on the lots. The tractor was small enough to move around the building sites without destroying anything, and I suddenly realized that perhaps with some additional equipment I could start a rental company.

I bought a larger, used backhoe, which I couldn't operate, and the Lake Oswego Equipment Company was open for business. Of course, it meant that I had to hire some additional help. My employee was Lee Stidd, Jr. During my days in the hospital, Lee used to come up and talk for hours about guns and police work. It was a topic his father, the local mayor, was not interested in, and because I was, Lee and I became good friends.

That summer, before he started his first year in college, I hired him as my backhoe operator. He dug the sewer connection ditches for thirty-six lots in the development and managed to put the backhoe in one of the ditches. When he told me about it, I thought to myself, if I had been operating it, I could have easily been killed. But he jumped from the equipment before it rolled over.

I had little time, however, to dwell on fate. As the development began to take shape, another friend, Virgil Solso, a local banker, had a business proposition he thought I might be interested in.

"A bowling alley!"

"That's right. I have a client who wants to open a bowling alley in this area. You own that property over on the south side of the lake and he seems to think that it's a perfect place to put a bowling alley."

I looked at him and shook my head. "I've got all my money tied up in this project," I groaned, "and it's going to be another five to eight months before we're done."

"Don't worry, Jess. I can take care of the financing. You build the bowling alley."

Our house sat on the property where the bowling alley was destined to be built, which meant we had to move the house, which meant we had to spend more money.

One night when reruns dominated the television schedule (yes, they plagued mankind even back in the good old days), Jeanne and I sat down and began adding up our debts. The final total numbed us. We owed a quarter of a million dollars—$250,000! This was at a time when premium gasoline sold for thirty-one cents a gallon and a gallon of milk carried the whopping price tag of thirty-three cents. A quarter of a million dollars of debts was staggering.

When I pointed out to Virgil the next day that we were growing concerned about our ability to pay the loans back, he just smiled and said in a knowing voice, "Jess, you're not alone. If any one of us stumbles, we'll all go down the drain. If you have a problem, we'll figure some way to work it out."

Since the banker wasn't overly concerned and nonchalantly shrugged off a quarter of a million dollars, I decided, "Why should I worry?" Armed with that philosophy, I went out and bought a heavy-duty cat with a three-quarter-yard four-in-one bucket. This type of bucket was a front-loader. It either operated as a regular scoop shovel or opened in the middle and could be used as a blade or scraper. It resembled a clam. You can dig up a lot of ground with it, and now I was in the excavation business, digging out basements, swimming pools, and anything else demanding big holes in the ground.

This particular piece of equipment could be fitted with hand controls, and I always looked forward to operating it. I guess it was a form of therapy, much like fishing. When I felt depressed or angry, I could hop on that machine and work until I was totally exhausted. The hostility, depression, or frustration of the day was gone, and I knew I had worked as hard as anyone with two good legs. It was an extremely satisfying sensation to see that at the end of a day there were one or two new basements, a swimming pool, or a cesspool dug out ready for the contractor.

One day, while I was working on a basement for a new eye clinic, Dr. Kimberly drove by. At first he just glanced at me on the tractor. I recognized him immediately and waved, but he drove on without acknowledging my gesture. But a minute or two later he came back and stopped the car. He rolled down the window and leaned out. There was a big grin on his face and he yelled, "Thatta boy, Jess!" I think both of us were proud of how far I had come.

I could operate about half of the equipment we had, but that meant the other half sat idle unless we could find a competent operator. By we, I mean Jeanne and I. Finding a good driver was difficult. Lee had returned to school and I found few workers whom I could trust to do good work and take care of the equipment. Still, I was growing fond of collecting machines. It's not unlike collecting records, bottle caps, or stamps. There is that constant urge to add to your collection, whether you needed to or not. And no matter how big a machine is, it is never big enough.

An acquaintance of mind owned a dump truck, but business had been off and he was in danger of losing it to the bank. He asked if I might be interested in buying it and my eyes lit up. I didn't have a dump truck. I also didn't have a need for a dump truck, but who's rational when it comes to collecting. I talked it over with Jeanne and she seemed to have some reservations.

"Absolutely not! Jess, I know what's going to happen! You buy that truck and I'm going to wind up driving it! No, we don't need a dump truck and we don't need another piece of equipment you can't operate!"

Jeanne was absolutely right. We didn't need that dump truck; I couldn't drive it; and she would undoubtedly wind up driving it. Her arguments were flawless, and it took me almost two weeks to work up enough courage to tell her I had bought the truck. She started becoming suspicious when she noticed that it was always parked out in front of the house.

"Why is that dump truck parked outside? You didn't buy it, did you?" she questioned in a rather icy tone.

"John parked it out there for a couple of days," I replied, trying to avoid a direct answer, and for a couple of days that response sufficed. But after a week the explanation wore extremely thin.

"You bought that truck, didn't you?"

"Well, I was just trying to help John out," I said defensively.

"No you weren't! You were helping Jess Roe add to his toy collection!" The words were spoken with a certain amount of hostility, and for the next few days Jeanne constantly reminded me that she was not happy with my purchase. But the incident finally faded away and would have been forgotten had we been able to find a driver for a load of sand. Unfortunately, it was in midsummer and everyone was working. And as Jeanne had predicted, she was the only one left.

"I knew it! I knew it! I knew I was going to get stuck with that monster!"

It's amazing how awful crow tastes, or how dry words can be when you have to eat them. But to Jeanne's credit, she did the job as well as any trucker, wheeling that big truck around building sites and dumping the sand right on target. I went to great lengths to compliment her on her driving skills.

Jeanne smiled at the compliment, but it was the kind of smile one normally associates with a shark. "We're selling that truck," she said softly.

"This probably won't happen again, Jeanne."

"We're selling that truck." She smiled again. I could almost see the dorsal fin breaking the surface. The next week we sold the truck.

So Jeanne removed herself from the dump-truck driving business and at the same time removed the Lake Oswego Equipment Company from the same venture. From then on, we just concentrated on digging out basements, sewer lines, and landscaping.

Mike was now eleven years old and growing more interested in the business. He used to come out to the job sites and watch me operate the tractor. After three weeks, he began pressing me about trying it. At first I said no. It just didn't seem possible that he could be old enough to do the work. But he never gave up, and pretty soon I came to the conclusion that it would be easier to let him try it than to have to listen to him keep asking.

Despite his youth, it was obvious that he had been watching me closely. Although he had some problems operating the backhoe, he understood the principle and with a little trial-and-error time managed to master the fundamentals. He quickly realized, however, that he wasn't strong enough or able enough to do a lot of work, and after proving to himself he could do it his interest drifted on to other things.

At that time baseball occupied a good deal of his time. Unfortunately he was tall for his age, and a bit uncoordinated. As a result, he spent as much time on the bench as he did playing, which didn't sit too well with him. Like all youngsters, he wasn't willing to admit that someone was better than he, and he became discouraged.

"Mike, you have to understand that regardless of how good you are, there's always someone else who at that particular moment might be a little better. That doesn't mean it will always be that way, but you have to accept it. If you sit down and stop trying you'll never find out how good you can be."

Mike listened, but you could sense the frustration of youth. "But, Dad, I'm trying as hard as I can! I practice all the time and I still don't get to play all the time."

He looked so serious and had such a deep frown on his face, I found it difficult not to laugh. I thought of Magda and tried to recall how she used to handle me when I was struggling or growing weary of the therapy.

"Mike, the secret to life is not to worry about today but look toward tomorrow. If you're honestly working as hard as you can, then don't worry about it. You're still growing. Some kids never have to struggle with coordination and it gives them an edge. You're still developing. All you can do is keep at it and don't give up."

And he didn't. I was proud of his determination but hadn't considered that his program of self-improvement meant I would spend a lot of time playing catch. Almost every afternoon we'd go out into the backyard and throw the ball around. The only drawback was Cindy.

Cindy was our German shepherd. Jeanne had bought her for Mike's birthday while I was in the hospital. Cindy was great with children and even better at fetching. Her only problem was being able to distinguish between fetch and catch. She was a bit like the Cookie Monster on "Sesame Street." As Mike and I tossed the ball back and forth she would lie there watching as if it were a tennis match. She was waiting for the moment when one of us would throw the ball a little too low. She needed only one throw and the game of catch was over. Cindy would leap into the air, grab the ball, and take off.

Unlike some dogs, Cindy didn't return the ball after an interception. If she caught it, it was her ball and you'd have to tackle her to get it back. She was also very clever at swiping footballs, softballs, and tennis balls. Basketballs presented something of a dilemma. She could only nose the ball around, so she was easier to capture, but she always gave it her best shot. There were times when the children would come inside crying that Cindy wouldn't give the ball back and Jeanne would have to spend a half hour tracking the dog down, prying the ball loose from her mouth, and then dragging her into the garage so the kids could play.

She was also very protective of youngsters, and our neighbors always knew that when she was around no harm could come to the children. This, of course, did have occasional drawbacks for the parents.

One afternoon one of our neighbors' children was playing in the yard. When his mother called him in for his nap, he was not interested. She called him twice and twice he said no, which of course angered the mother. But when she grabbed the youngster and was about to discipline him, Cindy let out a threatening, low growl and bared her teeth. The mother gingerly tiptoed out of the yard and securely locked the gate behind her. Then she spent the next ten minutes trying gently to coax her truant offspring out of the yard and away from Cindy's protective care.

To avoid Cindy's constant interruptions, we would spend a lot of afternoons practicing at the local ball park. Mike, his friend Frank Solter, Frank's father, Ray, and I would work out. Ray would pitch batting practice and hit the kids ground balls and flies and I would play catch.

Watching Ray work with the kids, I could feel those old twinges of envy and depression stirring deep inside. A year earlier I would have gone into a black tailspin, but now I could handle it. I knew that Mike wanted and needed me even if I couldn't swing a bat very well.

Jeanne

The momentum had shifted for the family. You could feel it. There had been moments when the sense of unity simply wasn't there. We were happy, still a family, but a lot of the spark or enthusiasm within the family was missing. Now things had returned to normal. Jess was providing that enthusiasm. He had a purpose, a direction to aim his life in.

He was becoming more and more involved in the development and equipment business. He became so proficient at operating the excavation cat that few of his customers realized he couldn't walk. Meanwhile, the children were rapidly growing up before our eyes.

In all families, at least from my own observation, brothers and sisters seldom get along for any great length of time. Mike loved to tease Chris and Sus. One of his favorite tortures was to take his sisters to a show he had already seen and then give them a play-by-play account of what was going to happen next. This always infuriated Chris, but the next time he offered to take them, they were ready to go.

It never failed that Chris, regardless of the bait Mike threw out, would bite, and the battle was on. Finally, in desperation, she would yell "Mom!" and Mom would unwillingly become the referee. Sus was another matter. When Mike started picking on her, she was absolutely delighted. Since she was the youngest, her brother hardly noticed her. So when he started, he quickly discovered he had a willing victim who thought being teased was great fun. Mike would quickly tire of a game where his intended victim was having more fun than he was. But if Mike had tired of the game, Sus was just warming up. She still wanted to be a victim and wouldn't let Mike alone. Invariably Mike would release a frustrated cry of "Mom!" and I was back in the game.

We also started back to church, or at least the children and I did. I tried on a number of occasions to get Jess to go, but he always refused. He had any number of excuses, but basically he still didn't like going out in public using his crutches or being pushed in his wheelchair. No amount of coaxing would budge him. He still felt as if everyone was staring at him when he sat in the wheelchair.

Still, he took an interest in what we were doing in church and always quizzed the children on their Sunday school lessons. He always enjoyed the girls' complaining about Mike's questionable singing ability.

"He was awful, Daddy," Sus complained. "He couldn't carry a note in his pocket!"

"You mean, he couldn't carry a note in a bucket." Jess laughed.

"He couldn't carry it there, either," she said disgustedly.

Unfortunately the girls were right. Mike was awful! He had a flat, nasal voice and, as if that wasn't enough, he loved to sing at the top of his voice. What he lacked in ability, he more than made up for in enthusiasm.

The same could have been said for Cindy. When Cindy was a puppy, we were very strict about her leaving the yard. Each time she went through the gate without permission, I'd take after her with a rolled-up newspaper. She learned quickly, but apparently didn't understand that the restriction was just for her.

One day after Sunday school, following a spring rainstorm, Mike came running into the kitchen and asked if he could go over to the neighbors' and play. He was twelve at the time and fairly big for his age. The ground was wet and muddy and it was only a matter of time before another rain hit, but I decided if he didn't go then, he'd be stuck inside all day. So, with a whoop of excitement, he dashed outdoors.

Fifteen minutes later, he came back inside, crying, his jeans covered with mud.

"What happened?"

"Cindy won't let me go!" he cried.

"Cindy won't let you go?"

"Every time I get to the gate," he sobbed, "she grabs my pant leg and drags me back inside the yard. I even tried to kick her, but I missed and fell down!"

Well, we called Cindy into the house and Mike took off again for the neighbors'. But Jess just couldn't resist. He couldn't imagine that the dog could drag Mike back in the yard, so he let Cindy out. Sure enough, as soon as she spotted Mike heading for the gate, she took off like a shot. She jumped up and hit Mike from behind, knocked him down, and started dragging him by the pant leg back into the yard. All the time, Mike was yelling, "Cindy, let go! Dad said it was all right! Cindy, darn it, let go!" Finally Jess called Cindy back in the house and Mike made good his escape.

In the evenings we watched very little television. For the first two hours the children had to study. No exceptions. The few shows we did watch were "Our Miss Brooks," "Ozzie and Harriet," "Father Knows Best," and some of the other family programs. But a lot of times we played games. Monopoly was popular, as were Sorry and five-hand solitaire. In five-hand solitaire each person played against everyone else. All the aces were placed in the center of the table and then it was a race to see who could play on our ace first. You have to be quick in spotting the play and even faster to play your card. If you were even a split second too slow, you either lost the play or got your hand smashed!

There had been those moments when I wasn't sure we'd be able to enjoy each other, I mean enjoy the family life, but that seemed to be behind us. Jess and I mentioned to each other how amazed we were at how fast Mike was growing up.

It seemed like only a few days ago that he had started school, then there were a few hours for Cub Scouts, Boy Scouts, Little League, and suddenly he was entering high school. Little did we know that within a few more years he would graduate, go to college, go to Vietnam, and become a policeman.

CHAPTER SEVEN

Before I realized it, Mike was almost ready to enter high school. His interests changed from baseball to cars. In a few more years, it would be cars and girls. Instead of wanting to be a quarterback or basketball center, he was now convinced that his future lay in race car driving. Chris and Sus, with their mother on the guardian council, joined Job's Daughters, a female branch of the Masons.

Meanwhile I continued to be pulled in varied and interesting directions. As the Cherry Crest project drew near completion, I began to wonder what I might do next. The excavation business was becoming a bit tiring. People would call at all hours wanting me to do this or give advice on that, or they would have an emergency that had to be taken care of immediately. As I pondered the future, a friend pointed me in a new direction.

Darrell Jones was a Clackamas County commissioner. He came over one night and asked if I'd be interested in becoming a member of the advisory council to the planning commission. Since I had participated in a lot of building in the county, at least in terms of digging basements, I figured I probably knew as much as the next guy and agreed.

Although it was not a decision-making group, we took the job seriously: we took a hard look at growth in the county and began setting up what we thought were important guidelines in terms of countywide development. We began looking at sewage treatment needs, water, police protection, school requirements, road developments, and industrial needs. It was a learning process for those of us on the advisory council. It afforded us a firsthand look at how government worked and at the extremely sensitive issue of striking a balance between the needs of industry and the quality of life each citizen had a right to expect.

In 1961 I was named to the planning commission and served for six years, acting as the commission chairman during the last twelve months. We made a lot of decisions during that time, but I'm extremely proud of the part I played in developing the county's first comprehensive land development plan. For the first time, development decisions could be made based on an all-encompassing countywide plan. It may be only a minor contribution, but it's one I'll always be proud of.

About the same time I was named to the planning commission, my future took another turn. Bill Knowles had been the Lake Oswego municipal judge for years and finally decided to retire. There were few people around with any type of legal background who were willing to devote time to the job. Since I had been a policeman and since I lived in the area, Mayor Lee Stidd asked if I would be interested in the job.

"It doesn't pay much," he warned, "but you'll get to see a lot of your friends."

He was absolutely right. Within a year many of my friends appeared before my court. It was held once a week in the city library. I listened only to traffic violations and general nuisance types of complaint. Criminal cases were always heard by county judges.

Hearing that I had become a municipal judge, an old police friend of mine, Johnny Roe (no relation) suggested I should enroll in some night law classes held in Portland. At first I resisted, figuring that the more legal background I had, the more confused I would become when trying to rule on a case. I had always tried to be fair in all decisions, even if my friends were involved, and I can say I never made a decision that cost me any sleep. My single guideline was "Be fair, seek justice."

This, of course, would never have sat well with the great Oliver Wendell Holmes, Jr. When an attorney pleaded for justice, Holmes shot back angrily, "This is a court of law, young man, not a court of justice!"

Well, after several weeks of Johnny's constantly hounding me, I gave in and decided to give it a try. In spite of the fishing trips with Davis, I was very sensitive about going out in public in my wheelchair. As a judge and a county planner, I made a point of being seated before anyone came in. I told Johnny that I was apprehensive about going, but he assured me everything would be all right and that I needed to get out more anyway. Jeanne agreed, and I decided that it did make sense. I had taken some aptitude tests while at the rehabilitation center and had scored well in the legal area. Now I had a chance to discover whether or not the designers of those tests really knew what they were doing.

From the moment I got out of the car, I knew I had made a mistake. First, the building was old, and the doorways and hallways were narrow, which meant I couldn't maneuver very well in my wheelchair and it wouldn't fit into the tiny elevator. Johnny had to fold it up and carry it up the stairs. I had to crutch-walk up those steep stairs while people tried to get around me. By the time I reached the third floor, I was exhausted. Johnny unfolded the wheelchair and pushed me to the room, but the doorway was again too narrow and I had to get out, refold the chair, and then crutch-walk into the room.

I was already embarrassed by having people waiting for me on the stairs; now I was holding up class as they watched me get the wheelchair through the doorway and then crutch-walk into the room. Halfway inside, I tripped over a pile of books and fell flat on my face. Johnny started to help me, but I angrily waved him off. Managing to get to my feet, I got over to a desk and sat there for the remainder of the class.

Afterward, I told Johnny that the entire misadventure was humiliating and that I wouldn't be coming back. He tried to talk me out of it, using every logical argument he could think of, but I had made up my mind. The episode had reconfirmed my opinion that, while I could do a lot of things, I really couldn't function out in a society designed for people with two good legs. For a number of years after that disaster, I avoided anything requiring me to move around in public.

Today, looking back, I realize I was wrong, but things are easier now for the handicapped. New buildings have to meet federal regulations, there are elevators in most buildings, and it has become relatively easy to maneuver a wheelchair around.

That experience ended my attempt at law school, but I continued as a judge. I really enjoyed the job, I enjoyed being active, and I enjoyed working with people—although there was one time when it became extremely painful.

The day before Thanksgiving, as I was crutch-walking into the courtroom, my right leg brace collapsed, forcing a tremendous amount of weight on the leg. I heard it snap as I fell to the ground. For a second I wasn't quite sure what had happened, but then the pain began to roll up my leg and I could feel the cold sweat beading on my forehead. It was obvious I had broken the leg, and the court clerk asked if I wanted to call off court.

Again, my pride overpowered commonsense. I was embarrassed by the fall and didn't want to admit that I couldn't control my own body. I told him no, and he and a man who was scheduled to appear before me helped me to my chair.

It was a fast session. Later, someone told me that I hung them all. I don't think I could have been that tough, but I had little patience for listening to excuses. The man who had helped me to the chair pleaded guilty to a speeding ticket and I gave him a strong lecture. But considering his aid to the court, I suspended his sentence.

Then it was off to the hospital. X rays showed that it was a severe fracture and that they would have to operate and set the break with a pin. It's funny, but until that accident I had always pictured a bone pin as something that did resemble a pin. I thought it would be small. I was wrong. The doctor showed me the pin he was going to put in my leg. It more closely resembled a rod than a pin. I was surprised and just a little bit apprehensive.

Thanksgiving Day I was operated on, and everything went perfectly. Two days later, Dr. Kimberly had me come to his office for a routine checkup before allowing me to go home.

He asked a lot of questions about my excavation business, told me to keep up the good work, and in between questions thumbed through my medical records. At one point he had to leave the office and was gone for some time. Meanwhile, my medical records were just lying there.

Neither Jeanne nor I could resist taking a look at those reports. The first couple of pages were rather boring: routine medical forms, much of the handwriting illegible. But then I came across a page that had a large space for "Doctor's Comments."

Dr. Kimberly's comments were rather chilling. "I expect this patient to attempt rehabilitation for a few months. He will make an honest attempt and then give up and confine himself to a chair and a sedentary life. I give him five to seven years' life expectancy."

When he returned I asked him about his observation and he just smiled. "Well, Jess," he said with his soft Scottish accent, "I'm glad you proved me wrong."

He urged me to continue to expand my life, and within a few months I decided it was time to try hunting again.

I had had a two-year running battle with Jim over deer hunting. From the moment we first set out in the *Little Jewel*, Jim started talking about a hunting expedition. I argued that all he wanted me there for was to keep the campfire going and do the cooking. He, on the other hand, argued that I was correct in my suspicion but that it would be a lot of fun anyway.

The idea of hunting appealed to me, but I found myself wrestling with another prejudice. I always sneered at so-called road hunters: hunters who drove to a likely spot, parked their truck, and sat there waiting for an unsuspecting deer to come trotting by. That was a poor-man's excuse for hunting, I thought. Now I realized that road hunting was all I could do, and I wasn't sure I really wanted to stoop that low.

Finally I decided to give it a try. But it wasn't Jim who convinced me, it was an old friend of mine, C. D. Thomas. Everyone calls him Tommy. He is a bona fide character. There is a constant flash of merriment in his eyes, a laugh in his voice, and a smile on his face. He is one of the best carpenters I have ever met. He can build anything and takes great pride in the quality of his work. He is a craftsman with tools and with a gun. Tommy takes pride in his shooting and hunting ability as he does in his work.

After months of talking, he finally convinced me that I had to get back out in the hills and away from the crazies—people who didn't hunt. Although I'm sure he liked my company, I always suspected that the main reason for his persistence in dragging us out into eastern Oregon was so he could devote more time to teasing the children.

He loved to give them a bad time. Mike was just beginning to notice girls, and every time Tommy spotted one, he'd drag her over and introduce her to Mike. Poor Mike, he'd die on the spot and mumble something about being pleased to meet her and turn beet red. Tommy would just smile and say, "Mike, you've got to come up with a better line than that or you're going to be a bachelor for the rest of your life!"

When Mike wasn't around, Tommy would pick on the girls. Once Sus showed him her new gerbil.

"That's not a gerbil," he said, after carefully studying the furry little animal.

Sus looked a bit perplexed. "It is too a gerbil!"

Tommy shook his head. "That's a rat. See the long tail? Jess, you shouldn't let Sus keep a rat. They get mean when they grow up."

"It's not a rat," Sus argued, but she took another look at her new pet. "Rats are bigger. Herbie's already grown."

"Nope. That's a baby rat. I can spot them a mile off. He's gonna start growin' pretty soon now. Just can't imagine why a pretty girl like you would want a pet rat!" Tommy said sadly.

Sus stuck out her chin and said defiantly that Herbie was a gerbil and not a rat and that was all there was to it. But for the next few days she kept a closer than usual vigilance on Herbie just to make sure he didn't start growing into a rat.

And while Sus watched over Herbie, I took the first step toward my first hunting trip since the accident. I decided that since I was going to be confined to the roads during the hunting season, what I needed was a good, solid, four-wheel-drive vehicle. After spending days looking over hundreds of four-wheelers, I found just what I was looking for. It was a 1962 Scout International. After making the selection, I spent the better part of the day fighting over the price and finally exhausted the salesman to the point where I got it for just about what I wanted.

I was so delighted with the deal I had gotten, I overlooked one important detail. When I got in to rig up my hand controls I discovered the Scout was a manual shift. Hand controls are designed for automatics, since there's no way a paraplegic can operate a clutch. I stared in disbelief, then looked at Jeanne. We had already signed the papers, and I knew the salesman would not be in any mood to forget the whole thing, so I had Jeanne drive my dream vehicle home while I brooded over being such an idiot.

A few days later, I could finally talk about it, and when I mentioned my faux pas to Tommy, he laughed and then told me about a mechanic who could probably rig up something so I could work the clutch. Tommy warned me that the man was a bit crusty and his language could make battle-hardened marines blush, but if you could ignore those minor foibles, he was a heck of a mechanic.

The next day I had Jeanne drive me and the Scout over to the man's shop and explained my problem. He listened quietly, thought about it for a second or two, and then let loose with a barrage of profanity that flowed as casually as if he were giving you the time of day. Basically what he told us was to leave the Scout with him for a few days and he'd come up with a solution to the problem. Actually, his explanation was considerably longer and certainly more colorful than what I have relayed, but that was the general thrust of the conversation.

Three days later, Jeanne and I returned and he had come up with what I thought was an ingenious solution. The man had taken the power steering cylinder out of an old Thunderbird and connected a vacuum tank from a windshield wiper to it. The tank would hold eighty pounds of air per square inch. To the tank he rigged up a small twelve-volt compressor and then attached a high-pressure air nozzle.

Every time I wanted to shift, all I had to do was push a button he had connected to the gearshift. The button released just enough air to activate the clutch and allow me to shift into gear. In three days he had invented and designed a pressurized gearshift. He might have been a tough-talking man, but he was also a mechanical genius. I kept that vehicle for almost eight years, and I never had any trouble with it. It survived rough mountain roads, hard driving, and a wreck and never failed.

In the fall of 1962, I made my first hunting trip. Jeanne and I took the entire family, loaded the Scout to the hilt, and took off for a small eastern-Oregon town called Prairie City, situated between the Strawberry Mountain range and the Blue Mountains. It's beautiful country, especially in the fall when the leaves turn in the scattered groves of birch and cottonwood.

It was warm, but you could smell fall. You didn't have to look for the bright red, yellow, or orange leaves or the V formation of geese moving quietly and effortlessly across the late afternoon sky. Each time the wind shifted and swirled around you, it announced that the season was here and in command.

Before the first day of hunting, Tommy, two of his friends, and I mapped out the area we'd be hunting in. Tommy carefully pointed out the various logging roads available, but warned me that if it began to rain or snow, I should get out as fast as possible. Even with a four-wheel rig, the elements could quickly turn the roads into an impassable muddy quagmire or a frozen surface hazardous even to ice skaters. They were roads in name only. In reality they were just trails designed for dry-weather use.

The first day, I decided to take Sus with me and Mike hunted with Tommy and his friends. Sus and I drove around the back roads, looking for signs of deer trails, as quietly as one can with a four-wheel-drive vehicle and a chattery ten-year-old. After two hours of bouncing over chuckholes and off giant boulders, we finally found a likely trail. The deer traveled on better trails than we did.

For four hours we sat in the car and waited. Sus was very quiet for the first five minutes and then became increasingly bored. Although I constantly admonished her to be quiet, the warning's impact was only good for five or six minutes. Then she would launch into "two thousand questions" or start singing catchy little tunes like "Three Blind Mice." What's that old Sam Levenson line about "Insanity is hereditary, you catch it from your children!"?

Next Sus wanted to know why I wanted to go hunting.

"Well, we go hunting so we can have meat," I answered in what seemed like a perfectly logical voice.

"I thought we just went to the grocery store?"

"Well, you can go to the store, honey, but you have to pay for the meat. Out here, if you're a good hunter, it's free."

Sus thought about that one for a second or two. "Mom said you paid lots of money for your gun." I ignored the question. "Wouldn't it be cheaper just to pay the store man?"

I made a mental note to take Mike with me the next day. "Well, you have to spend some money, but after that you don't have to buy another rifle."

"What about bullets and gas?"

"Want to sing a song, Sus?"

Somewhere between "Three Blind Mice" and the economics of hunting, I thought I spotted something moving in the brush. It took me a few seconds to focus my binoculars, but I finally zeroed in on two does. I stayed on them for a minute or so, and then a big, four-point buck came out from behind the trees and into a clearing.

Sus realized immediately that I had spotted some deer and wanted to see them.

"All right, but be very quiet, and hurry, or they'll leave."

She took the binoculars and started scanning the area. "I don't see anything," she complained.

"Move more to your right," I whispered.

"I still don't see anything," she cried in frustration.

"Move more to your right and up a bit."

"Everything is fuzzy."

"You have to focus, Sus," I said, trying to hide the frustration that was also building in me. They were drawing near the car, and Sus was talking loud enough for the deer to hear her.

Sus still couldn't find the deer and her last complaint spooked them. They made two or three wild jumps and were almost out of range, when in desperation I fired a shot without even aiming. It wasn't close and the deer went bounding up the hill.

"I see them! I see them, Daddy. I was looking too far to the right. Oh," she said dejectedly, "I can't see them anymore."

"Neither can I, Sus." I laughed. "Neither can I."

If our first outing was not successful, Tommy and his group fared no better. At least I got off a shot. They came back with clean rifles and plenty of ammunition. It was just like going fishing with Davis.

We hunted through the week, and the invigorating morning crispness changed into a day-long coldness. The blue skies gave way to threatening gray clouds that everyone knew carried snow. At best we'd have two more days of hunting before the first snows began to fall.

This time I took Mike with me. It was his first hunting trip where I let him carry a rifle. He had gone through the Boy Scout and State Game Commission hunting classes and had shown that he understood the power and danger his rifle represented.

The morning air had sharpened its bite as it rattled around the Scout and the gray clouds continued to roll in. We sat there for a couple of hours, but saw nothing but an occasional chipmunk scurrying around the forest floor stashing away its final bits of food before the snow hit.

Our unproductive vigil gave us time to talk on sort of a man-to-man basis. We talked primarily about his future. He wasn't exactly sure what he wanted to do, and it concerned him because he would be entering high school the next year.

"Well, what do you like to do?"

"I like cars." He grinned. "I'd like to be a race car driver."

"There's quite a bit of competition, Mike. That's not to say you couldn't make it, but have you thought of anything else?"

"Well, I like math and science. I do pretty good in those subjects. But I don't want to be a teacher."

I laughed. "There are other things you can do with math and science, Mike. You could be an engineer, or go into forest management. Or you could combine your interest in cars and science and math. You could become an auto engineer and design cars or something like that."

Mike looked seriously at me and nodded. "I'll think about it, Dad."

We talked for another couple of hours before the cold finally drove us in. Tommy had bagged a buck, so the hunting party was proclaimed a success, but it almost ended in disaster.

Despite the ominous clouds, we voted to go out one more day. Mike went with Tommy this time, and I headed out on a final patrol of the logging roads. After three hours of listening to my teeth chatter and watching the first flakes of snow fall silently to the ground. I called it quits.

When I got back to the camp, I learned that Mike was missing. He had gotten separated from the main group and had become lost. With the snow clouds darkening and the wind picking up, we began retracing the group's steps. I traveled along the roads in the area honking my horn and yelling at the top of my voice. Out in the woods, I could hear Tommy and the others shouting and occasionally firing their rifles. The snow picked up, the light was fading rapidly, and the temperature started dropping.

It was another four hours before we finally located him. I give all credit to those hunting courses he had taken earlier. As soon as Mike realized he was lost, he immediately stopped and built a fire. As darkness fell, he gathered up as much wood as possible and started building a shelter. For a fourteen-year-old boy, he showed a lot of poise. He didn't panic and he didn't forget his hunting instructions. Whether or not it saved his life is a matter for conjecture, but few people have ever survived a snowstorm without heat and some kind of shelter. I was very proud of him that day.

There would be a few more hunting trips, but after a while I discovered that I couldn't bring myself to hunt anymore. My views shifted dramatically after one incident. I had been sitting at a well-traveled deer trail for less than an hour when I heard four or five shots some distance away.

Because of the distance, I didn't give it too much thought and went on with some mindless daydreaming. Fifteen minutes later I heard another couple of shots, which were obviously much closer. Then I could hear some thrashing around in the nearby woods and I pulled up my rifle and waited.

Seconds later, two young does came crashing through the brush. As I drew my sights on them and waited for what I expected to be a buck following them, I became aware of the deer's faces. Their eyes were wide with fear, their tongues were hanging out from exhaustion as they desperately tried to escape the hunters' bullets. The buck came racing out into the open, wearing the same frightened expression, and even though I had a clear shot at him, I couldn't pull the trigger.

I can't condemn others who hunt. I don't feel that there's anything wrong with hunting except that I personally could never again kill one of God's creatures. I don't know who said it, but it's true. If we had to kill and butcher our own meat, the number of vegetarians would increase dramatically.

But I had some wonderful times and experienced some tremendous companionship and excitement during those hunting days. They were days I'll never forget.

Watching the children grow up was also a tremendous experience. In 1963 Mike entered the tenth grade at Lake Oswego High School. He was still a tall and gangly boy, still struggling to gain control of his body, make it go where he wanted it to go. His lack of coordination prevented him from doing very well in sports, but he tried. At times his lack of success would bother him and we'd talk about it.

Like all young people, he wanted to be good. He wanted to be recognized by his classmates as an athlete. At that age, sports are very important. It was difficult for him to admit that he wasn't going to reach that particular goal.

"I try, Dad, I really do, but I guess I'm just not good enough."

"Mike, being good is a rather vague term. We can't all be the best, the Mickey Mantles or Henry Aarons. Very few athletes ever make it to the big leagues of professional sports. That doesn't mean those who didn't make it weren't good. It just meant some others were better."

"I don't understand."

"Well, all anyone can ask of himself is, 'Did I try as hard as I could? Did I give it my best effort?' If you can honestly say yes to those questions, you have absolutely nothing to feel bad about. Even if you made the team, you'd find others who are better. There's always someone who's better. You just concentrate on doing the best you can. Always try to improve yourself. If you can do just that, you'll go a long way in your life. You'll have a great deal to be proud of."

Mike smiled and nodded. He made a few more attempts at athletics, but the results were about the same. It would be another couple of years before he developed his coordination. By then he'd be in Vietnam.

But before he reached that plateau he had to struggle with another problem of youth: honesty. It was a tough lesson that resulted in his getting a lot of exercise.

Just before Christmas of his senior year, Mike asked his mother if he could borrow the Scout one morning to go to school. It was our policy that the children could not take a car to school. Cars had a way of becoming an obstacle to studying. The kids either had to take the bus or one of us would take them to school. But this morning, Mike told Jeanne that he had taken some money out of savings in order to do some Christmas shopping and that, if he could have the Scout, he could get his shopping done on his way home from school.

Mike had never lied to us and Jeanne accepted his explanation, as did I when Jeanne told me later that she let Mike have the car.

Probably he started the day with good intentions, but somewhere between the house and school his good intentions took a route that led him and a friend away from school. On the spur of the moment, they decided it would be more fun to take the four-wheeler out into the hills than sit in English class.

Things were going swimmingly until they were traveling up a

hill, driving directly into the sun. Mike lost sight of the edge of the road, and the next thing he knew, he was in the ditch. The drop into the ditch smashed in the driver's side of the Scout, but fortunately neither he nor his friend was injured. After getting a wrecker to pull them out of the ditch, which took all of Mike's Christmas money, Mike took his friend back to the school and then came home. It must have been a long and torturous drive.

When he pulled into the driveway, Jeanne spotted him and wondered aloud why he was home so early. From the kitchen window she couldn't see the driver's side of the car. Mike came inside wearing an extremely long and guilty expression.

"Dad, I've got something to tell you and"—he took a long, deep breath and let it out slowly—"I sure wish I didn't have to tell you, but I have to."

Mike knew the Scout was one of my pride and joys. I really liked that machine. "What's the matter?"

"I wrecked the Scout," he blurted out.

I'm not sure if a frown crossed my face, but if it didn't, there was one inside trying to get out. "What happened?" I asked in the calmest possible voice. Actually, my calmness surprised me as well as Jeanne.

"Remember what you said about how you always pay for your sins? Well, it's sure true. I skipped school this morning and a friend and I went riding up on Pete's Mountain. I got too close to a ditch and went in. I banged up the driver's side pretty good."

Now it was my turn to take a long, deep breath and let it out slowly.

"I know I was wrong. I'll do anything you say to make it up. I'll pay for the car, anything. Dad, I'm really sorry it happened and it'll never happen again."

I sat there for a second thinking about it and poured a cup of coffee before finally answering him. "Well, first of all, you'll have to pay the insurance deductible. It's fifty dollars."

"That's fair," he sighed.

"And you're grounded for the next two months. No more car. If you want to go someplace, either your mother or I will take you or you'll have to walk. Understood?"

"Understood."

I'm sure Mike must have died a thousand deaths driving back

to the house that morning. He would have done anything to avoid facing me, but he came to me and laid it out. Again, I was proud of him for his maturity. I wasn't thrilled about my bashed Scout, but Mike showed me he had the courage to admit his mistakes. And for the next two months he put a lot of time in walking around the area. He seldom called for a ride. If the weather was halfway decent, Mike walked.

Later, after the grounding had been lifted, Mike went out and bought himself a '57 Plymouth. It was a real clunker, but he planned to overhaul it himself and take it to college that fall. The plan was sound, but the car was weak.

One Sunday afternoon, Jeanne and I and the girls returned from a drive in the country. As I pulled into the driveway, I was faced with a driveway covered with engine parts. In the middle of all those parts was Mike, carefully studying a car owner's repair manual for Plymouths.

"What is all of this?" I asked, pointing to what looked like metal litter.

Mike shook his head sadly. "It was my engine. I blew it up this morning. I'm going to rebuild it."

I shook my head. "Mike, you are not turning our driveway into a used-parts operation. I want this mess cleaned up and out of sight!"

Mike smiled and looked around at all the parts. "How 'bout giving me three days to put it back together? If I can't do it in three days, I'll junk the whole thing. Three days."

Against my better judgment, I agreed to three days and Mike immediately set about putting his engine back together again. At the time he was working for the county digging ditches, but as soon as he got off work he started on his engine.

At the end of three days, it was all back together again, but not tested.

He came running into the kitchen and announced that the engine was in one piece.

"But will it work?" I asked.

"I'll let you know in a few minutes," and he dashed back outside. For the next hour we heard Mike turn the engine over, then there would be silence as he made some adjustments, and then he would make another attempt at starting it. On the fourth adjustment, the engine caught hold and roared to life. He came racing in with an ear-to-ear grin on his face and proudly announced, "It's alive! The monster is alive!"

Mike would have one more problem with the Plymouth before heading off for college that fall. He was pulled over for doing eighty-five miles an hour in a thirty-five-mile-an-hour speed zone. This time I was extremely upset with him because he had been speeding in an area where lots of children played. I gave him a long and energetic lecture on speeding and told him how disappointed I was in his behavior.

Mike was totally crushed by my lecture and apologized for the incident. But I was upset enough that I wasn't about to let him off the hook that easily. Because of my past position as Lake Oswego municipal judge (I had quit in 1964), I was good friends with the county judge before whom Mike was appearing. I told the judge that I wanted Mike to learn a lesson, but that I didn't want him to go to jail.

The judge smiled and said he'd take care of everything. Mike's hearing was the first one out of the box and the judge read him the riot act. He lectured him about speeding, about how he was endangering not only his life, but the lives of others. The judge was putting on a great show and had worked himself up into a real desk-pounding lecture. He kind of reminded me of Jailin' Jake.

Finally, with a note of disgust, the judge told the bailiff to take this inconsiderate young man to one of the jail cells until he decided what to do with him. Poor Mike was absolutely petrified. As I mentioned, Mike was the first case before the court and it was another four hours before all the other cases had been heard. In the meantime, Mike sat all by himself in that cell figuring that the judge had thrown away the key. When he was finally released, the judge fined him a dollar for every mile over the speed limit, gave him another stern lecture on highway manners, and then let him go. I don't think I ever saw a young man so relieved to get out of a room in all my life.

After that, Mike's lead foot lightened up a bit. As for the old Plymouth, it never made it to college. Just before the fall term began, the engine blew again and this time Mike decided there was no hope of salvaging it. He left it in the yard and decided to take on college on foot. We tried to sell the car a number of times, but finally had to pay to have it dragged off for scrap.

CHAPTER EIGHT

As Mike walked down the aisle at his high school graduation, sporting a grin that consumed the lower third of his face, I also grinned: first as a proud father and then in disbelief. How had he grown so fast? It was only yesterday that he was born. I remembered his first steps, his first tooth, and his first day of school. His smile reminded me of the puzzlement on his face when he visited me at the hospital, the frustration that showed when Cindy refused to let him out of the yard, and the embarrassment when he announced he had wrecked the Scout. Now he was about to enter college.

To celebrate his graduation and acceptance at Oregon State University in the fall of 1966, Jeanne and I took him on a fishing trip out over the Columbia River bar. Since 1964 Jeanne and I had operated a commercial sport-fishing business out of Ilwaco, Washington, a small fishing port just inside the mouth of the Columbia.

We got into the business with the purchase of the twenty-six-foot power cruiser dubbed the *Ramblin' Roes'*. It was a beautiful, powerful, and sleek boat. I was in love with it, but after the first cruise I was ready to sink it.

It had been a beautiful Sunday morning when we launched the boat on the Willamette River in Portland, about twenty miles south of the Columbia. Jeanne and some of our friends drove down to Ilwaco, and we planned to meet them there in the late afternoon. On board the *Ramblin' Roes'* were Chris and Sus and a good friend of mine, Jim Reuther, and his young daughter, Patty.

But from the moment I fired up the engines, things went wrong. First we were low on gas, which meant I had to maneuver what seemed to me like an ocean liner up to the dock. Until the *Ramblin' Roes'*, the only boat I had operated was a modestly sized runabout.

Unsure of my ability to dock, I told Chris to get up on the bow and grab the tie-up line. When we drew near the dock, she was supposed to jump over to the dock and pull the boat up to the gas pump. It seemed like a good plan at the time. Unfortunately, just as I told Chris to jump, I accidently gunned the engine and the boat kicked away from the dock. This minor alteration in the boat's course left Chris's leap about two feet short of the dock. Instead of on the dock, she landed in the water. She was not excited about the ability of the ship's master. It went downhill from there.

We couldn't even get out of Portland without a struggle. As we headed downriver, we came to the Morrison Bridge—a drawbridge. The antenna on the *Ramblin' Roes'* was too high to pass under the bridge, so we had to have the bridge raised. The concept was simple enough; the execution left a great deal to be desired.

In order to get the bridge operator to raise the bridge, you were required to give the proper signal. In this case it was a series of boat whistles. Not just any boat whistle, but the exact boat whistle. However, since I had never had a boat that couldn't just go under the bridge, I wasn't too familiar with the whistling procedure. So for the next twenty minutes we circled in front of the bridge like idiots, blowing the whistle and thinking unkind thoughts about the attendant, who casually watched our progress as we searched for the secret code. Now I knew why trolls were always described in rather unsympathetic terms.

We tried everything from SOS to the "Hallelujah Chorus." My patience was wearing a bit thin, and if the *Ramblin' Roes'* had been a submarine I think I would have tried to sink that bridge. Finally either we hit the right combination or the attendant was becoming dizzy, because the bridge magically opened and we were on our way to the Columbia. We were confident that our troubles were now behind us.

That sense of security lasted about twenty minutes. Just after we passed a forty-foot cruiser moving downriver, the engine's red warning light started flashing. There had been some kind of malfunction in the engine that allowed all the oil to leak out into the bilge. The bilge didn't need oil, but the engine certainly did, and without it, I had to shut the engine down. There we were in the middle of the Columbia with no power. We were dead in the water and moved only at the whim of the current. My very expensive boat had been magically transformed into what was probably the most expensive raft ever to challenge the Mighty Columbia.

About ten minutes into what seemed like an eternity, a young man came chugging up in a tired old boat powered by a coughing and sputtering outboard that appeared to have been used in the off-season to beat moles senseless.

"You folks got some problems?" he asked cheerfully.

Ask anyone, there is nothing worse than a cheerful Good Samaritan. Anyway, we admitted that yes, we were having some problems, and he offered to tow us into Kalama, where we could get the engine repaired. Despite his sputtery old engine, that fellow managed to get us into the port. There was, of course, a certain loss of face in having a twelve-foot scow towing in my brand-new, shiny boat. It's something like having your brand-new Mercedes towed into the shop by a 1964 Studebaker Lark. It hurts.

By now we were already two hours late, and after we docked, Jim and the kids headed into town to find a mechanic and to call Jeanne and let her know we were running behind schedule. Unfortunately they couldn't make contact with Jeanne, but did manage to round up a mechanic who solved the problem and had us back on the river in about an hour. Again we began thinking that now surely our problems were behind us.

Again we were wrong. Fifteen minutes out of Kalama we spotted that forty-foot cruiser coming back upriver in what seemed like a big hurry, although I didn't give it too much thought, assuming they were just out joyriding. Of course I was wrong. They were in a hurry for a good reason. As we rounded the bend around which they had appeared we found ourselves facing a huge ocean freighter plowing its way upriver toward Portland. The ship was kicking up large waves as it churned upriver, and when they hit us, they started bouncing us around like a cork.

As if that weren't bad enough, the tide was going out. Although the waves were still coming, the water behind the waves was receding. We would crest a five- or six-foot wave, but then fall eight or ten feet to the new surface. Each time we would fall, the boat bottom would pancake on the surface, sending a jolting shock through the boat. This went on for about ten minutes, and I knew that at any moment the bottom would split open and we'd go down like a lead weight.

That little episode delayed us another hour, and the sun was deep in the west by the time we finally reached Astoria, near the mouth of the Columbia. We were also low on gas again, and I decided we'd have to top off the tanks before trying to make it across the river and into Ilwaco on the Washington side.

By now I was really concerned about what Jeanne might be thinking, since we were so late. But the telephone at the dock was out of order and the pumps were closed. So Jim and the kids took a ten-gallon can and set off on foot for the downtown area in search of a gas station.

Two more hours passed and the sun was gone and the wind had really picked up. The mouth of the Columbia can be extremely dangerous and the whitecaps were really riding high. After a few minutes of deliberation, however, I decided to go across anyway, since I knew Jeanne would be worrying and there wasn't any means of contacting her.

The trip across was one of the worst I have ever had. The wind continued to pick up and it was really tossing us around. To make matters worse, we were fighting a strong tide and making very little headway. Overhead we spotted a Coast Guard helicopter as it darted around the area, spending a lot of time in our vicinity.

I wondered if there was a boat in trouble in the area, but couldn't see any signs of distress, so we kept plowing on toward the port. The helicopter continued to stay in the area, and then I remembered we had a two-way ship-to-shore radio and asked Jim to try to tune in on the Coast Guard frequency. By now the river was really rough and the night pitch-black. The only thing you could see were the navigational buoys. All you could hear were the howling wind and the constant thumping of the helicopter prop.

Jim finally tuned in on the chopper just in time for us to catch part of a transmission.

"It's really rough out here, but there's a little boat trying to bang his way down the channel. We'll stick by and see if he makes it to Ilwaco."

There wasn't any other boat in distress, so they were simply waiting for us to go under! That did little to raise my confidence, but somehow we finally made it into port. We were six hours late, and Jeanne was absolutely beside herself with anger and relief.

"Why didn't you call and let us know you were going to be late? We thought you had all drowned or something!"

I explained that we had tried to call several times but couldn't make a connection.

"Why didn't you use the two-way?"

"What?"

"The two-way radio. Why didn't you use it? You knew I had one in the car."

I had completely forgotten about it, and after that disastrous shakedown cruise I was ready to forget about the *Ramblin' Roes'*. But in the morning, after an exhausted sleep, I felt a little better about the boat and decided to keep it.

Two years later, Mike, Jeanne, and I were out over the Columbia bar on a beautiful late-September afternoon. The water was extremely smooth and Mike was enjoying the tranquillity the ocean offered. Of course, part of the reason it was so tranquil was that there were no fish. We had been fishing for better than three hours and none of us had even had a bite. Earlier in the day there were a number of boats around us, but as their patience dried up, they headed south to the Oregon side. We decided to stay put, for what reason I can't remember

Around four, about an hour before we would head back into Ilwaco, I spotted a couple of seals thrashing about in the water and pointed them out to Mike.

"Seals, that's great. Aren't they supposed to travel ahead of salmon?"

I shook my head and continued to watch the two cavorting in the water, making a terrible racket. "Mike, those two are going to scare away any fish within two miles of this place—if there are any fish within two miles of here."

No sooner had I spoken than the water suddenly came alive with herring. They were literally dancing on the water and it began to boil with activity. None of us had seen anything like it. Mike and Jeanne stood there fascinated by the scene and I started to understand what was happening. The salmon were feeding on the herring, driving the smaller fish ahead of them in a frantic effort to escape.

About the time I reasoned it out, Mike began shouting and pointing out away from the boat. The ocean was churning and alive with salmon. Seconds later we were in the middle of a sea of fish. Everywhere you looked, there were salmon. It was another five minutes before any of us thought of fishing. We had been mesmerized by one of nature's miracles. Later we learned from a friend, who had spotted the school from a plane, that the school was roughly seven miles long and over a mile wide and we were sitting in the middle of it.

Finally Mike picked up a pole and broke the trance. From then on we fished until we ran out of bait. The salmon averaged twenty pounds apiece. If we had been using nets, we could have hauled thousands of them in. But with just fishing poles, it took each of us about ten minutes to land one. All the time the salmon continued to move past us, a seemingly inexhaustible supply.

After forty-five minutes, we ran out of bait. It was probably just as well. All of us were worn out from that concentrated period of fishing. We put down our poles and just sat there watching the salmon making their way toward the Columbia and the final leg of their three-year journey. It was one of the most amazing and beautiful things I have ever witnessed. When they finally passed by, the ocean became quiet again and we sat there sharing with each other the excitement and feelings each of us had experienced during that brief time.

It couldn't have been a better send-off to college. I'm very happy that we could share that moment together. So many will never have that experience, and we were able to experience it together. It would be one of the last really happy times we would share with Mike.

Mike enrolled at Oregon State, majoring in forestry, and for the first term, things seemed to go well. He studied hard and came home with a B-plus average. Over the Christmas vacation he told us that he had been invited to join Tau Kappa Epsilon.

He talked excitedly about joining the fraternity, but Jeanne and I were not enthralled. Neither of us wanted him to join a fraternity during his first year, fearing that his grades would suffer. But Mike was very convincing and finally we agreed he could join.

His grades didn't suffer, they died quickly and painlessly. Mike had discovered college could be a lot more fun if you didn't bother with classes, which he didn't. For the next three months, Mike carefully studied the world of alcohol and girls. He had a terrific time and promptly flunked out of school.

He came home during spring vacation, a bit embarrassed and not sure what he wanted to do about college.

"Dad, I'm not sure I want to go back to school. I don't think I'm ready for it yet."

"Well," I said, smiling, "you seemed to enjoy the last term pretty well."

Mike grinned. "Yeah, that was very interesting. I learned a lot, but I'm not sure it would be anything you'd want to put down on a résumé. Actually, I was thinking about maybe dropping out and thinking the whole thing over."

"What about the draft? You stay out more than a quarter, especially with your grades, and they'll draft you."

"I thought about that. Maybe that might not be so bad. It'd give me some time to think about what I really want to do with my life."

"How 'bout Vietnam? They're sending a lot of kids over there. That bother you any?"

Mike thought for a second before answering. "Well, I think the United States is doing the right thing. I got into a lot of arguments with some of the kids at college. They say we're interfering in a civil war, that we're really trying to protect some oil fields over there, or that the Communists would be better than the South Vietnamese government. I don't believe that.

"Where are we supposed to fight? Do we fight for Thailand, Australia, New Zealand, or do we wait until they try to take Hawaii? I just think we should stop them now and let them know we're willing to fight. A lot of kids are against the war because they'd rather get drunk than fight for their country, or they're afraid that if they spend a couple of years in the Army they won't get a good job. I think most of them aren't against the war as much as they'd prefer not to be inconvenienced."

Mike went on for quite a while, talking about his feelings toward Vietnam and America's involvement. There was no doubt in his mind that the country was right and that Vietnam was a good place to show the Communists we were willing to fight.

Still, I talked him into trying school one more time, and he enrolled at Portland State University. Instead of taking an apartment, he decided to stay at home in order to save money. A college education might be nice, but it wasn't fast. What he had in mind was something with four wheels, a huge engine with four carburetors, and a four-on-the-floor. Staying at home meant he didn't have to worry about paying the rent or buying groceries. That's what moms and dads are for. And if he didn't have to spend his money for such nonessentials, that fast car wasn't so far away.

But while he could save money for a car, he found it almost impossible to apply himself to his studies. Part of the problem was he wasn't ready for school. He could do the work when he wanted to, but most of the time he didn't want to. Then there was the Vietnam conflict. Antiwar sentiment ran high on the campus and Mike felt out of place. He got into a lot of heated arguments about Vietnam and finally decided that there was no reason for him to remain where he was considered a social outcast, a member of the establishment.

Less than a month after he enrolled, he walked out of an afternoon class and into the nearest army recruiting office. He had made up his mind. He was going to go to Vietnam.

He came back home and talked it over with Jeanne and me, but we both knew there was no hope of talking him out of enlisting. He was positive that college couldn't teach him anything at this point and that the Army could.

"I really don't have a direction right now. I want time to think and I should get a lot in the Army. They tell you what to do, you don't even have to think about it." He smiled.

He looked at both of us and must have read the concern we felt about Vietnam and the dangers he might face.

"Maybe we are wrong to be over there, but I don't think so. If I don't go and see for myself, I'll never know one way or the other. I know one thing, though. Those kids marching up and down the street screaming 'Hell no, we won't go' haven't got the foggiest idea what's happening. They're just repeating someone else's words. At least I'll be able to speak from experience."

The next morning he went down to the Armed Forces Examination Station and took his physical. One of the toughest fights he'd have was getting into the Army. First there was the problem of his dental retainer. At nine o'clock he called home and was obviously upset. The Army wouldn't take him while he was still wearing the retainer. He wanted us to call the dentist and arrange for a quick appointment to have the retainer removed.

It took a little pleading and some fast driving, but we managed to get Mike to the dentist, have the retainer removed, and get him back to the examination station in time to complete his physical. But that wasn't the end of his battle to get in.

As a youngster, Mike had been struck in the eye by a rock. The impact made a small puncture in the cornea, and at first the doctors insisted that he be rated 4-F. Thousands of draft-aged men would have leaped with joy at that news, but Mike was crushed. Immediately he began talking to various people and successfully argued his case to be classified as 1-A. A week later he was on his way to boot camp.

Fort Lewis, Washington, is located near the northwest port city of Tacoma. It is a sprawling 85,000-acre army facility dating back to pre-World War II. The same is true for many of the taverns that circle the camp. Just to the north of Fort Lewis is McChord Air Force Base, a Military Airlift Command center, which during Vietnam was a major shipping point to the Far East.

Most of the buildings were drab, sterile boxes, prefabricated structures that had been intended to last four or five years, until WW II was over. When Mike arrived, those old "temporary facilities" were still there, and they're still standing today. If you pass by the camp today, traveling on Interstate 5, you can see that those "temporary structures" have recently been given a new coat of drab paint.

For the first week after Mike enlisted we didn't hear anything. Remembering my first week in the Army during WW II, I wasn't surprised. The first thing drill instructors try to do is cut off your contact with the civilian world: no newspapers, no television, and little time for writing letters. Everything is done on the run; screaming is the normal tone of voice used when addressing new recruits; instructions and regulations come at you like machine-gun fire; and sleep is usually something from the "good old days."

So when the first letter arrived, I was prepared for the normal pages of griping and complaining about army life, army food, and army money. Jeanne and I were both surprised.

Dear Mom and Dad,

Hello from Camp Kuckamonga. Things are really going great! I must be nuts or something, because I really like Army life. Even the food!

We took tests yesterday and today. Out of 55 men, 7 of us were selected to take the Officer Candidate School test, 6 passed including me! Only two of us passed the Officer's Leadership test. I went in and talked to a First Lieut. He had me go down and check my eyes. Because of that puncture in my eye, they say I'm qualified for OCS but not combat, but I think I can talk my way out of it.

Could you start talking to Gilbert's as soon as prices come in on the Barracuda or 383 Satellites. I've got two goals driving me right now, officer's school and a car. They seem to be doing the job of motivating me.

Your son!

Pvt. M. Roe, RA 18960517

Mike's letters were like that all the way through boot camp. He seemed to love the challenge of the Army and got a tremendous kick out of all the attention his eye received. For three days running he was dragged into the hospital for examinations. Mike suspected they were not so much examinations as they were clinical study sessions for the inexperienced ophthalmologists. They were fascinated by the corneal puncture and would study Mike's eye, then cheerfully spend hours exchanging notes, observations, and theories for the rest of the afternoon.

Besides passing the Officer's Qualifying Test, Mike had scored 151 on the army IQ test and was being considered for the West Point Prep School, the first step toward enrollment at West Point.

But all of these options would take time and Mike was determined to go to Vietnam. He would consider West Point, he wrote us, after he returned and if he was still eligible, but he was going to "Nam" first.

His letters continued on a regular basis for the rest of his boot camp. It was interesting to see the change in Mike's opinion of the D.I.s, the drill instructors, and of their toughness and demanding attitudes. First there was a certain amount of wariness—not fright, but the kind of admiration one gives a tough adversary. Later, near the end of the twelve-week training, his comments reflected a growing admiration for those men's ability to take kids with different ethnic and social backgrounds and mold them into a team, to give them the kind of confidence needed to survive in a combat situation.

There was little concern noted about his own well-being. Mike believed he could take care of himself. You could call it self-confidence, or the youthful attitude that it never happens to you, but he never worried about himself. Still, he voiced a growing anxiety about the nation. He wrote angrily about the increasing number of antiwar demonstrations and the violence surrounding those demonstrations. Puzzlement showed when he referred to the race riots that were spreading across the country. He admitted no knowledge of conditions among the blacks or their frustrations, but he couldn't understand why they would burn down their own houses and businesses as a form of protest.

During those months at Fort Lewis, violence and destruction erupted in Tampa Bay, Cincinnati, Atlanta, and Buffalo. Then, during the final week of Mike's basic training, Newark, New Jersey, exploded with gunshots, fire, and death. Twenty-six people were killed, and Mike wasn't alone in his concern about the health of the nation. Before the ashes had even cooled in Newark, the skyline of Detroit was outlined by the fires of yet another riot, which continued until forty persons had lost their lives and millions of dollars in property had been destroyed.

While still watching for an available date to begin OCS, Mike completed his basic training and was reassigned to Fort Rucker, Alabama. The closest city was Montgomery, a three-hour drive. Again, Mike expressed his enthusiasm for the Army and the countryside of Alabama.

"You're going to be surprised, but I love it down here! The countryside is beautiful, the grass green and it actually rains. I'm surprised, it even looks like Oregon. But the food is terrible, the worst I've ever eaten. If this is what they mean about army chow, then I'm beginning to understand!"

Mike had been sent to Rucker to be trained as an aircrew chief and mechanic on Huey helicopters. He would be in Alabama for the next three months. Meanwhile, Jeanne and I were about to close out our participation in the commercial sport-fishing business. We'd been thinking about it for some time, but I have the feeling that our last fish-selling deal was the clincher as far as Jeanne was concerned.

We had been fishing all weekend and the results were not what you might call overwhelming. By Sunday evening we had landed the sum total of three salmon. Jeanne suggested we take them home and put them in the freezer, but I wanted to sell them. We already had a freezer full of salmon and I didn't think we needed any more. Jeanne complained that we were going to feel awfully silly pulling up in front of the salmon cannery to unload three fish.

The argument carried for about an hour, but I won out and we arrived at the cannery, taking our place behind the other fishermen who were unloading hundreds of pounds of salmon, while we established our "catch" at roughly fifty-five pounds.

When our turn came, Jeanne went inside and told the foreman we wanted to sell our fish. A few minutes later, a huge box was lowered from the processing room on the second floor down to the *Ramblin' Roes'*.

Jeanne

This was one of the silliest things I think I've ever let Jess talk me into. We only had three fish and they were only medium-sized. Jess was right in insisting that we didn't need the salmon, but to have to haul those poor fish over to the cannery was going to be an embarrassing situation.

That didn't bother Jess, of course, since he planned to sit inside the boat, and wait for me to conclude the transaction! Some help he was!

When I went inside, it was a busy afternoon. Other fishermen had been successful and there was a frenzy of activity as they sold their catches and headed for home before nightfall. When I announced we wanted to sell our fish, the foreman didn't bother to ask how many, which I thank God for, but just said to move the pickup around to the side and that he'd have the dump box lowered down to the dock.

I can still remember the way the foreman's mouth dropped as I approached the fish box, redfaced, carrying our three fish. They were swallowed up by the box and he kept looking at me hoping that I would indicate that I was going back for more salmon. We stood looking at each other for at least a minute, as I slowly died a thousand times over. I shrugged my shoulders to let him know there were no more fish.

He studied the box for a second, started laughing, then called over another worker or two. He began to laugh harder as he pointed to the box, to me, and then back to the box. His friends chimed in and then laughter began to echo around the cannery.

As embarrassed as I was, I couldn't help laughing either. Those fish looked so pathetic at the bottom of that box and I felt like a fool, but everyone seemed to be enjoying the situation immensely. After the laughter died down, I had to go inside to pick up the money for our fish. This proved to be just as embarrassing as putting them in the box.

I stood in line behind the other fishermen, and obviously word had filtered down about the crazy lady and her three fish. I tried to act nonchalant as I stood there listening to the money being paid out.

"That's $230," the foreman yelled out as he counted the money; "$185 for you; $265 for you, Charlie."

The sums continued to stay in the high-one-hundred- and mid-two-hundred-dollar range until it was my turn.

"Three dollars and eighty-five cents, lady. Don't you think it would have been simpler to have gone over to the restaurant and just ordered a salmon dinner?"

I smiled as calmly as I could, took the money, and hurried out. But I couldn't help hearing the chorus of snickers and guffaws growing as I headed for the boat. I was mortified, but Jess thought it was great. He laughed all the way home about the reaction of the foreman when he lowered the fish box down and I dropped our three fish in.

I did not find the episode as amusing as Jess did, but I

had to admit that we must have provided the cannery with at least a week's worth of laughter.

A few weeks later, we decided that it was time to get out of the fish business. Jess got no argument from me on that decision.

The *Ramblin' Roes'* was out of business. It was probably just as well. Another three dollars and eighty-five cents and it would have put us in another income-tax bracket.

As for Mike, he continued to thrive in the Army. He wrote once or twice a week. It was obvious that he was happy. In the Army he could see the results of his efforts: not in the form of a grade, but in terms of making machines perform correctly. He was feeling the experience of being on his own, responsible for his actions. He was also experiencing success, and there was a purpose for his getting up every morning. It wasn't theory, it was practical application. Today I guess the younger generation would say he was experiencing the first rush of adulthood.

Mike wrote excitedly about his classes, working on helicopters, and receiving ribbons for his uniform. The subject of OCS came up while he was at Fort Rucker and it was explained to him that, if he accepted, it would be at least a year before he would again be eligible for Vietnam duty. Given the option, Mike chose Nam. He wrote and told us of his decision and that we shouldn't worry. As soon as he returned, he assured us, he would go to officer's school.

He completed his maintenance training in early December and received a thirty-day pass before his reassignment to Vietnam. Mike and three of his buddies decided to travel with another soldier who lived in the Northwest and owned a car. Traveling together, they reasoned, they could save more than half of their travel money. They saved money, but it almost cost them their lives.

Traveling in New Mexico during a hard winter storm, they were hit head on by a semi. The truck had spun out of control after striking a patch of black ice. The impact destroyed the car, and when the truck driver walked over to it he was positive everyone was dead. Despite the destruction, none of them was injured. The driver received a few minor cuts, as did the other soldier in the front, but Mike and his friend in the back escaped unscathed. Both were asleep at the time of the wreck, and Mike said later the fact that they were asleep and relaxed probably saved them from injury.

When Mike recounted the accident, including the facts that the car had been demolished and that the state patrol investigator reported that he didn't understand how anyone survived, Jeanne and I felt that if Mike had survived the accident, he would survive Vietnam. I realize that may sound a bit odd, but both of us came to the conclusion that if God had wanted Mike, he could have had him then. Since he survived that moment, we assumed he would also live through Vietnam.

Mike's escape from that wreck brought extra cheer to our Christmas. Our relatives gathered for a family holiday partly as a tradition and partly to say good-bye to Mike. He was scheduled to report to the Oakland base for assignment to Vietnam.

I was surprised to see that Mike had changed little despite seven months of army life. He now made his own bed and picked up his clothes, which his mother thought was a major improvement, but overall he was the same as the day he had left for Fort Lewis.

Physically he was slightly heavier, and he seemed to have a more positive attitude about himself, but those were the only visible changes. He still laughed, teased his sisters, talked about fast cars, and movies and music had become an important part of his life.

He talked about bands I had never heard before, bands that sounded more like industries or zoos. There were the Beatles, the Turtles, the Animals, Led Zeppelin, and Steppenwolf. 1967 was also the year of movies such as *Bonnie and Clyde, The Dirty Dozen, The Graduate*, and *Cool Hand Luke*.

As for Vietnam, trying to involve Mike in a conversation about the dangers of combat was like talking to a wall. Nine thousand American troops had lost their lives that year, more than in the previous five years, and the United States was pumping two billion dollars a month into the war effort. But Mike felt no concern about going and was confident he would not be injured. He was going over to see for himself if America should be involved, he wanted to fight Communists, and he was going to save enough money to buy a fast car. That was the meaning of Vietnam for Mike. The thought of danger never seemed to enter his mind.

CHAPTER NINE

> Look not mournfully into the Past. It comes not back again. Wisely improve the Present. It is thine. Go forth to meet the shadowy Future, without fear, and with a manly heart.
>
> Longfellow, *Hyperion*

It's interesting that much of what has been written about Vietnam has been about the men and women who fought in that distant land and about those who fought in order not to go there. I suppose that is always the case with wars and protests.

But, looking back, I sometimes think that the parents of that era might be the source of an interesting story. They were forced to stand on the sidelines many times, one voice telling them that this is the way it must be, that the youth must fight for the good of the nation, that history has ordained this system of settling conflicts. There was always the eternal hope that the sacrifices made were not in vain. But there was another voice, a discomforting one, that told of the suffering, the death, the waste, and reminded them that despite the sacrifices, man would fight again. During those moments, you heard the cries of protest and wondered aloud: Why?

For Mike, that question never arose. He knew why he was going to Vietnam. He was going to help the Vietnamese defeat "Charlie," the Communists. He was going to show the Reds that Americans could fight and fight well. He wore youth's pride well. To many, Mike's enemies were merely windmills that posed no threat, and sane men do not battle windmills that pose no threats. But for Mike they were giants and there was no question of their existence or menace.

That confidence was put quickly to the test. Mike arrived in Vietnam on January 21, 1968, only a week before the Tet offensive caught the Americans by surprise. He had been assigned to the 114th Assault Helicopter Company, stationed in Vinhlong, about sixty miles southwest of Saigon in the Delta area. He immediately came under fire.

We knew he was in the Saigon area and read with growing concern about the offensive thrust of the Vietcong. Only a few days earlier the generals had been saying the Vietcong were on the defensive and things were under control. As the fighting raged on throughout the Saigon area, we waited for Mike's first letter. Each day we watched the road, anticipating the blue and white Jeep's appearance on the block. Each day we'd quickly shuffle through the bills, junk mail, and correspondence, looking for Mike's letter.

Finally, on February 8, it arrived and everyone breathed a sigh of relief.

4 Feb. 68
Dear Mom & Dad,

Greetings from exotic Vietnam where the natives are friendly and loaded—with explosives!

I guess it's time I wrote. I've got a legitimate excuse for not writing, though. There hasn't been any mail going out for a week. I hope you aren't worried.

Before I tell you all the news, there's something I'd like to discuss. You know how they say that anyone that's not scared is either crazy or a liar. Well, I'm not a liar, and I hope I'm not crazy, but since I've been here, I feel so calm, I don't know why. I feel almost as if I belong here. It's really a weird feeling.

I've now been in the company eight days and we've been under attack seven. It all started last Monday night at 3 a.m. with a hundred (give or take a few) mortar rounds. Since then, we've been mortared two to five times a night. We haven't been getting much sleep.

The first night, we took positions on the perimeter. I'd been there an hour when I almost got it. We were laying there and a V.C. machine gun opened up. Rounds hit within six inches on each side of my head! Take it for what it's worth, I'll be more careful from now on.

That's all for now
Mike

His initial letters always glowed with confidence as he relayed the daily activity, the fire fights and night battles. Everything was new, everything was a life-and-death situation, and youth has a way of believing in its invincibility. I imagine that the combat situation, the powerful machines, can get the adrenaline flowing. Given the circumstances, it could be very easy for a newcomer not to look too closely at the veterans with their faces drawn with worry. They had probably also experienced that first rush of confidence and sense of power, but it always gives way to fear that they might not make it back, that they might die for something they were not too sure about.

Despite the fact that his helicopter crashed twice in the first month, he still remained overtly excited and unconcerned about his own welfare. The first ship crashed on takeoff owing to an overload, but the second, on February 20, was brought down by enemy fire. According to Mike's letter, they were two to three miles out of the heliport when they were hit by machine-gun fire. The engine had been hit several times, but they managed to coast into the camp.

Mike referred to himself as "the Lucky Kid" for the first couple of months. After that, it was just "the Kid."

By March there was a noticeable change in his outlook. It was subtle at first. When he first began writing, his handwriting was sprawling, the words big, almost bold. But by mid-March you could see that his handwriting was becoming tighter, the words were growing smaller. I'm not a psychologist, but it was almost as if he was subconsciously becoming aware of the danger and that his mind was withdrawing, trying to shut it out.

His letters were becoming less optimistic. A conflict was beginning to emerge, one that must have affected everyone who served in Vietnam. He didn't put it in so many words, but he hinted at the thought. "If these people we are fighting for really want to be free, why aren't they fighting? The more we fight, the less they do."

> *15 Mar.—The next time someone says something about what a great army the South Vietnamese have, just laugh at them. Those soldiers are useless. They're old men and VC rejects! Two days ago, we took them into an area to drive*

off Charlie and both times we had to come back and pull them out because Charlie, though out-numbered, had them surrounded! We had to go back, take all that incoming fire to pull them out and for what!—nothing! They're worthless. They might as well get out of the way so we can do the job right the first time.

21 Mar.—It's tough going into an area and seeing all those hungry people. Sometimes I just want to sit down and cry, especially when I see the small children. They have nothing. I wish those anti-war protesters could see what wonderful people the Viet Cong really are. They tie hand-grenades to little three-year-old girls, pull the pins and then have them walk over to the G.I.s who are giving out candy. If those protesters had the guts to come over here, maybe they wouldn't be so quick to condemn what we're trying to do!

Mike

Build me straight, O worthy Master!
Staunch and strong, a goodly vessel,
That shall laugh at all disaster,
And with wave and whirlwind wrestle!

Longfellow, *The Building of the Ship*

The conflicts within Mike continued to grow as rapidly as the paradox of the Vietnam War. They were told to fight but not to win. They were only to return fire if fired upon, even though everyone agreed they were at war. The people they had come to protect didn't want to fight. Friends of Americans by day often turned out to be the enemy by night.

Mike's ambivalence continued toward the ARVN troops, as he complained that many times they would land and the troops would refuse to leave the helicopter. Often they would grab onto a metal post and cling to it until someone finally pulled them loose and literally threw them off the helicopter. And for every extra second it took for the crew members to unload the ARVN troops, it gave the Vietcong that much longer to zero in on the choppers.

I could understand Mike's frustration, but wrote and tried to explain that those troops were farmers who probably, until a few months ago, had never fired a weapon and had certainly never traveled in a helicopter. Obviously they were going to be terrified, and his anger should probably be directed at those responsible for training the troops rather than the troops themselves.

If my counsel had any effect, it was probably only momentary. It was hard for me to identify with the frustration he and his buddies were undergoing. Mike wrote of taking ammunition into an outpost and being surprised to see that for once the ARVN were eager to help. They were well organized and quickly unloaded the supplies and seemed to be in excellent spirits. It was only later that Mike learned the real ARVN troops had abandoned the position without notifying anyone, and in such haste that they left their uniforms behind. The eager and cheerful troops were Vietcong.

Another time, Mike's helicopter was ordered to take supplies into an outpost near the helicopter base. The outpost had been surrounded and they were running out of ammunition. Braving heavy ground fire, the helicopter got into the site, off-loaded the supplies, and got out. But later the ARVN pulled out, leaving the ammunition that the helicopter crew had risked their lives to deliver. After that night, the ammunition was used to shell the helicopter base.

Perhaps the worst indignity, which demonstrated, at least to Mike, that perhaps the United States was fighting a losing cause, came during a heavy seven-day battle near the Delta community of Mytho. It had been a heavy pitched battle in which the Army had sprung a trap on the Vietcong. Intelligence estimated that they had trapped at least two to three thousand regular troops.

Because of the intense fighting, Mike's squadron was ordered to evacuate civilians from the area. Night and day they ferried the trapped civilians out of the battle zone. After almost four days of continuous flying, their company commander received a thank-you note for their hard and successful work. Unfortunately the note was from a Vietcong battalion commander. If the note was true, Mike's unit had helicoptered a large number of the VC commander's troops out of the trap and had taken them to a safe zone, where they formed up and launched another attack behind U.S. lines.

Of course, it may never have happened. Many military officials insist that such publicized thank-you notes were merely propaganda, a means of undermining the resolution of American fighting troops.

The note didn't affect Mike as much as an article that appeared in an issue of *Time* magazine. He complained that even when they beat the Vietcong on their own ground, beat them at their own game, the American press swept it under the table as merely military exaggeration.

On the same day that direct peace negotiation began between North Vietnam and the United States, Mike wrote angrily about what he considered unfair reporting:

> *3 April—I just glanced at a* Time *magazine. In there they said they thought the V.C. figure (body count) was exaggerated. Ha! There's been somewhere around 500 to 1,000 V.C. killed in our area. We didn't even bother to count. I imagine this is going on all over. If anything, the count is higher. We can't win!*

Later in the week, Mike recorded his first confirmed kill. According to his letters, he spent a long time brooding over the incident. He had taken a life and it bothered him deeply. I could feel the emotional struggle that was going on inside him, but it was never directly expressed.

Pictures he sent home showed that he had changed little, except that the smile was different. I remembered the grin that had spread across his face at graduation. It was warm, genuine, and confident. In the pictures sent from Vietnam, the smile was tight, almost cold. If I hadn't known Mike, I would have said it was a sinister smile.

In retrospect, perhaps "callous" would have been a better term. He wrote of the gruesome medevac details when they had to fly into battle zones and airlift the bodies out for identification. It was one of the most difficult things he had to do during the war, and it seemed to harden him. Later he would write of "busting" someone, a euphemism for killing. I suspect it was another subconscious effort to protect his mind from the horrendous pressures that surrounded him. His handwriting became increasingly difficult to read, but the message was clear: he was becoming frustrated.

> *10 April—This sounds crazy, but I've got two urges. One is to throw five or six Viet Cong out of the helicopter at three thousand feet. The other is to really blast the ARVNs as we pull out of a landing zone. Maybe I'll do both before I leave this country.*

Some of his letters reflected a growing racist sentiment. He wrote about increasing racial tension between black and white American troops. They had formed their own gangs, the "Cobras," the "Knights," the "Outlaws," and so on. It sounded like something out of *West Side Story*.

I began to wonder what kind of a God would create a place like that where my son would have to go. I forgot that He sent His own Son into a sort of combat. All I could think of was that my son was there, exposed to all of the dangers, both physical and psychological, and I wondered what kind of benevolent God would allow this. That it might be considered a test never occurred to me.

No one would argue with the fact that the pressures on the troops were overwhelming. Each person has to deal with those pressures as best he can. Mike withdrew, it seemed, trying to close out the pressures mentally. He repeatedly wrote that he refused to let Vietnam get to him. But it got to others and many turned to drugs to erase, for the moment, the terrible tension that built up.

At first Mike wrote that the drug problem was overly exaggerated by the press, that it was not as widespread as reported. But later he wrote that he was wrong, that he had simply chosen to ignore the facts.

Shortly after a long battle in the southwest area near Saigon, where the official military body count showed that ARVN and U.S. helicopter forces had inflicted a heavy defeat on the Vietcong, Mike wrote that many soldiers were using marijuana and other drugs.

> *4 May—Remember my previous statement about drugs? Well, they have changed. Evidently, someone has found an easy way*

to get a hold of the stuff. Anyway, everybody and his brother is smoking that junk.

I'm sure glad I take care of my own aircraft. The jerks are smoking marijuana even while working on the helicopters and they've come out of the hangar really goofed up.

Over here, you've got to use every ounce of sense you've got and they're really asking for it by using drugs. One day, they're going to get nailed and it'll be their own fault. Oh well, it's their body. I just hope they don't take me with them when they self-destruct.

Chris and Sus, don't either of you mess with drugs! If you do, I'll never speak to you again!

Music at the time reflected the restless and questioning mood of the youth. Like others, Mike enjoyed the acid rock of Jimi Hendrix and the rebellious expressions of Steppenwolf. It was a strange mixture of the hard, acid rock and the emergence of what they called bubble-gum music. H. L. Mencken called television "chewing gum for the eyes." If that is the case, I will always think of bubble-gum music as chewing gum for the ears. Give me Benny Goodman anytime!

But while he shared the music, he disagreed with the antiwar movement. Letter after letter mentioned the war protesters and how they didn't have the foggiest idea of what they were talking about. You didn't have to read between the lines to know that he was struggling to control the frustration and anger he felt toward them. There were numerous references to what he and his buddies would do to the demonstrators if they ran into them when they got back to the States.

I think I understand the type of frustration Mike and the others were feeling. They were putting their lives on the line, they could never be sure who were the friendlies and who were the enemies. The humidity was almost sickening, and during the rice season, if you took a deep breath, you sucked in a half-dozen insects. To go through all of that and then to have others the same age telling you you're crazy, that you're a fascist or a killer, is not easy to accept. You want to reach out and hit someone. It's not unlike the frustration you might feel at a football game where your team is slowly losing an important game and you have to sit in the stands and watch it happen. Granted, the intensity is not the same, but the same helpless feeling is there.

By June, Mike had lost any hint of youthful invincibility, the romance of fighting had worn off, and his letters reflected a concern for his safety and the realization that his handwriting might be revealing something about him that he didn't understand.

> 1 *June—I don't know, but at times I think I'm going crazy. I get teed off at little things and then something big happens and it doesn't bother me at all.*
>
> *Everything I hear, any little sound when I'm flying, I start to shake. I'm nothing but a bundle of nerves. Maybe I'm beginning to hear footsteps and scared that they (law of averages) will catch up with me. I don't know.*
>
> *Yet, I couldn't stand not flying. It's worse when I'm on the ground. I feel trapped.*
>
> 3 *June—You probably wonder why I'm printing instead of writing. I can hardly read my own writing. It's gotten so small. I just wanted to write my letters a little different and eliminate some of the monotony for you. Probably the real reason lies deep in my subconscious. No, I haven't been reading any psychology books. I guess it's just me changing.*

Mike also changed his mind about OCS. He received his notice of acceptance, but decided to turn it down. At this point he was fed up with the Army and disgusted with the United States. He realized what others had known for some time, that the United States was not fighting to win, but rather to maintain the status quo. He couldn't accept that and wrote that he was seriously considering moving to Australia or New Zealand after his discharge.

I know he was serious at the time, but Jeanne and I didn't take his threats as the final word. After all, we reasoned, they didn't sell Roadrunners or Barracudas in Australia, or if they did, they were too expensive for Mike. We assumed that he would figure that out in a while and quietly cross those travel plans off his list of things to do.

Regardless of the mood he was in, he never failed to drop in a few lines about the latest in fast cars. He must have had a direct pipeline to *Motor Trend* or *Hot Rod* magazine because he was always up on the latest in engines. One month it was this car, then there was a sudden shift to another car, depending on the magazine article. All he really knew for certain was that the car had to be fast and have a four-on-the-floor. The rest of the details could be filled in later.

The war continued and he continued to fly. In July there was a change of command in Vietnam. General Creighton Abrams took over as U.S. military commander and General William Westmoreland returned Stateside. One of the first things Abrams did was revamp the way the United States was fighting. Westmoreland had believed in large forces sweeping across the countryside, but Abrams, with orders to de-Americanize the war as much as possible, went about forming fast, heavily armed, mobile units that could strike quickly when needed. This meant helicopters, which created more demands on all units, including Mike's.

Abrams also beefed up the ARVN forces, making sure they were better trained and better equipped. Although Mike still harbored ill-feeling toward the Vietnamese, he admitted once or twice that he had seen a few ARVN units that actually knew how to fight.

In the States, Richard Nixon had won the Republican nomination and Hubert Humphrey was preparing for the Democratic battle in Chicago. Most remember that the fight for the nomination didn't receive as much attention as the fight outside the convention hall.

Thousands of antiwar demonstrators arrived in Chicago to bring the war home to those they felt were responsible for it, the party of Lyndon Johnson.

There were violent and bloody battles between the Yippies (Youth International Party) and the Chicago police. During the heat of the confrontation, the police were accused of using excessive force in quieting the riot. News reports charged the police with using Gestapo-type tactics.

Mike read one article in *Time* magazine and exploded with anger. He wrote to the reporter, saying that the Yippies had repeatedly stated they were going to Chicago to disrupt the Democratic convention, that it was their goal to create total chaos. "Given this kind of attitude," Mike wrote, "I can't believe the news could take their side. The police were called every name in the book, they had bricks, bottles and other objects thrown at them and finally had to move in to establish law and order. That is their job! Yet, you made it sound like they were a bunch of Nazis picking on a peace-loving group of ministers or something!"

A portion of Mike's letter was printed in the next issue of *Time* and he received a letter from the reporter, who thanked Mike for his opinion but restated that all the reports indicated the police had exceeded reasonable force in bringing the situation under control. I know Mike didn't buy that explanation, but he seemed pleased that at least they were willing to print his comments about the incident.

On the same day that Denny McLain became the first major-league thirty-game winner since 1934, we got a letter from Mike announcing that for the fifth time his helicopter had gone down. Perhaps it wasn't as spectacular as winning thirty games, but it made an impression upon us. Three times he had been shot down, twice the aircraft had been forced down because of mechanical failures.

> 12 *Sept.—This afternoon we put in two more flights and went on a medevac. On the way out, we got hit. We took off downwind and couldn't get over a hundred feet. Charlie was waiting for us and hit us with a machine gun and we went down.*
>
> *We took hits in the pilot section, eliminating all radio and instrumentation. There were hits in the crewmember section, the fuel cells and most of the rest of the ship.*
>
> *It didn't take long for someone to pick us up and at last report, they said they're going to destroy the ship. The pilot was wounded in the leg, nothing serious though.*
>
> *Hey, I had a very small chunk of shrapnel go through the skin on my knuckle. Might get a Purple Heart. Wow! It will go well with my 17 air medals.*
>
> *Mike*

It was the last time one of Mike's flights was prematurely terminated. A few weeks after the last crash, he took his annual physical and the doctors once again discovered his punctured cornea and grounded him. Instead of flying, he was relegated to a position of "Hangar Rat," a mechanic.

Before, time passed quickly, but now, without the luxury of flying, without the excitement, time slowed to a crawl. To make matters worse, he was named acting platoon sergeant. He couldn't fly and he discovered the world of "pass the buck." Even as an acting platoon sergeant, he was expected to shape the troops up. Unfortunately, most of the troops were veterans and short-timers, those with only a short time left on their tour of duty.

Military discipline was lax, although Mike's unit was one of the most effective helicopter units in Vietnam. But as the 114th's base grew in size and importance, it drew more attention from the brass. Mike didn't see the value of a well-pressed uniform in 95-degree, 95 percent–humidity weather. Yet he was expected to enforce military dress codes. Before, they had done things as the situation dictated. Now he was told that things were to be done in "a military fashion."

The problem, of course, was that most of the men were used to their own way of doing things and resisted new routines and traditional military courtesies. Though Mike hated the job, he viewed himself as a sort of go-between between the regular military officers and NCO's and his own buddies. He took the heat and managed to keep the unit's "flexible approach" to military life.

But if the pressure of being a sergeant increased, the tension of combat eased. I'm not sure Mike realized the change, but both Jeanne and I saw it in his letters. Before the last crash, we could hardly read the letters; then after he was grounded, his handwriting began to open up. By November it had returned to normal and he was counting the days until he returned home.

To pass the time, Mike spent most of his off-duty hours rummaging through car magazines. He ran the gamut of fast machines. Each letter it was a new car, a bigger engine, or a new option. One letter, he'd tell us to order a Charger, then the next one would say, "Wait a minute, I think I want a Satellite." After that it was a Roadrunner, a Barracuda, and back to a Charger, and it would start all over again.

But without his dream of a new car, it would have been difficult for Mike. He sat there counting the days and trying to determine whether or not his year in Vietnam was worth it. He was bitter over the way the United States was fighting the war, angry at the antiwar protesters, and confused over why the Army decided his unit needed more military bearing.

20 Dec.—Dear Mom & Dad,

Well, hello from the pages of that great classic, "Mike In Wonderland." I've been over here 11 months and still don't know what is happening.

It's depressing as hell, plus everywhere you go some lifer tells you to do something, that your uniform isn't right. Boy, I'm glad I didn't decide to go to OCS.

Every time we turn around, they jump on us to do something else. One day, after the unit had been flying all day, some officer decided the road needed to be repaired, so we had to get out there and work on the road!

What bothers everyone is that this company has the finest combat record in the Delta. I just can't figure it out. We have a very high rate of hours flown, ships available and our accident rate is extremely low. Yet, they treat us like some detail company instead of a combat unit. No wonder we're losing.

34 days and I'm out!

Don't buy that Satellite. I've changed my mind again. Sorry. But this time I've really made up my mind. I want a Roadrunner with a 383 and a four-speed. I'll be home around the middle of January, so see if the dealer can have the car by then.

Mike

Every letter from that point on referred to the number of days left in Vietnam. And the closer he came to leaving, the better his handwriting became.

He became more philosophical about the war. As far as he was concerned, it was lost and all he wanted to do was to get out of Vietnam in one piece. Gone was the idealistic warrior who had wanted to save the world from communism. Gone was the young man who felt that a year was a small price to pay in defense of freedom. He saw young children living in squalor with little to eat while Vietnamese officials rode in Mercedes and lived in comfort. He read about the antiwar protesters who charged that American troops were no better than barbarians, then watched as the Vietcong turned small children into booby traps. The rich made money, the politicians gained votes, the poor retained their suffering, and little changed except that more than 25,000 U.S. soldiers had lost their lives.

Mike was discouraged and very tired. Now he just wanted to come home. But he wrote that he felt he could leave his experiences behind. He told us that Vietnam had deeply affected many of his friends, but that he would be able to blot the whole thing out of his life.

> *26 Dec.—This place is not going to get to me. I've made up my mind that I don't care about it. I am mentally turning my back on Vietnam, the war and those who I have grown to hate. I cannot see where it would do any good or accomplish anything to bring those feelings home with me.*

Finally his rotation orders came through and it was all over. He was on his way back to the United States. His last letter announced that he'd be in Oakland, California, on January 21, 1969, and would take the first available flight to Portland. He still had a year to serve, but he was out of Vietnam.

He added a P.S. saying that he was staying with his last choice in cars, the Roadrunner. He admitted that he could never come to any conclusions about Vietnam, but at least the quandary of which car had been solved.

Jeanne

Getting that last letter announcing that Mike was coming home lifted a tremendous amount of weight off of the family's shoulders. There was little doubt that God would send Mike safely back to us, but we held our collective breath anyway. Even if you're sure that nothing will happen, the threat is always there, always in the back of your mind.

His phone call from Oakland was cheerful. He talked excitedly about returning to the "Great PX in the Sky," the United States; he said he was taking an early-morning flight to Portland and would I call the car dealer to see how his Roadrunner was coming. The requests and comments came out as a steady stream of conversation. He allowed very little room for me to add any comments. He laughed when I finally mentioned it was a one-way conversation and said he'd give us all a chance to talk when he got home.

Mike arrived in Portland in the middle of a cold spell, when the streets were covered with ice. He called from the airport and told us not to bother trying to get out, that he would take a taxi and let the driver worry about wrecking his car.

I watched him get out of the car and was surprised to see that he had changed little. From the news reports about soldiers returning from Vietnam, how their whole personality, their faces, had changed, I had expected to see a much older-looking son. But the only real change was that he had lost so much weight. It was still the same Mike and he still had that mischievous grin on his face as he walked up the sidewalk toward the house.

It felt good holding him, knowing that he was safe back home again. But he refused to let us make much of a fuss about his return. The grin never disappeared, yet we knew he felt the same relief we felt. It was obvious that he was nervous as he talked rapidly, excitedly, about Vietnam, about his buddies, and about his trip back to the United States. Not once did he bring up any unpleasant aspects of the war. He told the traditional war stories about the funny things and ridiculous foul-ups that happened.

He paced as he talked, and finally after a couple of hours he asked if I would take him into town so he could look up some of his friends.

Of course, the first friend he wanted to talk to was the car dealer. Once we got into the car, all he could think of was his Roadrunner! He gave me a fast fifteen-minute dissertation on carburetors, transmissions, and something called solid lifters. I never understood a word he said, but he certainly enjoyed the talk.

He was crushed to discover that his car wouldn't be in for another fifteen days, but he resigned himself to the fact and spent the rest of the day talking to old friends.

When we returned in the afternoon, Chris and Sus were home and immediately cornered Mike. The three of them must have set a new world's conversation record, talking nonstop for the next three hours. The girls wanted to know everything about Vietnam, and Mike tried to catch up with what people his own age were doing.

"Far out" and "out of sight" were the current fad terms, and the big films were *Planet of the Apes*, *2001: A Space Odyssey*, and *Rosemary's Baby*. Mike's first choice was *2001* since he was a science fiction buff, and then he expressed some interest in *Planet of the Apes*, noting that he thought it was appropriate that mankind wound up subservient to apes.

In the area of music, he discovered a new world of "acid" or "drug" rock. Although Armed Forces Radio played most of the popular hits, references to drugs or strong antiwar sentiment were quietly deleted from the play list. He liked the music, but again he spoke out strongly and bitterly against drugs and warned his sisters to stay away from them. He also encouraged them to continue their education, saying that it was the only way of getting ahead.

When we sat down at the dinner table that evening, it was as if Mike had never left. He began teasing his sisters unmercifully and at one point licked his fork and promptly dropped it in Chris's glass of milk.

The familiar cry of "Mom!" was again heard in the Roe household.

But later in the meal we noticed that Mike was becoming increasingly quiet and nervous or high-strung. After dinner, he got up from the table, walked over to an easy chair, and sat down. We had a new dog then, a puppy (Cindy had died), and the puppy, Brandy, had been jumping on Mike all afternoon, trying to get him to play.

When Brandy started this time, Mike suddenly began to cry and asked us to keep the dog away from him. We asked him what was wrong, but he just shook his head and said he didn't know. He kept crying for a long time and finally went into the bedroom. I'm not sure he ever really knew what had happened, but I'm convinced it was just the sudden release of emotions that he had bottled up during his twelve months in Vietnam.

In the morning he was fine, but a bit embarrassed and somewhat puzzled by his behavior. But it was quickly forgotten and Mike settled down to a month's leave before reporting for duty at Fort Carson, Colorado Springs, Colorado. He reestablished friendships, caught up on the movies, and began dating. The most important event was the arrival of his new car.

After almost a year and a half of planning and saving his money, he had his car: a brand-new white Roadrunner with blue interior, a big engine, and a four-speed transmission. He wanted to give me another lecture on the function of the engine and transmission, but I managed to come up with a plausible excuse for missing it.

For the next week and a half, Mike all but lived in his car. It helped melt away the troubles and frustrations of Vietnam.

During the whole month that he was home, he talked very little about the war. Most of the time he just talked about the happy moments, but occasionally he would make a brief reference to the battles and the fear that crept into his mind. But then he would stop and smile and tell us that he didn't want to relive those moments. He just wanted to forget Vietnam and concentrate on his car.

In late February, Mike packed his bag and got ready for the long drive to Colorado. We hated to see him go, but I knew he was anxious to get out on the road and really give his new car a test. Both Jess and I counseled him on taking it easy on speed, and he smiled and nodded his head. We both knew we were talking to ourselves and that Mike was patronizing us. He had his travel plans already made out.

The last thing I told him was not to pick up hitchhikers, and he promised me he wouldn't.

Three days later, he called from Colorado Springs saying that the car ran perfectly and that it was a great trip. Jess asked him how fast he had driven, and Mike just laughed and said something about "flying low." He mentioned that he had picked up a hitchhiker and taken him as far as Denver. My motherly advice would have had more impact on my house plants.

CHAPTER TEN

While he was governor of Oregon, Tom McCall gained a good deal of national attention with an offhanded comment about the increasing number of people moving into the state and the growing resentment of native Oregonians.

McCall claimed it wasn't true that Oregonians didn't like newcomers. "Oregonians are friendly people," McCall said, smiling. "Every time we see an out-of-stater, we always tell them, 'By all means come and visit. But for heaven's sake don't stay! If you do stay, don't tell anyone where you've moved!' "

Many Oregonians feel that any reference to state weather that doesn't include the phrases "torrential downpour," "prevailing monsoons," and "Noah anchored here" is tantamount to treason.

It is with some trepidation that I note that the spring of 1969 was beautiful, sunny, and warm. I'm sorry, but it really was a nice spring and, with Mike safe and sound back in the United States, we could enjoy it. He had now been at Fort Carson about three months. It was better than Vietnam, although more boring and more "regular Army." Instead of complaining about fighting conditions, he grumbled about having to salute every time he turned around, having to keep his boots polished and his uniforms starched to the point where if he dropped them he claimed they would break.

There was little for him to do; and, in desperation, he volunteered for a tank maintenance school at Fort Knox, Kentucky.

Meanwhile, life went on in Oregon. Chris, after completing a secretarial business course, went to work for the registrar at Lewis and Clark College in Portland. During her spare time she took as many business classes as she could handle. Sus was completing her junior year at Lake Oswego High, and Jeanne and I were on the verge of becoming farmers.

Two years earlier, we had bought a 113-acre farm in the northwestern part of the state, near the small community of Carlton.

We were renting it out, but more and more we were beginning to like the idea of moving out to the peace and quiet of rural America.

We were getting a small taste of the life at our home on the outskirts of Lake Oswego. (We had moved in 1966 to a wooded two-and-a-half-acre site south of the city.) We were next to a bird sanctuary and spent a lot of time feeding the birds. The word must have gotten out that we were soft touches, because I swear we had more birds than the sanctuary. One day we counted twenty-seven quail and fifteen pheasants, plus a flock of smaller birds.

We'd go through a fifty-pound bag of bird feed a month, and I couldn't even claim the birds as dependents! Despite the injustice of the tax system, we spent a lot of hours watching over our brood.

"Jess, aren't they beautiful," Jeanne would exclaim. "They're so graceful. I wish we could bring them inside."

"Bad idea," I cautioned. "You let all those birds in here at one time, then someone scares them and they'll fly off with the house. That'd be a tough one to explain to the insurance company. I can see it all now: 'Honest, we were rolled by a flock of pheasants!' "

Jeanne laughed, and the birds ate their way through another fifty pounds of feed. I argued that they were beginning to take us for granted and that it was only a matter of time before they started frisking us for food as we came out of the house.

Jeanne wanted to tame them, while I was thinking in more practical terms.

"If we could just train them to mow the lawn or wash the car. Something useful."

She hit me with a wet dishrag, and I decided to switch to safer topics.

As the weather improved, we spent more time outside, watching the birds and working on the yard.

Our house sat well back from the road, about a hundred feet down a long driveway. It gave us the privacy we sought, but the position also seemed to discourage the neighbors from dropping in.

Every so often, when we were working out in the yard, I would spot a red-haired woman walking by. When she got to our driveway, she would peer down it for a second or two, then walk on. Finally, one day while I was working in the driveway building some flower planters, she came in and introduced herself as Marilyn Pavonne. She mentioned that she and her husband lived up the street and had wondered who the hermits were living next to the bird sanctuary.

After some friendly small talk about the neighborhood and the weather, the conversation got around to my wheelchair and the accident. I recounted some of the events, and my battles with Magda. She listened intently, then began praising the Lord for giving me the strength to meet the tests He had given me. She went on about how He must have spared my life because of the wonderful things He must have in store for me.

The more Marilyn talked about her God, the more uncomfortable I became. Although I felt I had a strong belief in God, I had never been around anyone who spoke so strongly about their devotion, except for ministers, of course. I felt that my relation with the Lord was a very personal thing and that it was something you just didn't discuss with others. I had never attempted to verbalize my belief.

People just didn't go around loudly expounding on their devotion to God and emotionally describing how influential He was in their lives unless they were ministers or religious zealots. I had always believed that, but now I was confronted by a person who seemed very warm and sincere. I couldn't classify her as a fanatic, and it puzzled me. She didn't fit the stereotyped role I tried to put her into.

Marilyn and her husband, Charles, became good friends and came over often to play cards and visit. Jeanne and I really enjoyed their company, and we would talk and laugh for hours. But invariably, sometime during the evening, the topic would shift to religion and they would again begin talking earnestly about God and how He daily entered their lives. Jeanne would eagerly enter into the discussion, but I held back, again feeling uncomfortable about expressing my thoughts.

I argued to myself that I didn't talk openly about my God because of the subject's personal nature. It never occurred to me that I might not be able to verbalize my beliefs because they were extremely shallow. In essence, I was only acknowledging the

Lord's existence, but I had never invited Him into my life and heart. It would take another two years and two heart attacks before I truly reached out and accepted Him.

While I was struggling with my faith, Mike was continuing to count the days until his enlistment was up. He wrote from Fort Knox describing his tank training and noted that he would never want to be in a tank if another war broke out. He described the tank as a motorized metal coffin speeding rapidly toward its own funeral.

His correspondence revolved around mundane army life, his training, his car, and dating. Since his arrival he had been dating a high school senior, Dee, whom he had met at a local drive-in restaurant. He seemed happy and talked excitedly about returning to college as soon as he was discharged. He felt that despite the major drawbacks of the Army, it had given him the maturity he lacked during his first attempt at college.

Both Jeanne and I were glad he had managed to leave Vietnam behind him and had moved so quickly back into a normal lifestyle. Articles continued to appear in the newspapers about men who were emotionally shattered by the war. We thanked God Mike escaped both the physical and the mental handicaps that many had suffered.

Mike continued to write about the Army and Dee. Chris decided she wanted to go to school on a full-time basis, and she quit her job and enrolled at Oregon State. She insisted that she was going to put herself through school and refused any help from us. Meanwhile, Jeanne and I kept thinking about that farm out near Carlton and began making plans to sell our house, let the birds fend for themselves, and become farmers.

In June, Mike returned to Fort Carson, but within three weeks he decided he wanted to get married. He called to talk to us about his decision. Both Jeanne and I tried to talk him out of it.

"Mike, you've only known her for a couple of months," I reasoned. "That's not enough time for this kind of commitment."

There was a pause on the phone. "That's what her parents said," Mike admitted. "But it doesn't make any difference if you've known someone one day or one year if you love them. I can't see any reason to wait."

"Yes, that's true. But on the other hand, Mike, if you really love each other, a couple more months won't make any difference."

"I still can't see any reason to wait!"

It was like talking to an echo. "This is a serious commitment, Mike. Take a little more time, that's all your mother and I are asking. Think about the responsibilities, the demands, and remember you're still young. Mike, you gave up a lot of youth going into the Army. I would think you wouldn't want any major responsibility right now. What about school?"

"Dad, if I could handle Vietnam, I can handle marriage and school. I know I can."

His mind was made up; the phone call was merely what he considered discharging his responsibility to us, to ask for our blessing. After a half hour, we knew there was no chance of changing his mind, and, faced with that situation, we wished him well and told him to come home as quickly as possible.

Mike took a leave, drove to Kentucky in late July, and married Dee. They returned to Fort Carson, and in September Mike managed to arrange an early discharge.

Mike and Dee came out to Oregon immediately after his discharge. Dee was a pretty girl, tall, with dark hair. Actually there was a striking similarity between Jeanne and Dee, and more than once during shopping trips the two were mistaken for mother and daughter.

Since Dee and Mike had arrived too late for Mike to enroll in the fall quarter at Oregon State, Mike decided to work a full year before going back to school. For the first month they stayed with us. Mike quickly found a job and they located an apartment and set up housekeeping. Meanwhile, we paid for Dee's tuition to a local business college where she was trained to become a keypunch operator.

For the most part they seemed to be happy, although there were times when it was obvious they were having difficulties. Arguments would occur, and relations between them would become strained for a while. But they always made up, and we wrote the arguments off as common to newlyweds adjusting to the give-and-take demands of marriage.

In the fall of 1970 they moved to Corvallis; Mike enrolled in engineering school while Dee found a job as a keypunch operator on the swing shift. It must have been difficult for them, since Mike went to school all day and studied in the evening while Dee worked. We saw them only occasionally and assumed they were happy.

Sus had graduated from high school, earned a scholarship, and enrolled at Oregon State, majoring in pre-med with hopes of becoming an ophthalmologist. Chris, meanwhile, remained determined to earn her own way through college. After a year at Oregon State, she began to run low on money and managed to get into a work-study program at Portland State. She worked extremely hard to get her education and we were very proud of her effort.

We all seemed to be managing our own lives, and things appeared to be running smoothly. During the Christmas holidays, we had an old-fashioned Christmas with everyone, including Mike and Dee, at our house. While everyone enjoyed the holidays, it was obvious to Jeanne and me that tension was growing between Mike and his wife. Neither said anything to us, and again we assumed it was something that would resolve itself.

Their problems intensified during the winter term, which was unfortunate because Mike was doing so well in school. He liked the challenge of his classes and his grades were high, but the stress of an unhappy marriage began to tell. Late one night he called us and asked if Dee was there. We told him she wasn't, and he said she hadn't come home after work. Growing concerned, he drove over to where she worked and found her car in the parking lot, but no one had seen her for a couple of hours. He admitted they had been arguing over finances and personal things, and now he was beginning to worry.

It was the first time Mike really admitted they were having trouble. Unfortunately there was little we could do but encourage him to work things out. We told him to talk over the problems with Dee and try to solve them calmly, in a logical manner. It was really all we could do since it wouldn't have been right to take sides after hearing only one side of the argument. Later, Dee went home and told Mike that she and a friend had gone out for a couple of drinks and she had lost track of time. I don't know how that situation was resolved—I never asked—but things did appear to calm down for the rest of the school year.

While Mike struggled with his marriage, we took a decisive step in making the transition from the life of suburban dwellers to that of pioneer farmers. Just how many pioneers had a pickup, central heating, air conditioning, television, and telephones isn't too clear, but the Roe pioneers were planning on it.

We put our home and bird-feeding center up for sale in the early spring and made arrangements to begin building a new home on the farm. Much to our surprise, and before construction on the new house got off the ground, our old home was literally sold out from under us. Construction was scheduled to be completed in mid-November, but unfortunately we had to move out of our present home by mid-June. Even without a pocket calculator, it didn't take us long to figure out that we were going to be homeless for about four months.

To solve the problem, Jeanne and I bought a thirty-one-foot trailer that would become our temporary living quarters while the farmhouse was finished. For two, this arrangement would not have been so bad, but it was going to be a crowded summer. Not only were there Jeanne and I, there were Chris and Sus (both home from college for the summer); our two dogs, Brandy and Gypsy; and our Siamese cat, Charlie Brown. The accommodations were going to be on the claustrophobic side.

Even the move out to the trailer was tight. Although we had stored all of our nonessentials, our pickup was piled high. We had to build in two small spaces for the dogs, and Jeanne, Sus, and I piled into the passenger cab with the cat. Chris followed in her car, also crammed to the limit.

On the way out to the farm, Brandy made an interesting discovery. She found that with a little perseverance she could unwrap a loaf of bread. For half the trip she happily munched on bread and watched the scenery go by. She must have been a little disappointed in her next discovery. Instead of bread, the next package contained flour, which was not at all interesting to eat but certainly spread to all corners of the pickup with amazing speed. Everything, including Brandy, was covered with flour when we arrived at the farm. What began as a brownish-colored dog wound up almost totally white and completely guilt-ridden.

We quickly came to appreciate the term "a close family." After three months I realized what a trying job Noah must have had trying to coordinate things in the ark. Still, he had more cubits to work with.

While we squeezed in and out of that trailer, Mike and Dee separated for the first time. Following spring term 1971, Dee flew back to Louisville to her parents. Mike said little about her leaving except to indicate that they just needed time away from each other in order to think things out.

While he was thinking things out, he joined the Oregon Army National Guard and was sent to Fort Benning, Georgia, for officer's school, but his punctured cornea caught up with him again. After about a week's training, doctors discovered his defective eye and washed him out of the program. To say he was upset would have been an understatement, since he had told medical officials in Oregon about the eye before he left for Fort Benning. Then to drive all the way down to Georgia just to be dropped from the program didn't sit well with Mike. But after a day or two of fuming over the situation, he chalked it up to the army way of doing things and washed his hands of the military.

I'm sure Mike had considered the closeness of Louisville to Fort Benning, and after being dropped he drove to the city and managed to patch things up with Dee. They returned to Oregon and for a while seemed to be getting along better. Mike decided not to go back to school and instead took a job assembling railroad cars. Dee got another job as a keypunch operator, and they seemed to settle down.

They came out to the farm on a regular basis, and each time they came we could sense that their relationship was growing more strained. Mike would occasionally complain that Dee refused to cook or take care of the apartment, but both Jeanne and I felt he was only describing the symptoms rather than really addressing the problem. Yet we both told him that he and Dee would have to iron out their own problems, that all we could do was encourage them to identify and talk about their problems and approach them honestly.

It hurt both Jeanne and me to see how unhappy they were and not be able to help them. We were probably as frustrated as they were as they struggled to make things work.

By this time, Sus had fallen in love and married, Chris had returned to college, and suddenly Jeanne and I were alone in that trailer. What had been a sardine can had magically become a spacious metal apartment. We were at a loss as to what to do with all the space now available to us.

Meanwhile, our new house was going up right on schedule. Dave Warlick, the foreman, was a wonderful person. Always cheerful, he kept things rolling right along and during his spare time would come over and talk to Jeanne and me. Like Marilyn and Charles Pavonne, he talked excitedly about his relationship with God and how He played such an important part in his daily life. Again I felt those uncomfortable feelings sweeping across me and would either attempt to change the topic or just withdraw from the conversation.

Occasionally Dave would notice that I had become quiet and try to draw me out.

"Talking about the Lord bothers you, doesn't it, Jess?"

I started to say no, then thought better of it. "Well, I just don't feel comfortable talking about religion. To me it's a personal thing, something that I like to keep close to my heart."

Dave smiled. "I understand, but remember what they used to say in school, Jess?"

I gave him a puzzled look and he smiled again. "They used to say that unless you could explain something clearly to another person, you really didn't understand the subject. There are a lot of people, Jess, who feel the same way about religion. The more you talk about it, the more you strengthen your faith. It's just a thought."

It was an interesting thought, and I gave it a lot of consideration over the next few months, as I did the subject of farming. I pondered the mysteries of farming, and after two months of pondering they were still mysteries. I had rented a tractor and excavated a site for the barn and cleared some brush around the house, but farming intimidated me. It probably still would if it hadn't been for our neighbor, George Stermer, and his wife, Barbara.

George wasn't a talkative person, but he was considered one of the best farmers in the area, and when he did talk, everyone listened. One of his first suggestions to me was that because the soil was poor, I should plow the ground and plant a cover crop the first year. He suggested hay, and that was enough for me. As for plowing, that was another question. The ground hadn't been tilled in years and, thanks to a hot summer, it was like concrete.

I bought an old tractor, and the first pass over that ground didn't even make a dent in it. Plowing with my rig was like taking your fingernails and dragging them across a blackboard.

I told George that plowing ground that hard produced about the same results as rearranging the deck chairs on the *Titanic*. I felt it was a futile effort and planned on waiting until it rained before trying again. He laughed and laid half of the problem on my tractor, saying that it just didn't have the power or weight to get the job done. Then he added that he was also somewhat suspicious of the driver. The last comment was said with a straight face, but his eyes were dancing with smirks.

The next day George arrived with his tractor and his smirking eyes, ready to do battle. He was going to give the novice pioneer a quick lesson on the art and science of plowing fields. He dropped the plow, gunned the engine, and took off in a cloud of dust. Twenty-five feet later, the wheels were spinning uselessly on the hard surface, smoke bellowed from the exhaust pipe, and the engine roared, but the ground refused to yield. George's grin faded slightly. Mirth gave way to determination.

George backed up to his starting point, studied the situation for a minute or two, and then got set for another go. His foot pushed more aggressively on the accelerator, he rode the clutch, and once more attempted to transform cement into furrows. This time he got thirty feet before the engine bogged down. The grin had vanished as he came back to where I was. With a morose sigh, he glanced at the clear blue sky and said dejectedly, "Think we ought to wait till the rain softens it up a bit, Jess."

It was a subtle admission of defeat, but only until the rain came. When it arrived, so did George. Since the ground had been softened by the downpour, George took little time plowing the twenty-five acres we wanted to plant. I was absolutely green with envy at the way his tractor cut through the soil. A few days later, the urge to own a new tractor became overwhelming, and I bought a beautiful and powerful rig, had hand controls installed, and moved out into the field. Within a short time I had disked and seeded our new pasture.

We were officially farmers—we had our first crop in. Now, with winter coming on, all we could do was sit back and wait for it to come up. There were times when watching hay grow was more exciting than watching television. Our friends from urban America would occasionally come out to visit, just to make sure we weren't starving to death.

Mike and Dee also continued to visit, but it was obvious that they had still not been able to put their marriage in order. We talked with them as much as we could, giving them subtle hints on how we solved our differences and jokingly talking about our arguments and how each of us would give ground until both of us could claim victory. We tried humor and encouraged understanding, but nothing really seemed to work. All we could do was hope and pray that they would find happiness.

Meanwhile, we were falling in love with our farm. The grass was coming up and warmer weather was on the way. The stand of sturdy oak trees was sprouting leaves and the rolling hills were turning that bright green which heralds the arrival of spring.

I had great plans of really working the land. My new tractor had sat idle for five months, and I was itching to get out there and get to work. I was ready to become a real farmer. As it worked out, I first became a true Christian.

The winter had been long and wet, and to pass the time I watched old movies on television. After eight or nine weeks of steady watching, you can become somewhat addicted to them.

John Wayne was my favorite, especially in the old war films. Jeanne, on the other hand, was not overly impressed with the Duke's single-handed rout of the Axis powers. One night in mid-March, I stayed up late to watch *Flying Tigers*, one of my favorites. Jeanne opted for bed, surmising that the good guys had the victory sewed up. She told me to call her if there was an upset.

Since my accident, I had taken a sleeping pill every night in order to sleep. A few days before John Wayne swept the skies clear of Japanese Zeros, Dr. Kimberly had changed my prescription, feeling that there was a chance I might become addicted to the old sleeping pill. Instead he prescribed Valium, which I took just before John bagged his first Zero.

Toward the middle of the film I decided to get up and get a snack. I locked my leg braces, but when I got up the left brace collapsed and I fell with my left leg twisted under me. As I hit the floor, I heard a loud snap and knew immediately the leg had been broken. But, unlike the time I broke my right leg, there was no pain. There had always been more feeling in my right leg.

I managed to get up, and at first I thought of calling Jeanne. But since I couldn't feel anything, even though I knew the leg was broken I decided to watch the rest of the movie. John Wayne would have been proud of me. Besides, it was the turning point in the story where John and his boys were about to save the world.

After making sure the world was in good hands, I went into the bedroom and took off the leg brace. As soon as I removed the support, my leg buckled between the knee and hip and there was a bulge above the knee where the bone was pushing toward the surface. Just behind the knee a large pocket of blood had formed, and I realized that it wasn't just a minor fracture.

After putting the brace back on, I woke Jeanne and told her what had happened. She was absolutely furious at me for not calling her sooner. Maybe John would have been proud of me, but I think she was seriously thinking of breaking my other leg.

Jeanne called our family doctor, Dr. David Grimwood, and he made arrangements for my immediate admission to the hospital. Then he contacted Dr. Kimberly and explained what happened; and Jeanne and Chris (she was staying with us for a couple of days) drove me to the hospital. Around 4 A.M. we arrived at the emergency room and everyone was there waiting for my grand entrance.

I was immediately taken upstairs for X rays. Not only was the bone broken, but it had snapped in half and the upper section had slipped downward past the lower section. I was very fortunate that there was no feeling: the pain would have been excruciating.

After X rays, I was brought back downstairs. At this point there was little to do until Dr. Kimberly called. No one felt there was any real problem, since I was obviously not in any pain or discomfort.

Around four-thirty Kimberly called. After a short conversation, a shot of morphine was ordered. The doctor treating me explained it was a precaution in case any delayed reaction or pain showed up. It was also supposed to help me get to sleep.

So while we all waited for the shot to take effect and put me to sleep, we continued our idle talk about the state of the world and how John Wayne should be hired to straighten things out.

I could feel the morphine taking effect, and I was really beginning to feel pretty good. The doctor smiled and decided that it was probably time to put me to bed. They put me on a gurney and began wheeling me down a dark hall while all the time I cheerfully chattered away, having a wonderful time.

Even when the nurse yelled, "Doctor, he's not breathing!" I thought I was still talking away, listening intently to every word I was saying. Before the sudden rush of activity could penetrate the drug-induced fog I was in, I found myself back in the emergency room with three or four people working feverishly around me.

Apparently I had had an adverse reaction to the morphine and had stopped breathing, but not talking. I was given another shot, which was supposed to neutralize the morphine. So while we waited for that shot to take effect, we took one more stab at solving the world's problems.

I lost track of time, but after another fifteen minutes I was again pronounced ready to go to bed and was put back on the gurney and trundled down the hall. This time I was careful to breathe.

Jeanne and Chris were told they might as well go home since nothing could be done until Dr. Kimberly had a chance to take a look at me later in the morning.

By the time I reached the fourth-floor ward, there were only a young nurse and a floor nurse around. After ten minutes of pushing and shoving, they came to the conclusion that the two of them would not be able to get me from the gurney to the bed. Finally I convinced them just to move the gurney close, saying that if they could get me up, I could swing myself over to the bed.

Halfway through that swing I felt a tremendous piercing pain rip through the left side of my chest. I screamed and collapsed onto the bed and started moaning as the stabbing pains increased in intensity. One of the nurses immediately called for the doctor.

When he arrived, I was still in agony and asked for something to kill the pain. But he couldn't do anything until the morphine had cleared itself from my body. I'm sure he realized I had had a heart attack, or at least suspected it. He reassured me that everything was going to be all right, and he checked some medical books, searching for a pain-killer that could be given in conjunction with the morphine neutralizer. Nothing was found, and I had to suffer through that pain for the next three hours.

Sometime around eight o'clock a heart specialist came into the room and talked to me for a few minutes, asking about the location of the pain, if I had ever had that kind of pain before, and if my family had a history of heart disease. I told him no and for the first time realized that I might have suffered a heart attack.

"Have you ever taken a nitroglycerin tablet before?" he asked.

I told him no, and asked if that question implied I had had a heart attack.

"Well, not all chest pains mean you've had a heart attack. But why don't you take this tablet, and let's see if it helps ease those chest pains."

I took the tablet, but a minute later, while the doctor was still in the room, pains that felt like lightning exploded across my chest. They seemed to explode in all directions at once. They formed a circle around my heart, and it felt as if someone had put my heart in a vise and turned it as tight as possible. The whole left side of my chest felt as though it were being torn apart.

The shock and pain were so overwhelming, I could hardly even scream for help. I heard the doctor yell, and the last thing I remember before blacking out was the doctor saying in a frantic voice, "Get some help in here, his blood pressure's dropped to seventy and it's still going down!"

Blackness filled my life for the next four hours. When I finally came to, it was *déjà vu*—clear plastic tubes, bottles hanging from chrome supports, and an assortment of wires attached to the chest area. It could have been 1956, but it wasn't. This time I was in the coronary care unit.

For the rest of the day I was aware of people running in and out of the room. Jeanne came in to talk, and it was obvious that she was shaken by the incident. She had brought me in for a broken leg, gone home assured that everything was under control, and then had come back to find me in intensive care.

Jeanne

That whole day was one of frustration. I doubt if I'll ever forgive the hospital for not keeping me informed of what was going on. I knew something had happened when we were walking down the hallway with Jess and suddenly the doctor and nurse turned the gurney around and headed back into the emergency room. I thought I heard something about breathing, but things happened so quickly I wasn't sure.

About ten minutes later the doctor came out and said Jess had had a reaction to the morphine but that things were now under control. Chris and I followed Jess up to the fourth floor, but we were told we couldn't go inside because other patients were sleeping. There were a couple of chairs out in the hallway, so Chris and I sat down and waited.

At first things were pretty quiet, then I heard a nurse calling for the doctor, and seconds later she rushed out of the ward. A minute later the doctor came racing in, and Chris and I sat there wondering what was going on.

When the doctor came out the second time, I asked him if everything was all right and he assured me that things were fine and that Jess was under good care. I told him that Chris had to get back to our house because she had classes. He almost insisted we leave and promised he would take care of Jess. I thought it was an odd statement considering that as far as I knew he was just suffering from a broken leg.

Later in the morning, after Chris had left for class, I called the hospital (this was after Jess's second heart attack) and asked for the fourth floor. By this time Jess was in the coronary care unit, but I was told there was no problem and that Jess was doing just fine. Since there seemed to be no problem and I was under the impression he was still there for a broken leg, I left a message that I had a few errands to run and would be there in the afternoon.

Just after one o'clock I arrived on the fourth floor and went to the ward where Jess had been taken a few hours before. When I couldn't find him, a nurse asked if she could help and the two of us tried to find him. Finally the head nurse came over and asked what the problem was. When I told her who I was and that I couldn't find Jess, she got a very puzzled look on her face.

"Didn't anyone call you?" she asked.

"What do you mean call?" I answered somewhat hesitantly. "I called this morning and was told Jess was fine!"

> The head nurse turned white and then told me that Jess had been moved to the coronary care unit. When I asked why, she just told me how to get there and said they would explain everything once I got there.
>
> I was in a state of shock. I must have looked as if I was ready for my own heart attack. I just couldn't believe that this could have happened. When I finally reached the room, the color had drained from my face and the nurse asked if I didn't want to sit down for a moment before seeing Jess.
>
> After composing myself, I went in to see Jess. Like me, his color was gone and he looked very tired, but seemed in reasonably good spirits considering all that he had gone through in the last fourteen hours. We talked for a few minutes, but he looked tired and I left.
>
> I was still angry about not being told of Jess's condition. I just couldn't believe that someone couldn't have taken the time to call and explain what had happened. But after allowing a few hours for a cooling-down period, I decided that instead of being upset I should thank God for sparing Jess.

The next morning the heart specialist came in to see how I was doing and I asked him just how bad it had been.

"Jess, you had two massive heart attacks."

"Well, I figured that much out. What does 'massive' mean?"

He paused for a moment. "You've come as close to dying as you'll ever come without actually going. Someone must be looking out for you, Jess." He smiled, patted me on the shoulder, and walked out.

There, alone in that room, I thought about what the doctor had said. It did appear that someone was looking out for me and I wrestled with the problem of who for a number of days. I knew the answer, but it was still difficult to accept. It is one thing to say you believe in God, it is another to actually feel it, to experience the Lord and know that He is a part of your life.

I wasn't there yet, but I was moving in that direction and I had a lot of help.

Dave Warlick came up to the hospital while I was still in the coronary care unit and talked with me for about a half hour. I'm sure he thought I was dying, although by that time I felt strong and was about to be moved back to the fourth floor. I was surprised by his visit. We were friends, but I didn't feel we were that close.

We exchanged small talk, discussing the weather, hospital life, and how the farm was coming. Finally he looked at me and asked the question that had obviously brought him to the hospital.

"Jess, are you a Christian?"

I nodded and assured him that I was.

"Are you a born-again Christian?"

I had heard the term before, but really didn't know what it meant and told Dave so.

"All you have to do, Jess, is publicly declare that Jesus Christ is your Lord and Savior. That He died for our sins and was raised from the dead in three days. Will you do that?"

Dave was so convincing and so sincere that before him I did take Jesus Christ as my Lord and Savior. After those emotional moments we prayed and then he left. Again I was left alone to consider what had been said, what had just taken place. According to Dave, I had been born again, and I did feel a certain warmth and security. But in the hospital there was no opportunity to explore these new feelings, this new awaking.

Jeanne came faithfully every day, and we talked about Dave's message and what it meant for us and our future. It was a challenge that wouldn't go away. There had been other times when I had thought about the Lord, but they were the times when I wanted something, or wanted Him to forgive me. It had never been a case of actually reaching out to God, of going to Him, but rather of expecting Him to come to me on my terms. When times were good, He was forgotten; when things went wrong, I suddenly rediscovered religion.

But now I wanted to learn more about my God and how He could become a part of my life.

For the next six weeks, while I waited for my leg to mend, we talked about the new direction in which religion might take us. Because of the heart attacks, Dr. Kimberly hadn't been able to get to the leg until after it had already started knitting. Eventually he decided it was useless to rebreak the leg, and finally he just put a cast on it and sent me home. He told me my left leg would be slightly twisted and shorter, but overall he felt it probably wouldn't cause me any trouble.

While I was still in the hospital, Jeanne met a group of people who would help us walk the last few steps to Jesus. Minister Layton Rogers; his wife, Rosemary; Tarlton Taylor; and his wife, Wanda, came over to the farm one afternoon, introduced themselves, and asked if there was anything they could do since they understood I was in the hospital. Dave Warlick had given the Rogerses our name and asked if they would see if Jeanne needed any help.

Jeanne thanked them, but said that Sus and her husband were staying with her and that everything was getting done. They never mentioned religion, but made Jeanne promise to call if she needed any help.

I got home in early May, just in time for our twenty-fifth anniversary. The cast prohibited me from doing much except watching television and supervising Jeanne and Sus and her husband.

About six weeks after my return to the farm, Layton Rogers, his wife, and about a half-dozen friends of theirs dropped by to see us. They had just come from a Bible study session and decided to see how the pioneer farmers were faring.

We were delighted to see them and invited them in for coffee and dessert. They stayed for more than an hour, talking about various topics. I kept waiting for someone to bring up the subject of religion, but no one did. Finally I couldn't stand it any longer and broached the subject myself.

"Layton, I understand you're the minister of a new church in McMinnville?"

Layton smiled softly. "Well, it's not exactly a church yet, Jess. We call it the Yamhill County Southern Baptist Mission. We meet over at the county fairgrounds. We're being sponsored by the Holgate Baptist Church in Portland. We're still a pretty small group, but we're growing."

We continued to talk about the mission and their plans for a while longer, until they said they had to leave. As they were on the way out the door, Layton invited us to visit one of their Sunday meetings.

I told them we would, and that was it. I had made similar promises in the past and didn't really think too much about my offhand commitment. But as the weeks passed, that promise began to nag at the back of my mind and I felt compelled to go just once in order to soothe my conscience. Finally, one Saturday evening, I told Jeanne to get ready for church because we were going the next morning.

It was one of the most important decisions of our lives. We went that Sunday, and both of us couldn't recall when we had felt so comfortable, so wanted. The people treated us like long-lost relatives, like part of their family. There was a genuine sincerity we had never felt before in a church.

Not only were we thrilled by the love that flowed among the members, but we were also deeply impressed by the sermon delivered by Layton. Actually, it wasn't so much a sermon as it was a discussion of God and how He was a part of all our lives. It wasn't theology exactly, but rather a talk about the personal relationship with Jesus Christ and how He is always with us.

For the first time I felt compelled to talk openly about my feelings toward the Lord, and I discovered that it generated a warm, tranquil glow inside me. Finally I had truly opened my heart; I was reaching out for the love of Christ. I now understood what it felt like being a part of His family. These emotions were new for me, but there was no doubt, no hesitation. The term "born again" now revealed itself to me. I had entered a new life, starting again, and I knew that nothing could ever take me away from the Lord's family.

Each day I could feel my faith grow. Before, while driving, I would become impatient with drivers who weren't driving the way I wanted them to. Now I found my anger had disappeared. I discovered it was difficult to hate your brother.

If there was joy in my heart for my personal discovery of Jesus Christ, there was even more for Mike and Dee. Mike had always faithfully attended Sunday school with his sisters while they were growing up (Jeanne had seen to that), but after high school he drifted from the Church to explore the temptations of youth and to fight a war.

But as Jeanne and I discussed the excitement that was now filling our lives, his interest in the Lord was rekindled. One Sunday, unannounced, he and Dee showed up in time for church and declared they were going with us. We were delighted.

Mike was immediately enthralled by the joy and happiness expressed by the congregation. He was pleased to discover that they not only found salvation in their faith, but also appreciated the Lord's humor. That was the clincher for Mike. As Jeanne and I had, Mike gave himself to the Lord. If possible, he opened his heart even wider than we did.

Occasionally, we would hold Bible study at our home, and Mike was always the first one there and one of the best prepared. He looked forward to the discussions and would talk excitedly about passages and how he related them to his life and his marriage. Dee wasn't quite so outspoken when it came to discussing their marriage, but seemed happy enough.

Mike couldn't wait to relate some humorous story he had discovered. He relished talking about situations that reminded him of his army days. One of his favorites was the story of poor old Gideon, whom God had commanded to defeat the armies of the Midianites and Amalekites.

To begin with, Gideon wasn't all that confident he could defeat his enemies, who heavily outnumbered the Israelites. But that turned out to be the least of his worries. God wanted to prove a point, and His example was driving poor Gideon close to tears. God wanted to demonstrate that it was more important for the Israelites to place their faith in Him than in their fighting prowess. He decided that a victory delivered by a ludicrously small army over a powerful one could only be attributed to the power of God. So the Lord ordered Gideon to send half his army home.

Gideon obeyed, but Mike figured there must have been a tremendous amount of gnashing of teeth and rending of clothes as Gideon watched half his army disappear.

"If Gideon had been a commander in Vietnam and ordered half his troops home, even with God's command in triplicate," Mike laughed gleefully, "the MP's would have thrown a net around him and dropped him in the funny farm."

Unfortunately for Gideon, the Lord wasn't through. Half an army might still claim sole victory, so He ordered Gideon to reduce his force to just three hundred men to meet an army that rivaled, in number, the sands along the shore. Gideon was getting nervous.

Mike enjoyed the quandary suffered by Gideon and the subsequent lesson of faith learned when victory was delivered.

He also enjoyed the Lord's dry sense of humor when seeking out Elijah, who had been ordered to destroy the four hundred and fifty priests of Baal and their idols.

Elijah completed his task, but in doing so managed to raise the ire of Queen Jezebel. It seems that the queen had grown quite fond of her priests and idols and had taken an immediate dislike to Elijah and his handiwork. In fact, she graphically explained what would happen to him when her soldiers caught him.

Deciding that discretion was the better part of valor, Elijah made a strategic retreat as fast as his legs could carry him.

When the Lord found Elijah hiding in a cave, He casually asked His servant, "What doest thou here, Elijah?"

Mike loved the story and its depiction of God's gentle sense of humor. But his growing interest in the Bible couldn't stop his marriage from withering.

Jeanne

I was mildly surprised but certainly pleased by Jess's reaction to our new church and friends and was delighted by Mike and Dee's interest. I felt the same warmth and love experienced by Jess, but for me the feelings weren't as new. I had been raised as a Christian Scientist and we were always a close, loving group. There was a strong, personal bond between us, and there was always joy in our worship.

The same feeling of joy, of love, was present at the Yamhill County Southern Baptist Mission. I couldn't believe there could be so much joy in religion! They believed in the love Christ offers, and they exhibited that love in their worship.

We appreciated the informality of the services, the fact that the congregation participated. It wasn't a routine or formula. The worship came from the heart. It took the direction dictated by the congregation's feelings at the moment. No one tried to channel those feelings into a prescribed program. That love and that joy were allowed to set the pace and to establish the mood each Sunday.

Jess's mood changed dramatically after we began going to the mission. Before, his temper was quick, his patience short

> when things upset him. But after we began attending the mission services, you could see the tranquillity in his face. There was no doubt he had found Christ, and I had reaffirmed my love for the Lord.
>
> Mike also seemed to be better able to handle the emotional problems of marriage. But Dee, after an initial warming, seemed to withdraw, and Jess and I noticed that the tension had returned.
>
> That still didn't dampen our enthusiasm for the church, and in September the whole family was baptized in the Southern Baptist Church.
>
> On the day of our baptism, Jess, in his excitement, almost forgot to take off his braces. He would have sunk to the bottom of the baptismal tank.
>
> Someone from the congregation laughed. "We would have added to the flock and gained a soul all in one step! Talk about efficiency!"

From the first Sunday we visited the mission, we never missed a service except for the day Belle gave birth. We had bought four polled Herefords and fell madly in love with each of them. Each had a personality of its own, and they were almost like family. We had to be with Belle when her calf arrived. However, it wasn't an easy delivery.

Instead of going out into the brush to drop her calf, Belle came in as close as she could to the house, lay down, and began bellowing. It was obvious that something was wrong and that she was having difficulty dropping her calf. We called the vet, and he told us to get her into a shelter and call again if the calf hadn't arrived in an hour.

In the meantime, George came over and had a look at the problem. The calf's feet had appeared, but it was big and causing the mother some real difficulty. An hour passed and the calf still hadn't come, so we called the vet again and he came right out. He took a look at poor old Belle and decided he'd have to perform some minor surgery in order to help her.

But while he went back to his pickup to get his instruments, George decided to give Belle a helping hand. By the time the vet returned, the calf was all the way into the world. Asked what happened, George grinned and said, "Well, I grabbed the calf's feet, and Belle and I each gave a grunt, and the calf just sort of popped out!"

Seeing that new calf up and running around in the afternoon was worth a missed Sunday with our friends at the mission. We had witnessed God's miracle of life and knew He'd understand. But it was our only absence. We looked forward to those Sundays.

My faith grew stronger each day. I became more at peace with myself. It was easier to accept people as they were and to accept myself as I was. Before discovering Christ, I never had the courage to go out into public using my crutches or wheelchair. But afterward I recognized that most people are wonderful and loving. They welcomed me into their midst as eagerly and warmly as they would anyone else. I forgot about the sensation of others staring at me because I knew the Lord was always walking next to me.

He was there the day I got down on my knees and prayed, and it was one of the most moving experiences of my life. Jeanne and I were watching Billy Graham on television and both of us had been moved by his sermon. As we listened, he began talking about giving your heart to Christ and that those out in the television audience could do the same.

"Christ loves you!" the Reverend told us. "All you have to do is get down on your knees and pray. Open up your heart to Jesus Christ and He will come to you."

Jeanne helped me out of the wheelchair and both of us got down on our knees and prayed. I felt the warmth and love of the Lord flow through me. It was an overpowering experience. Satan would never touch my life again and I felt the tears trickle softly down my cheeks. There was a time in my life when even the thought of crying would have embarrassed me. It would have meant that I wasn't a man. But now there was no embarrassment, and I knew that anyone who accepted God was a man. I was crying tears of joy and thanking the Lord for coming into my life.

More tears were about to enter our lives, but the Lord had prepared us. He would be there when we needed Him.

CHAPTER ELEVEN

> Let us therefore draw near with confidence to the throne of grace, that we may receive mercy and may find grace to help in time of need.
>
> Heb. 4:16; New American Standard Bible

By the summer of 1972 our farm was functioning with a reasonable amount of efficiency. The horizon seemed bright, the future secure as we drew closer to God. Through His will and our hard work, and with some expert advice thrown in by George Stermer, the pioneers were surviving. Our urban friends just shook their heads in amazement.

At the end of our third year, we were the proud owners of nine cows, two horses, two dogs, and a cat. It was hard work, and at times I worried about Jeanne. Although I did as much as I could, which was mostly plowing and running the equipment, it became Jeanne's responsibility to take care of the livestock. She worked harder than I thought was good for her, and I wondered aloud if we might have taken on more than we could handle. Yet she loved that farm and never gave any indication she wanted to leave. Before moving to the country, she had been susceptible to colds, pneumonia, flu, and migraine headaches. Those disappeared in the crisp, clean air.

It was unfortunate that the air didn't have the same cleansing effect on Mike and Dee's marriage. They visited us often, but the tension was still visible. However, at times there was a short but noticeable absence of animosity.

Wearing one of the silliest grins I've ever seen on a person, Mike announced that Dee was pregnant. It was obvious that both were delighted and excited by the event. Jeanne and I thanked God, hoping and praying that the baby would provide the catalyst needed to strengthen their marriage.

But their common bond began to weaken after a few months. The old frustrations and tensions began to creep back into their lives even before the baby was born. They struggled to solve their differences, and there would be infrequent moments when they were happy.

In December, after becoming dissatisfied with his job building railroad boxcars, Mike decided he wanted to become a policeman. He came out to the house one night and talked about his decision. He asked why I had joined the force, and I told him that it had probably been part accident and part fate. When I posed the same question to him, he just smiled.

"You'd think it was stupid."

"No, I wouldn't, Mike. I wouldn't have asked if I didn't want to know. Why do you want to become a policeman?"

He took a deep breath and exhaled slowly before answering. "Well, partly because you were a policeman. Partly, I guess, because it seems like an exciting job. It's not a nine-to-five routine like building boxcars. I mean, it's different every day, right?"

He looked at me for reassurance; I nodded my head and waited for him to continue. "And then, I'd be in a position to help others. I'd like that."

I thought back to those nights a few months before my accident and remembered how bitter I had been, how cynical and uncaring I had become toward society's needs. It hurt to recall those long nights when I tried to drink away the terrible, spiraling feelings of depression. Of course, drinking only fed the depression and nearly blotted out the love my family offered me daily. Only Jeanne's tremendous devotion and love had saved our marriage. It had been a nightmare, and now I sat there looking into my son's eyes, wondering what lay ahead for him. His marriage was on shaky ground, and Dee was six months pregnant.

"You say you want to help, Mike. You had those same feelings in Vietnam, and remember how frustrated and angry you became?"

Mike thought for a second. "It's different now, Dad. I mean, this is where I live. People didn't seem to care what happened to them over there. But here, well we have to care, don't we?"

Yes, I thought, we have to care. It was a logical conclusion. After all, if you don't care for your fellow man, then how can you be sure anyone will care for you? It was simply logical, but he would learn that many have yet to see the light. "There was the true light which, coming into the world, enlightens every man. He was in the world, and the world was made through Him, and the world did not know Him." (John 1:9–10; NASB)

"What about Dee? It's not difficult to see that you're having problems. There are a lot of pressures involved with being a policeman. You'll discover that people can be cruel, that they consider you an enemy. That can be very frustrating. People can call you a lot of names, they can express a lot of hatred toward you."

"There were a lot of pressures in Vietnam. I came out all right. And as for Dee and me, we'll be all right. I know we're having some problems, but we're still together. Maybe the baby will help settle us down."

I knew Mike had made up his mind, and I didn't feel it was my place to try to control his future. It was his decision to make. All I could do was warn him and pray.

A few days later, he took the police entrance exam and scored the highest out of some six hundred applicants. Mike was delirious with pride over his high marks and joined the department in January of 1973.

When he reported for duty the first day, they had a brief ceremony while handing out the rookies' badges. Just before they got to Mike, an old friend of mine, Elmer Brown, spotted him and told him to wait a minute. Elmer went into the back office area and came back out with another badge.

"This was your old man's badge," he told Mike, "number 206. He wore it with pride. You wear it the same way."

Mike did wear it with pride and couldn't wait to tell me that Badge 206 was back in service.

As in his initial experience with the Army, Mike found police work exhilarating, totally consuming. It offered him a new direction, a challenge for his life, and, I suspected, an emotional outlet for the troubles that plagued his marriage. The old enthusiasm and youthful exuberance resurfaced. He was sure he wanted to be a career police officer.

A month into his new career, he discovered a secondary vocation: fatherhood. On February 8, 1973, Dee gave birth to a beautiful daughter and our first grandchild, Jessie. She had beautiful big brown eyes and an infectious grin. Mike was overjoyed at her arrival, as was the rest of the family. He was the typical proud father, wearing a paternal grin and a camera wherever they went. Jessie's arrival seemed to have a calming effect on the marriage as Dee and Mike focused their attention on her.

Jeanne and I were happy for Mike and Dee. For once it seemed things were going well for them. As for us, our pioneer experiment was about to end. Despite Jeanne's love for the farm, it had been tough on her. Though it was a burden of love, I grew more and more concerned about the long hours she put in keeping the farm going.

We had gone through two very harsh winters during which the water pipes froze and daily Jeanne had to carry enough water in five-gallon cans to keep the livestock watered. She had to wade through ankle-deep mud during the rainy seasons, and I could do little to help her.

During the spring of 1973, while she was stringing barbed wire, the wire broke and lashed out like a bullwhip. A section caught Jeanne across the right leg, ripping open a terrible gash. Within seconds her white tennis shoes were red as blood spurted like a faucet. Jeanne managed to put together a crude pressure tourniquet. Fortunately Chris was staying with us at the time. While I got Jeanne into the pickup, Chris ran to the house to call the doctor and tell him we were on our way. It took more than twenty stitches to close the gap, and Jeanne was put out of action for more than a week.

Despite the problems, Jeanne was heartsick when I told her I wanted to sell the place. I knew that she loved that farm, but I also knew that it was just getting to be too much for us. I hated to disappoint her, we hated to move from our friends and our church, but I couldn't see any alternative. Even though it hurt deeply, Jeanne took the decision well.

Jeanne

Except for my tangle with the barbed wire, I had never been healthier. The colds, headaches, flu, and other ailments vanished in the clean air of the country. I looked forward to getting up with the sun each morning, going down to the barn and pitching hay and making sure the animals had water.

I even enjoyed the three-hundred-foot walk just to get the newspaper. It was so peaceful and beautiful. It made all the hard work worth while. The soil was poor and required a lot of attention in order to get anything to grow; I canned most of the vegetables and chopped the wood. And we could never go anywhere without first making sure the animals were watered and fed.

Yet when Jess told me he wanted to sell the farm, for the first time I cried over losing a home. The farm had become a part of me, and the animals had almost become family. I didn't want to lose it all, and yet I knew Jess was right. The farm had become too much for the two of us to handle.

In the spring of 1974 we sold it and moved to a big old farmhouse in another small farming community, Clatskanie on the Columbia River, about a ninety-minute drive from Portland. We both knew that the house was just a temporary stop, so we didn't bother unpacking most of our belongings.

Four months later we found a house on an acre overlooking a small valley between Newberg and McMinnville, Oregon. For years the small town of Dundee had been noted for its filberts, for a small but excellent-quality winery, and for being one of the infamous speed traps in the state. Our new home was a compromise between the amenities of suburban living and the freedom of rural farm life. Our neighbors' homes weren't stacked up against us, pheasants frequently landed in the yard and strutted about unafraid, and yet we could enjoy the convenience of supermarkets and shopping centers.

It was a lovely place, and I think I could have been very happy there. But soon it would have too many unpleasant memories to allow us to remain.

The move was difficult for Jeanne. We left a home we both loved and moved to Clatskanie, which we knew was only a temporary situation. We bought an old three-story farmhouse. The stairs made it difficult for me to move around in my wheelchair, but we had planned to stay only through the summer.

About the second week we were there, Mike drove up alone one afternoon. For the first time in months he seemed calm, a person who had managed to establish a kind of inner peace. I knew immediately that something had happened.

"You certainly look happy today," I said cheerfully.

Mike smiled awkwardly. "I don't know if 'happy' is the right way to describe it. It's more like someone released all the pressure that has been building up inside me." He looked at Jeanne and me for a second before saying what both of us had already guessed. "Dee and I are going to get a divorce."

It was a statement. He wasn't looking for our approval, but perhaps our support or reassurance. "I tried to make it work, really I did. But it was like traveling down a long road and when we got to the end there wasn't anything there. It was just a dead end."

There was no emotion in his voice. He could just as easily have been telling us he had decided to try a new brand of antifreeze. The lack of any emotion surprised me.

"That's a long step to take, Mike."

"But you're not surprised, are you?" he said, looking at us.

"No," I admitted, "we're not surprised."

"Would you advise me not to do it?"

I shook my head. "No. It's been obvious that neither of you was happy. I guess if you're going to do something unpleasant, it's better to get it over with rather than just standing around and continuing to be unhappy."

Mike smiled, but it was a cold smile. "That's the way I looked at it."

"Of course, you've got an added responsibility you can't just walk away from."

"You mean Jessie." This time there was a warm, loving smile. The emotion had finally surfaced.

"That's right, Jessie. You brought her into the world, and she didn't have any choice. Your mother and I would be terribly disappointed if you didn't take care of her."

"So would I. I love her. I really do. That's the toughest part of this whole thing." The emotion began to build in his voice. "She's really beautiful, isn't she?"

"Yes, she is. Have you and Dee worked things out?"

He nodded and took a deep breath. "Yeah. I'm going to keep paying for Jessie's support, and I think she should be with her mother. So we agreed to keep it that way. I'll be able to visit anytime I want and I can have her one week a month." He smiled again, but now the warmth had vanished. "It's kind of like Hertz Rent A Kid, isn't it?"

"Mike, we've never been through anything like this. There really isn't much we can say. You know we love you, but you have to work this out yourself. Both you and Dee are young. It's probably better to end it here, I suppose."

"I suppose," Mike said after a long pause. "But I did try to make it work. Really I did."

We viewed divorce with deep misgivings, but we also realized that there is a point where to continue would be useless, an exercise in self-torture. We believed Mike had tried. The outcome was regrettable, but we were relieved that the struggle was over. We encouraged him to put the divorce behind him, to get on with his life, to explore and discover what the world had to offer him. We hoped things would change for him.

Mike moved into an apartment in the north section of the city and during his spare time enrolled in a few classes at the University of Portland. Within a few weeks you could tell that he had found himself. He was happy again, he enjoyed school, and he still found police work challenging.

Jeanne and I, meanwhile, made the move to Dundee and settled in just as the leaves began to turn, heralding the fall of 1974. One of our first priorities was to locate a church that would give us the same satisfaction, the same expression of love and joy that we had experienced at the Southern Baptist Mission in McMinnville.

God must have understood the way we wished to express our devotion to Him, for we immediately came in contact with the United Methodist Church of Dundee and Rev. Dayton Loomis. The Reverend was in his mid-sixties, stood about five foot eight, had a slight build and pepper-gray hair. There was an inexhaustible twinkle in his eyes and his glasses were always perched on the lower portion of his nose, waiting, it seemed, for the right moment to drop into an unsuspecting bowl of soup or onto an innocent head. He kind of reminded us of actor Barry Fitzgerald, without the Irish accent.

He was a man who generated love and joy throughout the congregation. He didn't preach a sermon, he discussed it, constantly referring to events that happened in the community and relating them to the message of the Bible. His warm, comfortable style fit perfectly with the character of the church itself. It was a beautiful white board-and-batten structure that proudly supported a tall, sharp steeple. Each Sunday you could see Reverend Loomis in the entryway cheerfully ringing the steeple bell announcing the day's worship.

Many churches today have beautiful steeples, but all too often they are equipped with a transistorized sound system. Instead of a bell, there is a stereo cassette that plays "The Best Bell Notes Ever Recorded." Somehow it's just not the same, it doesn't offer the personal touch of having your minister joyfully ringing a bell to announce that God still loves you.

The cluster of oak and maple trees announced that autumn had arrived as the leaves began to explode with brilliant colors. The bright yellows, oranges, and reds produced a majestic backdrop for our little rural church.

In October, Mike began coming to services with us and took an instant liking to the church and Reverend Loomis. He looked forward to Sundays with the Dundee congregation and, like everyone else, to Reverend Loomis's off-the-cuff discussions about God. There were times when the Reverend would go off on a wild tangent, leaving everyone wondering how he could possibly tie his story in with the topic of his sermon. Regardless of how far afield he strayed, he somehow always managed to tie his saga to the point, and it always made perfect sense.

One afternoon, after another spellbinding story, I wondered aloud how such a small congregation had ever managed to procure such a wonderful man as Reverend Loomis.

Mike grinned and offered his theory. "Probably God figured that there were so many people in their golden years out here," he said, looking at both of us, "that they deserved the very best before they were finally called home."

"Golden years?" Jeanne responded. "Are you putting us in the golden years category?"

"Well, you're crowding the fifty-five mark, and we're not talking about the speed limit."

I laughed. "You make it sound like Gabriel has the chariot double-parked in our driveway!"

It was Mike's turn to laugh. "Just checking to see if you were paying attention. There's no use trying to second-guess God. He is about His work and we must accept it. Reverend Loomis is certainly a wonderful piece of work, isn't he?"

It was wonderful to see Mike's genuine, warm smile. We were so thankful that he was happy and living again. His studies were going well, and he was meeting new friends. Often he and his sisters would come out to the house for Sunday dinners, and many times he'd bring Jessie with him.

Seeing Jessie, who was almost two now, bouncing up the driveway, a huge grin on her face as she came to see Grandma and Grandpa, always made the day even warmer. She was growing into a beautiful child, and we loved every minute she was with us.

Since watching football in the afternoons consumed a lot of time, we would take turns spoiling Jessie between quarters and halves and during commercials. She had become a real part of our family, and it hurt when we learned that Dee was moving to Arizona.

The divorce had become final the last week in December. Right after New Year's, Dee came out to the house and we said goodbye to both her and Jessie. Her leaving depressed Mike, but he still felt that Jessie should be with her mother. He wished them well; and Dee promised to keep in touch.

In the middle of January, Mike came out to the house one night and seemed very pessimistic about his future. He wanted to have a serious discussion with us about what we should do if anything happened to him. He told us he had just changed his insurance policies, naming us his beneficiaries, and made us promise that we would make sure Jessie got a good education in case he wasn't able to take care of it. He explained that he had put all of his personal matters and papers in order and wanted us to understand how he had arranged everything.

We had never seen him so concerned about his future before. Even in Vietnam, he gave little thought to his safety and believed he was immune to danger. It was almost as if he had a premonition of what was just a week down the road. I felt a chill as I recalled that I had the same feeling after learning that two fellow officers had been killed. I had known I was next.

CHAPTER TWELVE

January 21, 1975, was a typical cold, wet Oregon winter's day. The wind drove sheets of rain across the landscape at a sharp angle and with enough force to penetrate even the toughest rainproof garment. The dark gray clouds seemed to hang only a few feet off the ground and moved quickly from west to east when the gusts of wind exploded.

By late afternoon the downpour had dumped almost an inch of rain on the Willamette Valley. The clouds exhausted themselves by nightfall, allowing the natives a few hours to wring out their raincoats and dry out their waterproof boots.

Jeanne, Chris, and I went over to friends of ours, Dr. Gordon Higginson and his wife, Margaret, to see their new home. The Higginsons had sold us our polled Herefords, and I jokingly claimed the profits paid for their house. It was a pleasant evening and time passed quickly.

Around ten-thirty we returned home. About ten minutes after we arrived, the doorbell rang. It was unusually late for a caller, but my mind touched off no alarms as I answered the door. I was surprised to see my nephew, Al Roe. He was a detective on the Portland police force, yet still no bells began to ring. My first thought was that he was out in the area working on a case and had decided to stop by.

That theory quickly vanished and the bells finally sounded when I noticed his ash-colored face and how nervous he was. I knew something was wrong.

There was a sudden urge to slam the door in his face, as if the door could bar whatever threatening news he was bringing.

He came inside and drew a deep breath and released it slowly before speaking. He glanced down at his feet; then his eyes met mine. I felt a cold chill race down my back. He quickly glanced toward Jeanne and finally Chris.

"Ah, Mike's been in a car accident."

There was dead silence in the room for a second or two, and I saw Jeanne and Chris stiffen. We knew Al would not have been sent if it hadn't been serious. The moisture in my mouth vanished, and I could feel a cold clamminess racing over my body. A voice began speaking from a distant point in my mind. I immediately recognized it as the same voice that almost twenty years earlier had screamed "Why me?" when I was told I would never walk again. Now it was saying, "Don't ask how bad he is! Don't ask!" Yet there was nothing I could do.

The tongue tends to stick to the roof of your mouth when it's dry, and for a moment I found it difficult to speak. When I did, my voice was thin and shaky.

"How bad is he?" I swallowed hard. Jeanne held her breath and waited. The wait was unbearable, and I saw Al lick his lips nervously while trying to find the right words.

"It's serious. I won't lie to you. They were hit head on by some drunk. Mike's side took most of the impact." He took a deep, shaky breath and swallowed. "I'm sorry. If you want, I'll drive you in to the hospital. He's at Emmanuel."

Jeanne and Chris were crying, and I could feel the muscles in my back seizing up into a knot. The tension moved swiftly up to my neck, creating a fierce headache that engulfed my mind. Things seemed to go gray and fuzzy, and I heard myself say, "No, I'll drive us there," but there was no real connection between my voice and me. I had withdrawn as I fought to keep control of my emotions.

Within a few minutes we were ready to go. Chris decided to go with Al to keep him company. On the way out the door, I absentmindedly picked up my .38 snub-nosed revolver, which I always carried when we went out at night. I felt that since I was limited in my movement, it made sense to carry the gun as protection. Al saw me put it in my coat pocket, but didn't say anything at the time. Once we were in our cars, he told Chris he wished I hadn't taken the gun and was obviously worried I might do something foolish.

I admit that as we drove into Portland, the thought of revenge occurred to me. I was angry and emotionally upset. Jeanne was crying, and it seemed as if our whole world had come crashing down upon us. I couldn't believe that it was happening. Mike had been so happy the past few months. It just wasn't fair. The voice agreed and kept reminding me of the fact all the way to the hospital.

Arriving at Emmanuel, we found the emergency room in what appeared to be a state of confusion. Policemen were standing around trying to look useful, doctors and nurses rushed purposefully in and out of doors, and, over in the far corner, a young woman wearing a green operating gown was giving orders. My first impression was that she was a high-school volunteer since she looked so young.

For a brief moment or two no one noticed we had arrived and we stood there stunned by the frantic activity. Our fears ran wild as we realized we were helpless bystanders who could do no more than watch and pray. Jeanne and Chris, already overwhelmed by the events of the night, caved in completely as they watched the desperate rush of people. The tears flowed unchecked. There was no effort even to wipe them away. Our world came crashing down upon us.

Finally Sus and her husband spotted us (we had called them before leaving the house) and came rushing over. Sus tried to comfort her mother and sister while the situation seemed to grow more chaotic for us. We still had no idea whether or not Mike was alive.

I caught a police uniform out of the corner of my eye and turned to see the police department's night commander, Captain Frenchie Brouillette, come into the room. His eyes swept the room and came to rest on our huddled group. I knew him when he came on the force as a rookie. He shook his head sadly when he saw me and walked slowly over to us.

"Jess, I can't tell you how sorry I am that this happened." He glanced over at the rest of the family and stared at them for a moment, searching for his next words. "I don't understand how this could happen to your son after what you've already gone through. I'm really sorry. I know that seems so inappropriate, Jess," he said, shrugging his shoulders, "but there's nothing else to say."

I nodded slowly, fighting back the tears. "How is he?" Again the question was difficult to ask. My voice was weak and uncertain.

Brouillette shook his head. "I honestly don't know, Jess. The doctors say he's in critical condition, but what does that mean?

Everything that can be done is being done. He's in good hands. A half hour ago this place was in total confusion. Dr. Stone came in, knocked a few heads together to clear the air, and things are functioning pretty well right now."

I looked at the mass of activity and couldn't imagine worse confusion. Yet, later on, I began to recognize the activity was coordinated and being guided by a strong hand. "Which one is Dr. Stone?" I didn't really care. The question was asked to prevent the unbearable silence that occurs during crisis periods. I didn't want to have time to think.

Brouillette pointed to the young woman I had pegged for a high-school volunteer. "That's her. Elizabeth Stone. The one in the operating gown."

I was amazed that such a young-looking person could, first, be old enough to be a doctor and, second, have the confidence to create order out of chaos. I watched, for the first time with interest, as she continued to give directions and coordinate the efforts of the staff.

Jeanne and Chris still had not been able to regain control of their emotions, and I was fighting back a desperate urge to start screaming. I felt the old bitterness of being tied to a wheelchair, of not being able to get up and physically release the pressures that were building inside. I struggled desperately to hold on, but the anger came through in my voice. "Al said the guy who hit them was drunk." The words were clipped and harsh.

Brouillette nodded. "Yeah. According to the investigating officer, the guy was drunk out of his mind. He didn't even know what had happened. From what I understand, Mike and Carl Witt—he was Mike's partner—were traveling east on Columbia Boulevard, and this guy was traveling west. I guess he was doing about seventy, lost control, the car hit a street divider or something. The car launched into the air, crossed the highway, and hit Mike's car head on."

My stomach churned as Brouillette described the accident, and I had to swallow hard to prevent myself from throwing up. I took a couple of deep breaths. Hot flashes swept across my forehead and sweat beads moved down my temples. It took a minute before I regained control enough to ask another question.

"How's Mike's partner?"

"A minor miracle. He received a slight concussion and some cuts and bruises. Other than that, he's fine, although he doesn't remember what happened."

"What about the guy driving the other car?" The frustration and anger returned to my voice.

Brouillette's face clouded and appeared troubled for a brief second. "Well, he's fine. He broke his leg. That was it." He must have seen the rage flash across my face because he grew uneasy and quickly added that the department was going all out to get him. "Jess, this one won't get away with a slap on the wrist. I can promise you that. He was obviously drunk, he's got a long traffic record including several DWI's [driving while intoxicated], and had a suspended driver's license."

"Then why was he driving?" I yelled in frustration.

"I can't answer that, Jess, you know that. All I can say is we can make sure he doesn't have the opportunity to do it again for a long time."

I knew Brouillette was trying to reassure me, but the words had little comfort. It just wasn't fair. Mike had gone through Vietnam without a scratch, had just gone through a divorce, and was just starting to enjoy life again—then, while on duty, got hit by some drunk who had no business being in a car and, as far as I could see, had no business living.

Someone mentioned that the driver was in the next room receiving medical attention. About that time his family arrived and were quickly moved into another room so there wouldn't be any contact between our family and theirs.

Al must have told someone I had a gun with me because when I rolled myself over toward the door where he was, two police officers stepped in front of me and quietly suggested it would be better if I went back and talked with Brouillette.

Trying to seek revenge wasn't on my mind any longer. I was angry, the rage boiled inside me because of my helplessness, but, unlike before, I had the Lord to lean on. A few years earlier, perhaps even a few months earlier, with the gun in my pocket, I probably would have tried to impose my own justice or, more accurately, my own revenge. But I could feel His influence and His guiding light. Revenge would be His, and I could live with that knowledge, which helped to ease the pain.

Later, Father Bill Curtin came over to talk with us. When he first introduced himself, I thought I must have misunderstood him. He was wearing jeans and a sweatshirt and looked nothing like the priests I had seen.

He noticed my amazement and smiled. "We don't always wear white collars. Mr. Roe, I just wanted you to know that Mike and I were good friends. In fact, we were together a few nights ago. I know he's going to make it. I was up with him earlier this evening, and while I know you're not Catholic, I prayed for him. I'm sure God didn't mind, I hope you don't."

I smiled weakly and thanked him for his efforts. He sat and talked with us for more than an hour, mentioning that his father was my sergeant back in the East Precinct. He was a very warm and sensitive man. It wasn't until a few days later that he told me he had done more than just pray for Mike. When he arrived at the hospital, Mike's condition was so unstable that he gave him the Last Rites. We deeply appreciated the bond of friendship he displayed in expressing his concern for Mike's fate. As he left, he turned to us and told us he knew there were no words to express what we were going through. But he wanted us to know that God was here and we must trust His will. The words were spoken with such sincerity that they gave us the comfort and strength we needed for that traumatic night.

As the hours dragged on, more and more of the pieces to the puzzle of what had actually happened began to fall into place. My memory of that night is somewhat foggy, and I'm not sure I really want to dig too deeply into those trying hours, but I was able to inspect the traffic accident reports that were filed. I have omitted the names of those filing the reports, but this is a verbatim account of the accident as seen by two eyewitnesses and the first officer to arrive on the scene.

First eyewitness—I was traveling eastbound on N. Columbia Blvd., and observed the police vehicle behind me. I looked at my speedometer and noted I was doing 40 mph. I was in the right lane of the two eastbound lanes and the police vehicle was in the left lane. Just shortly before the collision the police vehicle slowly passed and was approx. two car lengths ahead when I observed a big flash and a car up in the air which then came down on the police vehicle. I stopped my car alongside the accident and ran to the passenger side of the police car and could observe the police officer in the passenger seat [Mike's partner, Carl Witt]. He was unconscious, as was the driver.

Second eyewitness—I was westbound on N. Columbia, traveling at about 45 miles an hour. I did not see the car until it suddenly flew up in the air and then landed on the police car traveling in the eastbound lanes.

Officer report—I received a call from radio division at 8:27 pm to cover an injury accident at 2030 N. Columbia Blvd. Upon arrival, I observed the front of a vehicle bearing a license plate beginning with the letter "E" designating it as an official car, although I was unable to read the full license number or see much of this vehicle due to the position of a second car resting on top of the first auto. However, upon turning on the floodlights atop my patrol vehicle, I observed the remains of the Push Bumper Guards [extra heavy guards only on city police cars] indicating that this was a police vehicle. I went to the vehicle and observed one police officer sitting upright in the front seat of the vehicle, that he appeared to be unconscious and bleeding from the mouth. I immediately approached the left side of the vehicle and felt the neck of the officer whom I recognized as Officer Roe and tried to determine if there was a pulse. The pulse seemed to be quite strong and I called for two ambulances and backup assist.

There were other reports indicating that the driver was traveling between sixty-five and eighty miles an hour when he lost control of his vehicle. The car struck an overpass support, traveled about thirty feet, then flipped up and came down on top of Mike's car. Blood samples later showed that the driver had an alcohol reading of between .26 and .27. Police will usually file an intoxication charge once the reading reaches .10. At the reading reported on the driver who hit Mike, he must have been in a near-unconscious state.

Mike's partner, Carl Witt, reported that normally he (Witt) drove, but they had just come from a case and Mike volunteered to drive so Carl could write out the report. The accident occurred exactly six years to the day after Mike arrived home from Vietnam.

A lot of "ifs" crossed our minds that evening as we waited for the doctor's report, but the ifs couldn't change what had happened. The man who had caused the accident received a broken leg, Mike's partner needed to write a report, and Mike now lay on an operating table somewhere upstairs fighting for his life.

Portland Mayor Neil Goldschmidt came in sometime during the long night and expressed his sorrow. He stayed for a while and talked with Deputy District Attorney Kim Frankel before leaving. She later came over and explained that she was here to make sure all of the evidence and statements were accurately recorded in order to eliminate any possible legal loopholes when the city took the driver to court.

By three in the morning, Jeanne, Chris, Sus, and I were emotionally drained. Dr. Martin Johnson, the neurosurgeon who had been operating on Mike, and Dr. Stone, the young plastic surgeon who had pulled the emergency staff together during the first few hours, came down from surgery and spent a few minutes with us. They looked as tired as we felt.

Dr. Johnson spoke before any of us had a chance to ask the obvious question. "He's still in critical condition." Tears streamed down Jeanne and Chris's faces. "He's received very serious head injuries, and, if he survives, he'll need extensive plastic surgery. He took most of the impact of the car."

The phrase "if he survives" was not lost on anyone. "What are his chances?" I heard a distant voice ask. It was a moment before I realized it was my own.

Dr. Johnson rubbed his hand across his jaw and thought for a second. "Right now, I'd say he has a fifty-fifty chance. But if I were betting, I'd say he's going to make it. If he can make it through the next forty-eight hours, I'm sure he'll live. But I want you to understand there is extensive brain damage and I have no way of knowing what condition he will be in mentally, if he survives. I'm sorry to be so blunt, but I want you to understand the situation."

There were another few minutes of discussion, and finally Johnson asked if we wanted to go up and see Mike. Jeanne was in no condition to undergo such a traumatic experience, so I went alone.

Rolling my wheelchair down that dimly lit hallway was like pushing time back two decades. The sounds and smells of those long days in the hospital came rushing back, hitting me like an express train. It had been so long ago, yet nothing had changed. The sterilized atmosphere hung heavily in the air, the quiet was ominous. Whispers drifted down the hallway, sounding foreboding and threatening. Even the squeaky rubber soles came back to haunt me.

It was the saddest day of my life. It is not easy to suffer, but to experience the suffering or injuries of those you love is more difficult, more painful. As I approached the door, I could hear the oxygen system working efficiently, providing Mike's fragile link with life. Then I saw the bottles hanging high over the bed and the plastic tubing leading to a motionless body. I fought back the tears as I drew near. I gazed down upon my son's face and couldn't fight any longer. I buried my head in my hands and wept.

The thought kept running through my mind: "Dear God, why him? He's so young. Why couldn't it have been the drunk? He caused it and he only suffered a broken leg." There was no bitterness in my thoughts. I was just trying to understand.

As the tears fell, I thought of those days when Mike was smiling, those wonderful hunting trips, the time he put the Scout in the ditch, and the joy we felt when he returned safely from Vietnam. Now he lay there so quietly, his jaw shattered, broken in six places. His head was grotesquely pushed out of shape, his face unrecognizable. Instead of his breathing on his own, a thin, clear plastic tube had been pushed through the base of his throat and carried life into his lungs. I don't remember how long I stayed there, but I recall the eerie quiet, broken only by the steady hum of the unconcerned respirator.

I could feel the pity and resentment beginning to stir in my soul and knew I had to find the answer in God. I searched my mind and faith for reassurance that this was God's will and that it served His purpose. I recalled how Job, Jeremiah, and Paul suffered and that their suffering had enhanced the word of God. Later, I found the following passages and would lean heavily upon them: "I want you to know, brothers, that what has happened to me has really served to advance the gospel." (Phil. 1:12; NIV) "For to you it has been granted for Christ's sake, not only to believe in Him, but also to suffer for His sake." (Phil. 1:29; NASB)

You cannot question God's will. You must believe there is a purpose and that it will enhance His word. It was a terrible feeling to sit and watch Mike struggle for life and not be able to extend my hand. Everything was now up to Mike and God. I could only pray.

Though the experience had been shattering for me, it grew worse when I returned to face Jeanne and the rest of the family. There was no way of hiding my feelings. I wanted to be strong, but I couldn't be. There was no way of reassuring Jeanne that everything would be all right.

The ride home that morning was long and tense. There were no words that seemed appropriate, no encouragement that seemed sincere. Both of us knew that even before we reached home the Lord might have called Mike. It was the lowest ebb of our lives.

For the next forty-eight hours, we waited and prayed that Mike would survive. Again and again, the question of what the Lord had in store for Mike and for us turned in our minds. Alone, perhaps, the burden might have been unbearable, it might have been difficult to keep faith with our Savior. It might have been easier to give in to the temptation of condemnation, of doubt of our Lord, to accuse Him bitterly or reject all that we truly knew to be right.

But we were never alone. Christians always have their family, always have those who care and help carry the burden. Early on the first morning following Mike's accident, friends and neighbors who heard or read about the accident began calling and offering their love and prayers.

Reverend Loomis came over and spent the day with us, helping us reach out to God, helping us reaffirm our faith, allowing Him to guide us through the dark hours that lay ahead.

"Remember what Lamentations 3:56, 57, 58, tells us: that regardless of what happens to us, if the faith is kept, we will be saved," Loomis reminded us. "For whatever reason, this is God's will. It is difficult, I know, to understand or accept, but how can we possibly question His work when He willingly gave His only Son to save mankind? Jesus' death was God's will, and no other life had such an impact upon this world. Now we must be patient and pray that God's will is done. We can only wait for Him to reveal what He has chosen for Mike."

Reverend Loomis's words were a great comfort during that trying and challenging moment of our lives. He had gently pointed out how important God had become in our lives. I began to realize that His will had helped me through those long days of struggling with my handicap. I had always thought I had done it on my own, but now I knew that it was His hand, His Spirit, that pushed away the self-pity and drove me to reconstruct my life. Even when I had neglected Him, when I was busy making my way in the world, He did not abandon me. He was there by my side showing the way.

When Jeanne and I returned to the hospital in the afternoon and I gazed on Mike, I still cried, and the tears that fell were tears of sorrow, but I no longer asked why.

Those haunting ifs we had raised in anguish the night before were forgotten. Instead, I recalled Romans 9:20–21; (KJV):

> Nay but, O man, who art thou that repliest against God? Shall the thing formed say to him that formed it, Why hast thou made me thus?
>
> Hath not the potter power over the clay, of the same lump to make one vessel unto honour, and another unto dishonour?

God was telling me not to question why one person received minor injuries and Mike was critically hurt. I was not to question His wisdom but to accept the form of His will. Mike's fate was the will of God and would serve the Lord's purpose in some way. I now prayed that whatever purpose it served, it would have meaning. Perhaps, I thought as I sat near Mike, someone might turn away from drinking or perhaps another might decide to become a policeman and turn away from a life of crime. There were a myriad possibilities that Jeanne and I discussed as we watched over Mike. Yet we both knew that we might never understand or realize what purpose Mike's sacrifice served. But at least we could accept the Lord's will.

It didn't make the pain go away. Our hearts and souls cried for Mike. The pain and suffering of one you love will hurt regardless of the reason; that can never be avoided. But the knowledge that that person has been chosen to enhance the gospel, to do God's work, is reassuring. Not to have that knowledge would be infinitely more painful.

Mike survived the first forty-eight hours, and we thanked God for His love and protection. Now, we believed, God had not planned to call Mike home. Whatever the purpose, we felt it served with Mike near us.

Within a short time after the critical forty-eight hours had passed, Mike had grown strong enough to be taken off the respirator and breathe on his own. He was still unconscious, but his body was mending, although he got a helping hand from Dr. Stone. Ten days after the accident, she rebuilt Mike's face. She had to reconstruct his jaw, restructure his teeth and cheekbones, which had been heavily damaged by the impact.

Her work was almost a miracle in itself. Before, we only saw the shattered hulk of what had been our son, but she restored his physical presence to us using the knowledge and skill the Lord had given her. The rest, we were told—meaning whether or not he would emerge from his coma—was up to Mike and God. There was little medical science could do but wait as we were doing.

The wait would last almost three months. We maintained a near round-the-clock vigil, waiting for any sign that indicated Mike was attempting to fight through the black shroud that had closed around his mind. Through this long wait, Mike's right arm was clinched tightly across his chest and the doctors could do little to loosen the grip. It was another indication of brain damage.

Many of our friends and relatives came, called, and offered prayers for Mike. A third-grade class in Mike's district sent a huge letter made by the children expressing their hopes that he would soon return to his duties. Policemen from his district stopped by often to check on his progress, and letters of good wishes poured in from around the state.

One card carried the message of Psalm 56:11, "In God have I put my trust: I will not be afraid. . . ." (KJV) It was a wonderful and thoughtful message. From the mission in McMinnville the congregation sent us an inspirational book of verses. I think this verse was my favorite:

> But he who makes a sacrifice,
> so another may succeed, Is indeed
> a true disciple of our blessed
> Savior's creed— For when we "Give
> ourselves away" in sacrifice and
> love—we are laying up rich treasures
> in God's kingdom up above.

Jim Davis came as often as possible. It was the second time around for him, and he offered the same friendship and encouragement that had seen Jeanne and me through our first challenge. There were others, of course. Jeanne's parents were always there, and Carol Perta, Sue Howell, and Al Aaronson, all good family friends, gave us so much support. These were just a few of those who rallied around during the long vigil.

Perhaps Mike's biggest supporters were Chris and our nieces Kathy Downey and Charlotte Dickson. The four had grown up together and were very close, loyal friends. The three girls spent hours sitting next to Mike's bed, talking to him as though he were conscious. They discussed what they had been doing that day, read the newspapers and magazines aloud, and tried to keep him informed on world events.

They knew there was a chance Mike couldn't hear them, that their voices couldn't penetrate that shroud, but they also felt there was a chance he could hear. Even an outside chance, they felt, justified the extra effort.

Jeanne watched them a few times and mentioned how amazed she was at how cheerful they were and how excited they would become while describing the events of the day. They refused to give up, and their tenaciousness gave Jeanne inspiration. It was a hard period for her. She sat there watching her son and feeling so helpless, and the tears would begin again. The ache in her heart grew as she watched him sleep on.

But after seeing the girls talking so happily to Mike, as if he were only confined to bed because of a sore throat, Jeanne decided to try. At first she spoke in a low, soft voice, letting Mike know she was there and that she loved him. The sense of doing something, the feeling of communicating, gave her new hope and determination. As the days passed, her voice grew stronger and more positive. Early in March she began telling Mike that Easter Sunday was approaching and that she wanted only one thing for Easter. She wanted him to say "Hi, Mom" on Easter Sunday. Every day from then on, she would remind Mike that Easter was drawing near and that she wanted him to say "Hi, Mom."

Occasionally, Dr. Stone would join Jeanne or the girls while they were talking to Mike and she would join in. She was a wonderful person and gave Jeanne and me a tremendous amount of encouragement during those long days and nights. We've lost contact with her, but we think of her often and pray that God continues to guide her in her work and life.

Mike slept on through the cold and rain of winter and still had not responded when the first leaves of spring began reaching out for the warmth of the sun. Meanwhile, Jeanne continued to remind Mike that Easter was near. "Remember, Mike, you've got to say 'Hi, Mom,' please."

As Easter drew near, there was an occurrence that at first totally confused us. Letters began pouring in from the southern states. Letters and cards containing prayers for Mike overwhelmed the hospital staff. We were amazed and so thankful for that outpouring of love and Christian fellowship, but we couldn't understand how it was happening.

Finally we discovered that Mike had become the recipient of a chain prayer started by our friends Mamma and Pappa Foutch of Trenton, Georgia, and my sister Edna Stibbs of St. Petersburg, Florida. The two families, after hearing about Mike's accident, began contacting Southern Baptist churches in their areas and told the congregations about Mike's plight. Immediately the members took up Mike's cause. Thousands of wonderful Christians began praying for our son, and we could feel their faith and warmth pouring into Mike's room.

No one could ever deny the strength of Christ's family. Its love and power dominated Mike's room. It brought to mind one of Jeanne's favorite psalms:

> But the godly shall flourish like palm trees, and grow tall as the cedars of Lebanon. For they are transplanted into the Lord's own garden, and are under his personal care. Even in old age they will still produce fruit and be vital and green. This honors the Lord, and exhibits his faithful care. He is my shelter. There is nothing but goodness in him!
>
> (Ps. 92:12–15; Living Bible)

It was such a beautiful feeling to know that people who didn't know, would never know, Mike would offer their prayers to God. Of course, we should have known that this is what God means when He talks of the Christian family. When people are drawn to Christ, they are also drawn to each other. Being born again means having the sensitivity, the understanding, and the love to become more aware of the agony and ecstasy of human life. This was pointed out in Galatians 6:2: "Bear one another's burdens, and thus fulfill the law of Christ." (NASB)

The Foutches had become family friends after we met at the National Southern Baptist Convention that had been held in Portland. We met them and their daughter and son-in-law and immediately struck up a friendship. We invited them to our home for dinner and created a lasting Christian friendship.

As the letters continued to pour in, we began to understand more clearly the meaning of "Church." So often we think of a building as a church. But the true Church is a living body, not a structure made of cement and timber. The Church is the people of God, the warmth, love, and fellowship that allow us to be free, that offer us redemption.

The Lord was demonstrating to us that by being a part of His family, you are never alone, you can never be forgotten. Our Christian brothers and sisters were reaffirming their membership in the Lord's Church by sharing our burden. "But if we walk in the light, as he is in the light, we have fellowship with one another, and the blood of Jesus, his Son, purifies us from every sin." (I John 1:7; NIV) That love and concern for our fellow man was clearly expressed when Paul wrote to the Philippian community of faith about how the Lord wanted His children to relate to one another. "If therefore there is any encouragement in Christ, if there is any consolation of love, if there is any fellowship of the Spirit, if any affection and compassion, make my joy complete by being of the same mind, maintaining the same love, united in spirit, intent on one purpose. Do nothing from selfishness or empty conceit, but with humility of mind let each of you regard one another as more important than himself; do not *merely* look out for your own personal interests, but also for the interest of others. Have this attitude in yourselves which was also in Christ Jesus." (Phil. 2:1–5; NASB)

That our brothers and sisters were looking out for the interests of Mike there is no doubt. Their prayers gave us the strength to accept the will of God and keep our faith strong. As the letters continued, so did Jeanne's reminder that Easter was coming closer. "All you have to say is 'Hi, Mom.' Just two words, Mike, and you've only got a couple of weeks to practice, so you better get busy."

Nurses moved in and out of Mike's room on a regular basis. One morning in mid-March, a nurse thought she caught, out of the corner of her eye, a slight movement of Mike's eyelid. She took a second look, watched closely, but nothing happened. It was such a small thing, but when the nurse mentioned it to us, our spirits soared!

As soon as we got into the room, Jeanne began talking to Mike, gently reminding him of the few days that were left until Easter. She talked on for about fifteen minutes and then we saw his eyelids flutter!

He was coming out of his sleep. We were ecstatic. God was awakening Mike. By nightfall his eyes were wide open. However, there was no indication that he was actually experiencing any visual sensation.

Dr. Johnson explained that it was possible Mike was starting to fight his way out of the coma, but he warned us not to expect too much. He said there was still no indication of the extent of the brain damage. His recovery could range from the occasional eyelid movement now being experienced to full recovery. There was no way of really knowing.

Within a few days we noticed that his eyes were now following movement, and when we talked to him, his eyes would concentrate on whoever was speaking. Occasionally he would attempt a smile, but it was faint and quickly vanished. But even the slightest movement sent our hopes soaring. We were sure God was preparing Mike for a full recovery.

We thumbed through magazines carrying stories about brain-damage cases and drew encouragement from those that told of complete recovery and where the subject returned to a normal life. We were trying to determine God's will for Mike instead of waiting and praying for guidance. We did pray, but we were praying for Mike's recovery, not God's will to be done.

Dr. Johnson continually warned us to slow down and gain control of our emotions, to look realistically at what lay ahead for us and Mike.

"Mike is like a prizefighter who has taken about a hundred too many punches to the head. Actually, you can magnify that comparison a thousand times. There is an envelope of blood surrounding the brain, putting a great deal of pressure on it. Until that blood is gone, assuming it ever goes, little can be done. It all takes time. You have to understand that."

We listened patiently, but in our hearts we were sure God would provide a full recovery. We intensified our efforts, took heart at the constant flow of cards and letters, and continued talking to him, trying to push back the shroud that had cut him off from his family. The intensity of the expression in his eyes increased, and there were indications that he was moving out of the darkness. At times he would move his lips slightly as if trying to respond, but then would drift off into a semiconscious state and the intensity in his eyes would dim.

"Easter is almost here, Mike," Jeanne would say softly. "There're only a few days. Promise me you'll say, 'Hi, Mom.' Please, Mike, just for me." Tears would trickle slowly down her face as she coached Mike.

When Easter came, we went to church first and prayed that God would answer our small request. Reverend Loomis asked the congregation to pray for Mike. I can remember when I was in college wanting to win a particular basketball game very badly. It was very important to me and I worked hard all week, but on the day of the game I wasn't sure I wanted to play. I had worked so hard, had mentally prepared myself to the point where I realized that if we lost I might not be able to cope with defeat.

We felt that same paradox now of wanting Mike to speak and yet fearing that if he didn't it would make us face questions we had avoided asking. They were questions like: "What if Mike doesn't recover? What will become of him? How will it affect our lives?"

As we approached his bed, his eyes were shut. Jeanne pulled a chair up next to the bed and sat down.

"Mike," she said quietly, "it's Easter."

At first there was no response, and Jeanne spoke his name again.

This time his eyes fluttered and then opened. For a moment it seemed as if he found some difficulty in focusing. But then his eyes found Jeanne and the intensity burst forward. For the first time he smiled strongly. He didn't move, but the smile and his eyes told us that he was alive mentally as well as physically.

"It's Easter, Mike," Jeanne repeated.

He smiled again and began moving his mouth. It took a tremendous amount of concentration and effort, but after what seemed like an eternity to us, first we heard the air escaping through his mouth as if he was mentally trying to remember the steps involved in speaking.

Finally, in a weak and extremely thin voice, we heard our prayers answered. "Hi, Mom." His eyes danced with excitement. He had been able to deliver his Easter present.

Jeanne's face lit up with happiness and for the first time I saw tears of joy instead of tears of sadness. We both started laughing and crying, releasing the pent-up emotions that had been building over the last three months.

"You did it!" I laughed. "Mike, you're going up from here! Keep it up!" It was as if he had scored the winning goal in that game I had wanted to win so badly years ago.

At this point we felt our prayers had been answered. God had given us a sign that Mike's mind could function, that he could respond to his world. He had taken a major step toward leaving the hospital.

EPILOGUE

December 25, 1979

Jess and Jeanne finished building a new home in the late summer of 1979. It is a modest but comfortable three-bedroom home with a daylight basement and sits on the back corner of their 17 acres. Interstate 5, just a mile to the west, puts them only fifteen minutes by car from downtown Portland.

On Christmas Day, driving along the potholed road passing in front of their home, you could easily see the living Christmas tree sitting out on their sun deck. Even from the road, fifty yards away, you could tell it was a noble fir. The tree lights sparkled brightly, the ornaments swayed with the eastwardly breeze. The rain had stopped, but the moisture-laden wind and the gathering clouds in the west served notice the reprieve was of short duration.

Inside, the aroma of turkey and pie commanded the entire house. The fireplace blazed away, and wrapping paper was strewn around the living room as if the gifts had been opened with a Rototiller.

Chris and Sus were handling the cooking chores while their husbands, Sus's two-year-old daughter, Lindsay, Jeanne's parents, Jeanne, Jess, and Mike were gathered around the television set. It was the typical scene Christian families around the country were repeating on the day of their Savior's birth.

Jess and Mike's wheelchairs were close together as they watched the football action. Jess has aged little since that Easter Day almost five years ago when Mike first broke out of his coma.

Mike is heavier than before the accident, his nose still shows the effect of the crash, and there is a small scar on his neck left from one of Dr. Stone's incisions. Of course, Mike is in a wheelchair, but other than that he looks very much like the Mike Roe who went on duty on January 21, 1975. He can use a walker and can at times walk without support aids, but there were really too many obstacles Christmas Day for him to navigate around.

Mike looked around the living room in wonder. "This is really a terrific house, Dad. Who built it?"

"Your mother and I did. Along with your cousin Al's help."

"Really a great place." Mike nodded, then smelled the aroma of turkey wafting through the air. "What time is it?"

Jess glanced at his watch. "About two-thirty."

"When we gonna eat?"

Jess looked over at Chris and she held up five fingers. "How does five o'clock sound?"

"Too long! I'm hungry. I haven't had anything to eat all day."

"Nothing to eat?" Jess challenged. "What about all that breakfast you put away, not to mention the pie and sandwich about an hour ago?"

Mike grinned. "Oh yeah, I forgot. But I'm still hungry."

"You're always hungry, Mike." Jess smiled.

They turned their attention to the game and watched for about five minutes. After the quarterback rifled a perfect strike to his receiver in the end zone, Mike got an inquisitive look on his face.

"Hey, is Bart Starr still the quarterback for the Packers?"

Jess shook his head. "Don't you remember? He retired. He's the Packers' coach now."

"Oh."

A few plays later, the quarterback, trapped behind the line of scrimmage, scurried in desperate circles, hoping to find a miracle. It was a bad day for miracles, and a host of defensive players buried him.

Mike laughed gleefully. "That quarterback reminded me of Gideon when the Lord told him to send all his troops home. Old Gideon thought he was gonna get clobbered!"

"Only Gideon didn't get clobbered and the quarterback did," Jess replied, laughing.

"Yeah, that's right." Mike grinned. "Actually, the quarterback looks more like Elijah when he was hiding in that cave except this cave is four two-hundred-and-fifty-pound linemen." Mike laughed again. He was in a good mood. Since he is still an inpatient at a veterans' hospital, this was the first time he had been in the new house.

"What time is it, Dad?"

"About two-forty, Mike."

"When we gonna eat?"

"Oh, around five," Jess answered.

Mike nodded and began to fidget. He was always a nervous person and that trait seems to have intensified after the accident. He rolled his wheelchair over to the TV set and changed the channel.

"Mike, the others were watching the game."

Mike thought for a second. "Oh, I'm sorry. I just wanted to see what else was on."

He switched back to the game and watched, but really wasn't interested. "Boy, this is a nice house, Dad. Who built it?"

"Your mom and I, Mike."

"Oh. Sure did a great job. What time is it?"

"'Bout two forty-five."

The quarterback fired a desperation pass, which was picked off by a defensive back and returned fifteen yards. Mike sighed in disgust. "Bart Starr wouldn't have done that. Is he still playing for the Packers?"

"No, he's retired. He's their coach now."

Almost five years from the day his police car was hit head on, Mike has made a significant recovery. More than one neurologist predicted he would never walk again. Yet he has demonstrated on numerous occasions that he is capable of walking without support aids.

Most physicians felt he had suffered such extensive brain damage that he would never be able to speak, or if he did, he would not be able to carry on a coherent conversation. Mike again proved their diagnosis wrong. He continually exhibits a bright, functional mind capable of rational, insightful thinking. He is aware of his surroundings, of his injuries, he keeps up with current events and has never forgotten that he is a born-again Christian.

But there are also some major problems for Mike to overcome, and the road may be long. He has difficulty retaining information. The problem is not unlike senility. He will repeatedly ask the same questions, especially questions pertaining to time or age. He seems to have an obsession for knowing the time of day and how old people are. It is almost as if he realizes he has lost three months of his life and is trying to determine when it occurred. He has no memory of the accident or the three months that followed.

He has a compulsive urge for food. While this is not an unusual symptom for patients with brain damage, the intensity of that compulsion seems abnormally high. He had to be removed from two institutions because he would steal food from other patients.

Mike also exhibits periods of emotional instability. One neurologist described him as a person with a high intelligence, but with the emotions and frustrations of a six-year-old.

Initial progress after Mike emerged from his coma was impressive and encouraging for Jess and Jeanne. But later, the problem of recall, his obsession with food and cigarettes, and his lack of emotional stability began to surface. It became obvious that recovery would take time.

Mike is currently a patient at the veterans' hospital in Roseburg, Oregon, about a hundred and eighty miles south of Portland. Jess and Jeanne have been told that, from now on, Mike's continued progress will be slow. His advances will be small, and he will have to fight the emotional problems of depression and frustration.

"Mike has periods when he becomes extremely positive about his recovery," Jess says. "Then he hits a slump and his emotions spiral downward. He gives up. He begins to believe he'll be institutionalized forever. He becomes confused and loses his mental concentration. It's as if his mental circuits short out under stress.

"There are conflicting theories about Mike's condition. Some say it is a matter of brain damage and can never be corrected. Others insist his symptoms reflect emotional rather than physical problems, and that if the right key is found, he can be freed from his emotional prison. We will never give up hope that a key can be found. And that search has brought us closer to our God.

"That his future, like ours, is in the hands of the Lord is very clear. We found a new life in our Lord, but we understand that it has not made us saints. There was a time, when Mike was still in a coma and just after he awoke, that we prayed only for Mike's recovery. In other words, we were praying for God to implement our will rather than seeking His will. Today, instead of miracles, we pray for understanding and guidance.

"Like everyone who enters a new life, who is born again, we wobble at times like a child struggling to walk. We misunderstand what God wants from us and become impatient. Occasionally we fall, occasionally we forget to include God in our lives, but as Christians we have the faith to get back up and continue our journey with Christ.

"We know, but at times forget, that handicaps and burdens are not burdens but opportunities to share Christ with others. If we are to follow Christ, then we must be ready to carry the Cross and bear its weight with the knowledge we are serving God's will.

"To say we have stopped praying for Mike's full recovery would be misleading. To have Mike with us again as he was before the accident would be a miracle, a sign of God's divine power. Those hopes always enter our prayers. But our prayers are to do God's will. If we continue to seek Him, if we never lose faith in His role for Mike, then others will see the true power of the Lord. Our family, as a member of God's family, has been offered the opportunity to allow the Holy Spirit to use our lives to reach others.

"If all the tears we have shed and will undoubtedly continue to shed, if all the pain we have experienced and might experience in the future, guide just one soul to our Lord, then it is worth it. My wheelchair and Mike's challenge are the tools of the Lord, and I am excited He has chosen us to help carry His word."